PENGUIN BOOKS

# NATIONAL DISH

**Anya von Bremzen** is one of the most accomplished food writers of her generation: the winner of three James Beard Awards; a contributing writer at *AFAR* magazine; and the author of six acclaimed cookbooks, among them *The New Spanish Table*, *The Greatest Dishes: Around the World in 80 Recipes*, and *Please to the Table: The Russian Cookbook* (coauthored with John Welchman). Her memoir, *Mastering the Art of Soviet Cooking*, has been translated into nineteen languages. Anya has been a contributing editor at *Travel + Leisure* and *Food & Wine*, and has written for *Saveur*, *The New Yorker*, and *Foreign Policy*, among other publications. Her work has been anthologized in several editions of *Best Food Writing* and in *The Best American Travel Writing*. A former concert pianist, Anya is fluent in four languages and when not on the road divides her time between New York and Istanbul.

## Praise for *National Dish*

Named a Best Book of the Year by the *Financial Times*,
*The Guardian*, *The Observer Food Monthly*,
*The Spectator*, and BBC's *The Food Programme*

"Spectacularly intelligent and funny." —*The Guardian*

"If you've ever contemplated the origins and iconography of classic foods, then *National Dish* is the sensory-driven, historical deep dive for you. . . . [An] evocative, gorgeously layered exercise in place-making and cultural exploration, nuanced and rich as any of the dishes captured within."
—*Boston Globe*

"Expansive, terrific . . . an ode to the thrill of eating dishes that personify a culture." —*Bloomberg Businessweek*

"This book feels like a continuation of Anthony Bourdain's work, full of insight and curiosity. And it'll make you so damn hungry."
—Gary Shteyngart

"Revealing and richly detailed . . . Fans of food and travel writing will want to sink their teeth into this." —*Publishers Weekly* (starred review)

"Whether she's getting lost in loud, crowded Italian streets while searching for the most exquisite pasta, dining on ramen amid Japanese septuagenarians, or making mole for an unexpected fiesta in Oaxaca, von Bremzen nimbly separates fact from 'fakelore' to divine what is important behind the association of cuisine with geography—the character of a place and the memories of those who live there." —*The Washington Post*

"Engrossing . . . A fascinating reflection on the connection between food, place, and what flavors mean to the people who prepare them and those who travel to seek them out." —*Travel + Leisure*

"A fast-paced, entertaining travelogue, peppered with compact history lessons that reveal the surprising ways dishes become iconic. Reading this book is like traveling with someone who knows the best places to eat and the right people to meet, but who can still find joy in humble, improvised meals. . . . Our beloved dishes may not always tell a happy story about who we are, but they tell us what we have to give."
—*The New York Times Book Review*

"Von Bremzen's writing is rich, urgent, and redolent of her literary heritage. . . . A book that deserves to be devoured." —*The Irish Times*

"On a whirlwind tour of six cities . . . von Bremzen celebrates the colorful histories of canonical dishes. [Her] prose is . . . as bold and richly textured as a steaming bowl of shoyu ramen." —*Saveur*

"Incisive, spirited, and mouthwatering."
—Howard Chua-Eoan, *Bloomberg Opinion*

"So enlightening—as well as well so much fun to read . . . von Bremzen is a superb describer of flavours and textures." —Bee Wilson, *Financial Times*

"Von Bremzen is a delightfully engaged and engaging writer."
—*The Observer Food Monthly*

"A sparklingly intelligent examination of, and a meditation on, the interplay of cooking and identity." —*The Spectator*

"Vivid . . . for readers who appreciate a sensorial journey and eschew arriving at easy conclusions, this will hit the spot." —*Booklist*

"In this piquant platter of a book, von Bremzen tackles questions of culture, history, and the meaning of a good meal. . . . Her vivid narrative is packed with intriguing characters, and in some countries, conversations about the food can be as important as the dish itself." —*Kirkus Reviews*

"This voyage into culinary myth-making and identity is essential reading. Its breadth of scope and scholarship is conveyed with such engaging wit. I couldn't love it more." —Nigella Lawson

"Anya von Bremzen, already a legend of food writing and a storytelling inspiration to me, has done her best work yet. *National Dish* is a must read for all those who believe in building longer tables where food is what bring us all together." —José Andrés

"Nobody writes about food like Anya von Bremzen. In this smart, personal, and compulsively readable book, she takes on history, politics, love, and flavor to show us the real meaning of what we eat." —Ruth Reichl

"Enchanting, fascinating, thought-provoking, and humorous. Storytelling that brings people, culture, and history together through the lens of food." —Claudia Roden, author of *Claudia Roden's Mediterranean*

"Every dish tells a story. A powerful storyteller herself, Anya von Bremzen blends historical research and beautiful writing into this absorbing crazy-smart book about how food defines who we are and where we come from. Whether she's decoding pizza in Naples or tortillas in Mexico, Anya is your perfect guide to the profound subjects of nationalism, food, and identity. And she's often funny as hell."

—René Redzepi, chef and co-owner of Noma

"A playful, erudite, and mouthwatering exploration of ideas around food and identity. With the help of a diverse group of characters and dishes, Anya von Bremzen highlights the intricacies and contradictions of our relationship with what we eat." —Fuchsia Dunlop

"It's a great pleasure to follow Anya von Bremzen as she brings her characteristic wit, curiosity, and agility as a prose stylist to make sense of this current moment in which what we eat has become so closely bound to identity. She writes with the intimacy of your most erudite friend telling you a story. This is a masterfully woven study, both edifying and entertaining, from one of the finest writers on food today."

—Mayukh Sen, author of *Taste Makers: Seven Immigrant Women Who Revolutionized Food in America*

"Any new book by Anya von Bremzen is cause for celebration for curious cooks and readers. Whether she's writing about the hidden restaurants of Cuba, the modern chefs of Spain, or telling deeply poignant stories of the table of the Soviet Union where she grew up, she always balances the pleasures of the palate and the mind. In *National Dish*, she explores not just why people care about their food, but how food makes us a people."

—Francis Lam, host of *The Splendid Table*

"In this eye-opening book, Anya von Bremzen travels the world to search beyond the clichés of iconic foods like ramen, pizza, or tapas—showing us how their stories are tied to colonialism, nationalism, religion, race, and more. Full of delicious scenes, colorful characters, and fascinating historical facts, *National Dish* is both thought-provoking and hugely entertaining to read." —Kwame Onwuachi, chef, author, and restaurateur

"Anya von Bremzen's tour of world cuisines, from France to Japan to Turkey to Mexico, is written as both an elegant entertainment and a love letter to those cuisines. But it's also a meditation on the paradox of national identity that will seduce the gastronomic curiosity of any world traveler." —Lawrence Osborne, author of *The Forgiven* and *On Java Road*

"Anya von Bremzen's *National Dish* is a revelation, giving us hard truths about where our food traditions really come from. What we cherish about great food cultures—the genuine origins, the long historical roots—turns out to be in no small part myth, and of surprisingly recent vintage, yet *National Dish* is an exceedingly hopeful read."

—Dan Barber, chef and co-owner of Blue Hill and author of *The Third Plate*

## ALSO BY ANYA VON BREMZEN

*Paladares: Recipes Inspired by the*
*Private Restaurants of Cuba*

*Mastering the Art of Soviet Cooking:*
*A Memoir of Food and Longing*

*The New Spanish Table*

*The Greatest Dishes!*
*Around the World in 80 Recipes*

*Fiesta! A Celebration of Latin Hospitality*

*Terrific Pacific Cookbook*
(with John Welchman)

*Please to the Table: The Russian Cookbook*
(with John Welchman)

# NATIONAL DISH

Around the World in Search of
*FOOD, HISTORY, and the*
*MEANING OF HOME*

ANYA VON BREMZEN

PENGUIN BOOKS

PENGUIN BOOKS
An imprint of Penguin Random House LLC
penguinrandomhouse.com

First published in the United States of America by Penguin Press,
an imprint of Penguin Random House LLC, 2023
Published in Penguin Books 2024

ISBN 9780735223172 (paperback)

THE LIBRARY OF CONGRESS HAS CATALOGED THE
HARDCOVER EDITION AS FOLLOWS:

Names: Von Bremzen, Anya, author.
Title: National dish : around the world in search of food,
history, and the meaning of home / Anya von Bremzen.
Description: New York : Penguin Press, [2023] |
Includes bibliographical references and index.
Identifiers: LCCN 2022049211 (print) | LCCN 2022049212 (ebook) |
ISBN 9780735223165 (hardcover) | ISBN 9780735223189 (ebook)
Subjects: LCSH: Food habits—Social aspects. |
Food—Social aspects. | Nationalism.
Classification: LCC GT2850 .V66 2023 (print) |
LCC GT2850 (ebook) | DDC 3941/2—dc23/eng/20230309
LC record available at https://lccn.loc.gov/2022049211
LC ebook record available at https://lccn.loc.gov/2022049212

Printed in the United States of America
1st Printing

Designed by Amanda Dewey

For Larisa and Barry

And in memory of my brother, Andrei

# CONTENTS

# INTRODUCTION
## Paris: Pot on the Fire

On a gray fall morning in the days sometime before the pandemic, my partner Barry and I arrived in Paris, where I planned to make a pot-au-feu recipe from a nineteenth-century French cookbook. It was for a book project of my own, one that had begun to bubble and form in my mind, about national food cultures told through their symbolic dishes and meals, which I would cook, eat, and investigate in different parts of the world.

Dumping our luggage in our apartment swap in the multicultural 13th arrondissement, we immediately rushed across the wide Avenue d'Italie—to begin sabotaging French national food culture by ingesting a frenzy of calories. *Non*-Gallic calories.

At a petite dive called Mekong, a stupendous curried chicken banh mi was prepared with something like love by a tired Vietnamese woman who sighed that Saigon was *très belle, mais Paris? Eh bien, un peau triste* . . . At a halal Maghrebi boucherie there was mahjouba, a flaky Algerian crepe aromatic with a filling of stewed tomatoes and peppers. And a mustached butcher being tormented by a middle-aged Parisienne, prim and imperious. After she departed with her single veal escalope, he exhaled with a whistle and made a "crazy" sign with his finger.

Which pretty much summed up how I'd always felt about Paris.

Ever since my first visit back in the 1970s, as a sullen teenage refugee from the USSR newly settled in Philadelphia, my relationship with the City of Light had always been anxious and fraught. Other people might swoon over the bistros, rhapsodize about first encounters with platters of oysters and crocks of terrine. Me, I saw nothing but despotic prix fixe menus, withering classism, and Haussmann's relentless beige facades—assembly-line Stalinism epauletted with window geraniums.

But *right now*, onward, for pink mochi balls at a Korean épicerie on the main Asian artery, Avenue de Choisy, after which I frantically stuffed our shopping bag with frozen Cambodian dumplings and three huge Chinese moon cakes at the giant Asian supermarket, Tang Frères. Just nearby, at a fluorescent-lit Taiwanese bubble tea parlor, was where I discovered the Vietnamese summer roll–sushi mashup. Behold the sushiburrito.

It was the happiest Paris arrival I'd ever had. The 13th arrondissement comforted me right back to where I'd just left, my buoyant polyglot New York neighborhood of Jackson Heights, Queens. The postcolonial profusion of lemongrass, fish sauce, and harissa helped soften my Francophobic unease.

Sending Barry off to settle into our apartment swap—whose tiny cramped kitchen, by some astounding kismet, featured a large poster of Frederick Wiseman's documentary *In Jackson Heights*—I carried my purchases to our petite neighborhood park. South Asian and North African kids were kicking a soccer ball by the hibiscus bushes. On a bench, a Koranic old man with a wispy beard and a skullcap put his hand to his heart to greet me: "As-salaam alaikum!"

With this blessing and a test bite of moon cake (funky salted egg filling), I pondered that which had brought me to Paris—a place unbeloved by me, but historically crucial to the concept of a national food culture. My journey could hardly start anywhere else.

NATIONAL CUISINES, one food studies scholar observes, suffer from "problematic obviousness." The same could be said for the very idea of "national." Most of us take a view of nations as organic communities that have shared blood ties, race, language, culture, and diet since time immemorial. Among social scientists, however, this "primordialism" doesn't hold water. Scholars from the influential mid-1980s "modernist" school (Ernest Gellner, Eric Hobsbawm, Benedict Anderson) have persuasively argued that nations and nationalism are historically recent phenomena, dating roughly to the late Enlightenment—and to the French Revolution in particular, which supplied the model for our contemporary concept of the nation, as France's absolutist monarchy of divergent peoples and customs and dialects was transformed into a sovereign entity of common laws, a unified language, and a written constitution, ruled in the name of equal citizens under that grand idealist banner: Liberté, égalité, fraternité!

Inspired by the French example, the long nineteenth century would see the rise of ethnonational self-determination from colonial empires, until the first and second world wars released flood tides of new nation-states from the ruins—some of their current borders, of course, blatant carve-ups by European colonial powers.

The final wave of nations arrived in the early 1990s with the dissolution of Yugoslavia and the USSR. It was in the latter where I was born in the sixties, to be raised on the imperialist scarlet-blazed myth of the fraternity of Soviet socialist republics—as diverse as Nordic Estonia and desert Turkmenistan—all wisely governed by Moscow, my hometown. The food we relished was the disparate cuisine of an empire: Uzbek pilaf, spicy Georgian chicken in walnut sauce, briny Armenian dolmas; they relieved the quotidian blandness of Soviet-issue sosiski (franks) and mayonnaise-laden salads.

Then in 1974 my mother and I became stateless refugees, emigrants to the US.

I still remember my ESL teacher lecturing grandly in a loud, nasal Philadelphia accent about how proud we students should feel being part of a glorious melting-pot nation. And me trying to imagine myself somehow as a slice of weird Day-Glo–orange Velveeta melting away in the cauldron of gloppy chili of our school lunches. Instinctively wary of the great American assimilationist model, I didn't melt in very well. My overbearing patriotic Soviet education made me cynical about states and their identities.

Though now I sometimes wonder how it would feel to belong to a small, close-knit nation—Iceland?—I feel most at home in my Jackson Heights barrio of 168 languages, where I can have Colombian arepas for breakfast and Tibetan momos for lunch, and nobody cares about my identity. I'm a Jewish-Russian American national, born in a despotic imperium long deleted from maps. I speak with a heavy accent in several languages, lead a professionally nomadic existence as a food and travel writer, and own an apartment in Istanbul, former seat of the multiethnic Ottoman empire. At table my mom, Barry, and I are passionate ecumenical culturalists. We make gefilte fish for Passover, Persian pilaf for Nowruz, and a ham for Russian Orthodox Easter. The Polish philosopher Zygmunt Bauman has a great phrase for this very common postmodern—globalized—condition, of not committing to a single identity or place or community:

"Liquid modernity," he calls it. A life where "there are no permanent bonds."

So why then would someone like me set out to explore *national* food cultures?

Because with the rise and domination of globalization, nations and nationalism somehow seem both more obsolete and more vital and relevant than ever. There's hardly a better prism through which to see this than food. From Kampala to Kathmandu we confront the same omnipresent fast-food burger, while from Tbilisi to Tel Aviv the same "global Brooklyn" community of woolly hipsters protests such corporate/culinary imperialism with craft beer and Instagrammable sourdough loaves. In a way, both the craft brews and the burgers are different political flavors of transnational food flows. Such full-flood globalization, you'd think, would have wiped away local and national cravings. But no: the global and local nourish each other. Never have we been more cosmopolitan about what we eat—and yet never more essentialist, locavore, and particularist. As the world becomes ever more *liquid*, we argue about culinary appropriation and cultural ownership, seeking anchor and comfort in the mantras of authenticity, terroir, heritage. We have a compulsion to tie food to place, to forage for the genius loci on our pilgrimages to the birthplace of ramen, the cradle of pizza, the bouillabaisse bastion. Which is what I've been doing myself professionally for the last several decades.

What's more, as a national symbol, food carries the emotional charge of a flag and an anthem, those "invented traditions" crucial to building and sustaining a nation, to claiming deep historical roots. While in fact, often, they are both manufactured and recent.

And so here I sat on a bench in Paris, unwrapping my hyper-globalized sushiburrito while contemplating a super-essentialist quote from the great scholar Pascal Ory. France, wrote Ory, "is not a country with an ordinary relation to food. In the national vulgate food is one of the distinctive ingredients, if not *the* distinctive ingredient, of French identity."

Italians, Koreans, even Abkhazians would certainly wax indignant that their relation to food is every bit as special. But if our identities, at their most primal, involve how we talk about ourselves around a dinner table, it was France—and Paris specifically—that created the first explicitly national discourse about food, esteeming its cuisine as an exportable, uniquely French cultural product along with terms such as "chef" and "gastronomy." It was France that in the mid-seventeenth century laid the foundation as well for a truly *modern* cuisine, one that emerged from a jumble of medieval spices to invent and record sauces and techniques the world still utilizes today. To create "restaurants" as we know them, and turn "terroir" into a powerful national marketing tool.

Of course (to my not-so-secret glee, I admit) this Gallic culinary exceptionalism had taken a terrific beating over the past couple decades. So where was it now? And where, and how, did the idea of France as a "culinary country" come to be born?

. . .

The pot-au-feu that was to occupy me in Paris, my symbolic French national meal, came from a book by a deeply influential nineteenth-century chef whose fantastical story befits an epic novel. Abandoned on a Parisian street by his destitute father during Robespierre's terror, Marie-Antoine Carême would have been invented—by Balzac? Dumas père? both were gourmandizing fans—if he didn't already exist. Self-made and charismatic, he rose to become the world's first international celebrity toque (in fact he invented the headgear). Not only was Carême the grand maestro of *la grande cuisine*'s architectural spun-sugar spectaculars, he also codified the four mother sauces from which flowed the infinite "petites sauces," sauce being so essential to the French self-definition. And cheffing for royalty and the G7 set of his day, he spread the supremacy of Gallic cuisine across the globe. Or to put a modern spin on it, Carême conducted gastrodiplomacy (our au courant term for the political soft power of food) on behalf of Brand France.

Even more influential was Carême's written chauvinism. "Oh France, my beautiful homeland," he apostrophized in his 1833 seminal opus, *L'Art de la Cuisine Française au Dix-Neuvième Siècle*, "you alone unite in your breast the delights of gastronomy."

How then *are* national cuisines and food cultures created? The answer, as I'd come to learn, is rarely straightforward, but a seminal cookbook is always a good place to begin. And as the influential scholar of French history Priscilla Ferguson observed, it was Carême's books that unified La France around its cuisine and food language, at a time when French printed texts had begun making the ancien régime's aristocratic gastronomy accessible to an eager, more inclusive bourgeois public. "Carême's French cuisine," Ferguson writes, "became a key building block in the vast project of constructing a nation out of a divided country."

As the Chef of Kings addressed his public: "My book is not written for the great houses. Instead . . . I want that in our beautiful France, every citizen can eat succulent meals."

And the succulence that kicks off his magnum opus is the pot-au-feu, "pot on the fire." Broth, beef, and vegetables, soup and main course all in one cauldron, it's a symbolic bowlful of égalité-fraternité that Carême anointed *un plat proprement national*, a truly national dish. Pot-au-feu carries a monumental weight in French culture. Voltaire affiliates it with good manners; Balzac and even Michel Houellebecq, that scabrous provocateur, lovingly invoke its bourgeois comforts; scholars rate it a "mythical center of family gatherings." Myself, I was particularly intrigued by its liquid component, the stock or bouillon/broth—the aromatic foundation of the entire French sauce and potage edifice.

"Stock," proclaimed Carême's successor, Auguste Escoffier, dictator of belle epoque haughty splendor, "is everything in cooking, at least in French cooking."

Stock was homey yet at the same time existentially Cartesian: *I make bouillon, therefore I cook à la française.*

"CARÊME . . . POT-AU-FEU . . . such important subjects." Bénédict Beaugé, the great French gastronomic historian, saluted my project. "And these days, alas, so often ignored."

In his seventies, his nobly benevolent face ghostly pale under thinning white hair, Bénédict radiated a deep, humble humanity—the opposite of a blustery French intellectual. His book-lined apartment lay fairly near the Eiffel Tower, in Paris's west. Walking up his bland street, Rue de Lourmel, I noted a Middle Eastern self-service, a Japanese spot, and a wannabe hipster bar called Plan B.

"Ah, the new *global* Paris," I remarked, to open our conversation.

"And a chaos, culinarily speaking," Bénédict said. "A confusion—reflecting a larger one about our identity—lasting now for almost two decades . . . Though a constructive chaos, perhaps?"

He wondered, however, as I'd been wondering, about the "overarching idea of Frenchness, of a great civilization at table." In Paris nowadays, he said, only Japanese chefs seemed fascinated with Frenchness, while Tunisian bakers were winning the Best Baguette competitions.

"Yes, immigrant cuisines are changing Paris for the good," he affirmed. "But the problem? In France, we don't have your American clarity about being a melting-pot nation."

Indeed. Asking journalist friends about the ethnic composition of Paris, I'd been sternly reminded that French law prohibits official data on ethnicity, race, or religion—effectively rendering immigrant communities like the ones in our treizième mute and invisible. All in the name of republican ideals of color-blind universalism.

"Ah, but pot-au-feu!" Bénédict nodded approvingly. "That wonderful, curious thing, a dish entirely archetypal—meat in broth!—and yet totally national!"

As for Carême? He smiled tenderly as if talking about a beloved old uncle. "An artiste, our kitchen's first intellectual, a Cartesian spirit who gave French cuisine its logical foundation, a grammar. *However* . . ." A finger was raised. "The rationalization and ensuing *nationalization* of French cuisine—it didn't exactly begin with Carême!"

"Ah, you mean La Varenne," I replied.

In 1651, François Pierre de La Varenne, a "squire of cooking" to the Burgundian Marquis d'Uxelles, published his *Le Cuisinier François*, the first original cookbook in France after almost a century dominated by adaptations of Italian Renaissance texts—and the first anywhere to use a *national* title.

Hard to imagine, but until the 1650s there really wasn't anything remotely like distinct, codified "national" cooking, anywhere. While the poor subsisted on gruels and weeds (so undesirable then but now celebrated as "heritage"), the cosmopolitan cuisine of different courts brought in delectables from afar to show off power and wealth. All across Europe, cookbooks were shamelessly plagiarized, so that European (even Islamic) elites banqueted on pretty much the same roasted peacocks and herons, mammoth pies (sometimes containing live rabbits), and omnipresent blancmanges, those Islamic-influenced sludges of rice, chicken, and almond milk. Teeth-destroying Renaissance recipes often added two pounds of sugar for one pound of meat, while overloads of imported cinnamon, cloves, pepper, and saffron made everything taste, one historian quips, like bad Indian food.

*Le Cuisinier François* offers the earliest record of a seismic change in European cuisine. Seasonings in La Varenne's tome mostly ditch heavy East India spices for such *aromates français* as shallots and herbs; sugar is banished to meal's end; smooth emulsified-butter-based sauces begin to replace the chunky sweet-sour medieval concoctions. *Le Cuisinier* brims with dainty ragouts, light salads, and such recognizable French standards as boeuf à la mode. One of La Varenne's contemporaries best summed up this new *goût naturel*: "A cabbage soup should taste entirely of cabbage, a leek soup entirely of leeks."

A modern mantra, first heard in mid-seventeenth-century France.

"Then following La Varenne, in the next century," said Bénédict, a frail eminence among his great piles of books, "the Enlightenment spirit fully took over, while print culture exploded." Fervent new scientific approaches teamed up with Rousseau's cult of nature, whose rusticity was in fact very refined and expensive. Among other things, this alliance produced a vogue for super-condensed quasi-medicinal broths.

And the name of these Enlightenment elixirs?

Restaurants.

As historian Rebecca Spang writes in *The Invention of the Restaurant*, "centuries before a restaurant was a place to eat . . . a *restaurant* was a thing to eat, a restorative broth." Restaurants as places—as attractions that would be exclusive to Paris well into the mid-nineteenth century—first appeared a couple of decades before the 1789 Revolution, in the form of chichi bouillon spas, where for the first time in Western history, diners could show up at any time of day, sit at their separate tables, and order from a menu with prices. By the 1820s Paris had around three thousand restaurants, and they already resembled our own. Temples of aestheticized gluttony, yes—of truffled poulet Marengo and chandeliered opulence. But also, crucially, social and cultural landmarks that inspired an innovative and singularly French genre of literary gastrophilosophizing—attracting Brit and American pilgrims who assumed, per Spang, that France's "national character revealed itself in such dining rooms." Which it did.

"Of course national cuisines don't happen *overnight*," cautioned Bénédict, as I made ready to leave him to his texts and histories. It was a long process that mirrored developments in culture and politics. But one uniquely French hallmark, he stressed, going back to the mid-1600s, was a culinary quest for originality and novelty, made even more insistent by the advent of restaurants and the birth of the food critic. And pretty much ever since La Varenne, each triumphant new generation of French cuisiniers has expressed a recommitment to the ideal of goût naturel, to a more inventive and scientific—and more expensive—refinement. Carême? He, too, professed the "vast superiority" of his cuisine on account of its "simplicity, elegance . . . sumptuousness." Escoffier boasted of simplifying Carême—to be followed by an early-twentieth-century cuisine-bourgeoise regionalist movement that ridiculed Escoffier's pompous complexities. Then the 1970s nouvelle cuisine rebels (Bocuse, Troisgros, and the like) attacked the whole Carême-Escoffier legacy of "terrible brown sauces and white sauces" to raise the conquering flag of their own (shockingly expensive) lightness and naturalness.

But why—why, after the nouvelle cuisine revolution, did this uniquely French narrative of reinvention and rationalization flounder and tank spectacularly?

"FERRAN."

Nicolas Chatenier pronounced the culprit's name with a somber flourish. Nattily dressed, a handsome fortyish businessman-boulevardier, Nicolas was, at the time, the French Academy chair for the enormously influential San Pellegrino 50 Best Restaurants, Michelin's archrival.

He meant Ferran Adrià, the avant-garde Catalan genius of the erstwhile El Bulli restaurant on Spain's Costa Brava. In the late twentieth century Adrià appeared seemingly out of thin air, a magician cum scientist who, just like that, brilliantly and wittily challenged, deconstructed, and reimagined established French culinary grammar and logic—the way Picasso and Salvador Dalí upended and electrified the world of art.

Nicolas and I were hashing over the apocalyptic toppling of the cuisine française edifice at a burnished haute-bistro called La Poule au Pot, which charged sixty bucks for a portion of pot-au-feu's poultry cousin.

Nicolas grew up in a bourgeois Parisian family and remembers their festive excursions to France's grand dining temples as utter enchantments. "That bonbonnière that was Robuchon's Jamin . . ." he reminisced dreamily, as a bearded hipster garçon apportioned our yellow heritage Bresse chicken in broth with a cool millennial irony. "Those fairy-tale desserts chez Troisgros . . ." Maybe that's why as an aspiring food journalist in the early aughts, he became so troubled by the raging French gastronomy *crise*. So he wrote a long magazine article laying out the facts. Which nobody wanted to hear. "People accused me," he chuckled, "and I'm not making this up, of *being a British spy!*"

His eyes turned doleful. "France, a great food empire for centuries. Best training, best products, best chefs. And then . . ." He lifted a tragic hand. "The national *humiliation* of that *New York Times Magazine* story with Ferran on the cover about France declining and Spain ascending!"

"But come, Nicolas," I chided, "that article was almost *twenty* years ago!"

"And people here still talk about it," he assured me gravely.

It saddened him how the Spanish had displayed "amazing" unity around Ferran, while France's contemporary generation, led by Joël Robuchon and Alain Ducasse, were fighting each other.

"It was different with the seventies nouvelle cuisine guys," he insisted. "Troisgros, Bocuse, Michel Guérard, they were clever, authentic—*united*."

Sure, theirs was a radical 1968 rhetoric; revolution was in the air. But they seized upon that moment, a moment that was part of a sweeping larger cultural energy. "Everything was nouvelle and in-novative in France then. Nouvelle Vague cinema, nouveau roman literature, a new angle on cultural criticism. We were the capital of culture and fashion—Godard, Truffaut, Yves Saint Laurent!"

He paused for a mournful slurp of chicken bouillon. "Followed by twelve years of stagnant immobility under Chirac. A slow, bor-ing [sigh] . . . *decline*."

So the culinary crisis wasn't really because of Ferran?

Nicolas gave a Gallic shrug of assent. "It was a cascade of crises."

Crises such as outmoded, unsustainable Michelin standards of luxury that bankrupted some chefs, drove others even to suicide; the thirty-five-hour work week introduced in 2000, plus a draco-nian 19.5 percent VAT (lowered since) that put a further impossible strain on restaurants; at lower-rung places, scandals that erupted about pre-prepared dishes and frozen ingredients; in the country-side, chain supermarket and factory farms that threatened local tra-ditions. *Plus* the global fast-food invasion arrived.

"France, the exporter of a glorious civilization at table, became hooked on McMerde!" Nicolas lamented. "Even our baguettes be-came terrible. Prebaked, frozen, *industrial*."

But now, apparently, now all was ending well. Baguettes were spectacular once more and millennials were crazy for organic and farm fresh, as if channeling Rousseau's nature cult. The new vibe, in eastern Paris especially, brought Brooklynesque coffee bars, creative cocktails, Asian-influenced restaurants. "Currently all lines in Paris are blurred," Nicolas declared, "and that's really fun! Okay, we got thrown off for a while by the vitriol from abroad—but we have an open mind now! We may have lost the idea of a *national* cuisine, but we've opened up to outside. Go to Cheval d'Or," he admonished, "this Japanese guy doing this supercool neo-Cantonese food . . ."

"So wait—you're saying the Paris restaurant scene became interesting because chefs *ditched the idea of Frenchness*?"

Nicolas swallowed hard. He looked cornered. As the 50 Best head for France, he had to defend national values. "Well, yes, for a bit," he allowed. "But now people are sentimental again—about bistros! The céleri rémoulade and poulet-au-pot we just had. Look around: every table is full, every night. At *these* prices."

Terroir, he mused, poking his fork into the carcass of our poulet de Bresse, its graphic, scary claw still sticking out. Maybe that was always France's answer, her true *national* narrative. France's incredible products . . . and how the French talk so superbly about them, feeding the global appetite that they effectively created.

After dinner I wandered along the moonlit Seine, ignoring that romantic riverside Francophiles swoon over so tiresomely, to ponder my conversation with Nicolas. Priscilla Ferguson argues that French cuisine reigned supreme because of the food itself—the proof in the pudding. But, as Nicolas contended, also because the French were such aces at *discourse*: their conversation, their writing and philosophizing, had elevated gastronomy from subsistence or even a show of class power to a cultural form on par with literature, architecture, and music.

But *their conversation*, it occurred to me, was what ultimately hurt French cuisine.

Because it became bogged down and essentialist. As progressive ideas erupted elsewhere—the new imaginative science in Spain, the focus on sustainability in California and Scandinavia—the French became fixated on the anxiety of losing their storied supremacy. Their narrative turned nostalgic, defensive, rigid with hauteur and heritage. I recalled a star-studded chef conference in São Paulo about a decade ago. The young Catalan pastry wiz Jordi Roca presented a magically levitating dessert. Brazilian chef Alex Atala passionately discoursed on Amazonian biodiversity. And the French? I still remember rolling my eyes along with the audience when a kitchen team of the gastronomic god Alain Ducasse came onstage to pompously lecture about the importance of . . . *stocks*. Which is like going on about fountain pens at an AI summit.

Yet here I was in Paris myself, knee-deep in bouillon, researching pot-au-feu along with the history and science of stocks—fishing for broader connections between cuisine and country. It amazed me, for instance, how an eighteenth-century cup of restorative broth sat so smack at the French Enlightenment's intersection of cuisine, medicine, chemistry, emerging consumerism, and debates about taste, ancienne versus nouvelle. While a century later, broth represented democratization of dining, as inexpensive canteens called bouillons—the world's proto–fast-food chains—sprang up in fin de

siècle Paris, serving beef in broth plus a few simple items to disparate classes in hygienic, gaily attractive surroundings.

Now in the living room of our apartment with its clutter of
Balzacian bric-a-brac, I reexamined once again Carême's opening
recipe in *L'Art de la Cuisine Française*: "pot-au-feu maison."

*Put in an earthenware marmite four pounds of beef, a good
shank of veal, a chicken half-roasted on a spit, and three liters of
water. Later add two carrots, a turnip, leeks, and a clove stuck into
an onion . . .*

A straightforward recipe, if a little weird. Why the half-roasted
chicken?

What made the recipe a landmark, Bénédict told me, was
Carême's *Analyse du pot-au-feu bourgeois*, his opening preamble.
For here was the Chef of Kings, who'd dedicated his pages to Bar-
oness Rothschild, explaining the science and merits of bouillon for
a bourgeois female cook—bridging the gap between genders and
classes, praising his reader as "the woman who looks after the nutritional pot, and without the slightest notion of chemistry . . . has
simply learned from her mother how to care for the pot-au-feu."
This preamble, according to scholars, was what truly nationalized
the dish, leading generations of writers and cooks to start their own
books with this one-pot essential.

But how else, I asked myself, and for what other reasons, do dishes
get anointed as "national"?

There was unexpected economic success abroad (pizza in Italy);
tourist appeal (moussaka in Greece); nourishing of the masses during hard times (ramen in postwar Japan). Even, sometimes, top-down

fiat: see the strange case of pad Thai, a Chinese-origin noodle dish (like ramen) that got "Thaified" with tamarind and palm sugar and decreed the national street food by the 1930s dictator Phibun—part of his campaign that included renaming Siam as Thailand, banning minority languages, and pushing Chinese vendors off the streets.

Among all the contenders, of course, one-pot multi-ingredient stews made the most convincing national emblems with their miraculous symbolic power to feed rich and poor, transcend regional boundaries, unite historical pasts. In Brazil, feijoada was canonized for supposedly melding Indigenous, colonial, and African slave cultures in a cauldron of black beans and porkstuffs, while in Cuba the exact same thing was said about the multi-meat tuber stew, ajiaco. Or consider (if one must) the creepy Nazi promotion of Germany's eintopf ("one-pot") for forging some mythical völkisch community. Never mind that the word "eintopf" never even appeared in print until the 1930s. (A not-uncommon sort of situation, I would discover.)

And so here was my pot-au-feu with its very genuine historical roots. Although hardly a dish of the peasants (for whom meat was once a year) it was still easily mythologized as the perfect embodiment of French republican credos, a fraternal pot for *toute la France*. Even that towering snob Escoffier praised it as a "dish that despite its simplicity . . . comprises the entire dinner of the soldier and the laborer . . . the rich and the artisan." By Escoffier's belle epoque reign, France's Third Republic ambition to aggressively nationalize its citizenry through universal education, military service, regional integration, and rural modernization was almost fulfilled. Although women remained second-class citizens—unable to vote until 1944—"teaching Marianne how to cook," as one scholar puts it, "had become a national issue of paramount importance." And pretty much every domestic science textbook for girls began with pot-au-feu, which was also the name of a popular late-nineteenth-century domestic advice magazine for bourgeois housewives. Why, pot-au-feu even perfectly illustrated the era's embrace of regionalist "unity in diversity," since every region in France had its version (garbure in Languedoc, kig ha farz in Brittany), all now celebrated as parts of a grand, savory *national* whole.

The more I thought about it, the more pot-au-feu seemed like an obvious master class in "national dish" building.

E<small>XCEPT</small>...

People I questioned talked about it in a perfunctory nostalgic past tense—*ah, grand-mère*, ah, Sunday pot-au-feu lunch back in the countryside—before breathlessly recommending a bao burger hotspot or a très Brooklyn mezcal bar. The two important chefs advertised to me as pot-au-feu experts were both on some extended Asian trips and, judging from their gleeful Instagram feeds, not planning to return anytime soon.

Even Alain Ducasse, that éminence grise of Gallic gastronomy, seemed to be shoving the exemplary "national dish" under the bus.

"Carême . . . pot-au-feu . . . hmm . . ." mused Ducasse, in response to my question, when I called on him at his flagship Hôtel Plaza Athénée restaurant.

Clad in an impeccable tan suit and his signature Alden high-top shoes, Ducasse, now in his sixties, with his glut of Michelin stars and a restaurant empire across several continents, loomed in my mind as a kind of modern corporate Carême. A grand cultural entrepreneur and gastrodiplomat who entertained heads of state at Versailles on behalf of Brand France.

"Pot-au-feu . . ." Ducasse shook his silver-maned head. Having converted to a Rousseauian-sounding *cuisine de la naturalité*—that evergreen Gallic recommitment—he was nowadays focused on the health of the planet. Red meat? he frowned. Bad for environment.

"Stocks, *fonds, les sauces classiques françaises* . . . Carême, Escoffier . . ." Ducasse summed up my questions distractedly. "*Bien sûr*, it's our French DNA . . . they inspire us still." Though he didn't sound exactly passionate. "In our work we've kept"—he paused to calculate—"about ten percent. Maybe less."

Ten percent?

I thought of that stage show in São Paulo, the hoary air of presumption of the eternal ultimacy of French stocks.

Then again, my friend Alexandra Michot, food editor of French *Elle*, had been much more ruthless a few days before. "It took us a full hundred years," she sputtered, "to shake off the Carême-Escoffier legacy, to unlearn that overbearing French cuisine grammar. And now," she proclaimed, "we're finally free! And the future is beautiful."

Which was more or less the substance of Ducasse's line.

Ten years ago the French food scene was, Ducasse admitted tactfully, *un peu* depressed. But today? "Today there's so much talent, so much diversity—Asian, North African, new interpretations of bistros. So many new stories all unique, individual, personal."

This was verbatim what I'd been hearing from Nicolas and others and experiencing myself—but coming from Alain Ducasse, *the* establishment, it was, I guess, the new official French narrative: universalism is dead, long live particularism. And Gallic haute cuisine itself? Pretty dead, too—because some months after my visit, Ducasse would be evicted from his prestigious but unprofitable Plaza Athénée address and would collaborate on a pop-up with Albert Adrià, the kid brother of his historic archnemesis, Ferran. Last I heard he'd opened a high-end vegan burger stand.

SO WHERE did all this leave my Carême/pot-au-feu project—the logical starting point, or so I'd figured, for probing French food and identity—in this birthplace of Gallic gastronomy that no longer seemed interested?

Even my devoutly Francophile elderly mom, who'd just landed in Paris en route to New York from a visit to Moscow, was eyeing the underside of the proverbial bus.

"But Anyut . . ." she wondered, using my Russian diminutive on our way to the neighborhood butcher after a morning snacking on Tunisian "pirozhki" and Cambodian "blini." "Why pot-au-feu? As the French national dish, shouldn't we be making couscous or something?"

A description I'd just read, by an Algerian political activist, came to my mind: France was a "McDonald's-couscous-steak-frites society." *Mondialization* prevailed. Had I absurdly fallen into some tourist authenticity trap, expecting a cuisine frozen in amber? Was I being naïve, pursuing some hoary archival dish and its supposedly *national* narrative in the transcultural capital of a country whose grand official color-blindness was no longer able to whitewash its diversity?

And where, indeed, *was* pot-au-feu in surveys of *les plats préférés des Français?*

About a decade ago le couscous in fact topped the polls, provoking the usual chauvinist outcries and inevitable taunting headlines in Britain about "la France profonde choking on its soupe à l'oignon." (Britain, please note, savvily replaced roast beef with chicken tikka masala as its own edible symbol to show off its multiculturalism.) The latest French results looked more calming for nationalists, with couscous ranked eighth and magret de canard (but how's duck breast even a *dish*?) in first place. But still, these days France's best-loved malbouffe (junk food) was a gooey, steroidal love child of burrito and shawarma known as "French tacos."

THE ONLY PERSON in all of Paris, it seemed, truly enthusiastic about my pot-au-feu, besides the august Bénédict Beaugé, was Monsieur Larbi, the Moroccan butcher.

"*Donc, alors, pot-au-feu, Madame Anya?*" He was practically rubbing his hands in excitement when I came in with my mom, doggedly, to order the meats.

"Pot-au-feu, ooh-la-la, bravo!" approved Madame Fatima, a Berber regular buying two kilos of quivering sheep's brains.

Monsieur Larbi ran the most convivial of the halal boucheries on Avenue d'Italie. It was a throbbing cumin-scented community center crowded with men in cheap leather jackets, girls in torn jeans, matrons in headscarves, all gossiping about the vagaries of Parisian life in French, Berber, and Arabic. Portly and gray haired, M. Larbi radiated a gruff joie de vivre. He'd been an engineer back in Essaouira, but here in Paris, who'd give him a decent job? "Paris," he would lament, "where is its humanity? It's cold, classist, unaffordable." And naturally halal butchers were best. Because? "Because the French are too lazy to get up at dawn, and have lost any connection to animals."

And, he'd hint darkly, halal issues brought out the worst of French xenophobia.

"Madame Anya, soon they'll force us to eat *jambon*!" Monsieur Larbi would whisper.

But now he was all pot-au-feu. "*Gite, paleron, plat de côtes.*" He slapped the classic (and untranslatable) cuts of beef on the scale, then flourished two giant marrow bones and started sawing them in half.

"*Mais pardon, Monsieur Larbi*," I bleated. "*Pas de gites ou plat de côtes pour moi . . .*" Instead I asked for Carême's particular five pounds of tranche de boeuf (rump), a veal shank—and a half-roasted chicken.

M. Larbi looked surprised. Even mildly offended. His expertise, his participation in the civilizing mission of France, was being questioned. And by whom? By someone who mangled the phrase *au revoir*. "But, Madame Anya"—he shook his head gravely—"*ceci n'est pas un vrais pot-au-feu*. French cuisine, *il y a des règles*." There are rules.

A chicken in a pot-au-feu? *Jamais!* pronounced Madame Fatima. Never!

On my phone, I showed M. Larbi Carême's landmark recipe. He still looked unconvinced. My phone was passed around the store. Opinions were aired. Women in headscarves were giggling, rolling their eyes.

And suddenly I had an unsettling feeling of being the "other" in this shop full of immigrants, an uncivilized and unassimilated intruder, ignorant of France's rules. Yes, belonging, identity, they could be *liquid*, too, contingent and transactional. Here were people who had bashed France only five minutes before now defending its *patrimoine culinaire* as their own, at least for a moment.

"What a strange scene," said my mom as we headed home with the meats. "I can't imagine Mr. Nacho, our Colombian butcher in Jackson Heights, lecturing on any *American* dishes."

EVER ATTEMPTED A MONUMENT de la gastronomie française in a five-square-meter kitchen with no counter space as a sudden autumn heat wave kicks in, sending Parisians flocking to outdoor cafés for tequila cocktails and cooling Asian salads?

Oh, and I wasn't just intending a modest little pot-au-feu family supper. No, *mesdames et messieurs*: for my project, and in honor of my mother's presence, I'd decided on the whole grand shebang as a setting. The certified "gastronomic meal of the French."

What's that?

In 2010, when nation-branding with food was already lucrative business—as Peru, Thailand, Korea, Japan, and Mexico were all busily capitalizing on the soft power of their cuisines to promote tourism and exports—*le repas gastronomique des Français* was inscribed on the UNESCO Intangible Cultural Heritage (ICH) list after years of intense lobbying by the Mission Française du Patrimoine et des Cultures Alimentaires. It was the first time that the ICH list—established in the early aughts to "decolonize heritage" but quickly appropriated by various state players for their own image-building agendas—had recognized foodways, along with the usual stuff, such as Peru's Scissor Dance. ("Traditional Mexican Cuisine" got a nod, too, that year.)

The UNESCO description of France's repas gastronomique

begins with windy talk of "togetherness, the pleasure of taste . . . the setting of a beautiful table . . ." Then it hails that timeworn oh-so-French alimentary grammar: the "fixed structure, commencing with an apéritif . . . and ending with liqueurs, containing in between at least four successive courses, namely a starter, fish and/or meat with vegetables, cheese and dessert."

Voila, my dutiful plan.

The UNESCO honor was a big cultural deal, greeted by nationalistic headlines like "France Offers Its Gastronomy to Humanity" and "The World Is Envious of Our Meals." The global reaction, however, was summed up by another British (of course) newsprint jibe, to the effect that while French cuisine might have acquired UNESCO status, its "artery-clogging richness and prissy presentations went out of vogue, along with the old fashioned red-and-white tablecloth."

And yet here was an inveterate anti-Francophile, me, sitting down now at last, sweat wiped off, at our cramped kitchen table cleared for our "fixed structure" repast . . . experiencing, perhaps for the first time in my life, a pang of affection for France, for Paris. It was a beautiful museum piece of a meal. We started with apéros of Lillet with œufs mayonnaise and Rousseau-worthy ruby-red radishes with sunshine-yellow butter. Our appetizer proper was that French millennial Instagram darling, pâté en croûte—an architectural Caremian pastry case from the sleek food hall of Galeries Lafayette, housing a mosaic of pork *farce*, truffles, and foie gras. "Mmmm," approved my mom as we slathered globs of artery-clogging bone marrow on an award-winning baguette from our local Tunisian baker. Carême's amber pot-au-feu broth followed, in dainty porcelain cups, succeeded by M. Larbi's excellent halal boeuf, chicken, and veal, all overcooked by me but not tragically—and concluding with oozy Camembert (France's "national myth," as one anthropologist called it) and glossy darkly chocolaty éclairs decorated with gold leaf.

"Remember . . . in Moscow?" Mom panted softly, as she and I sat in the bibelot clutter of the living room, while Barry cursed from the kitchen at the mountain of dirty dishes.

Yes, I remembered . . . I remembered it well . . .

BACK IN SOVIET MOSCOW, Paris had featured intensively in my mother's dreamlife. It was a mythical Elsewhere beyond the implacable Iron Curtain, a neverland desperately dear to her from Flaubert and Zola and her precious Proust, but so unattainable it could have been Mars. She was a yearning, romantic Francophile stuck in our ghastly Moscow communal apartment reeking of alcohol and stale cabbage. When Mom made her own thin cabbage soup, she'd call it pot-au-feu, announcing that she'd read about it in Balzac's *Cousin Pons*. She hadn't a clue what a "bon pot-au-feu" tasted like, but the name was aromatic with her yearning.

"Remember in Moscow?" she repeated. "Eating my make-believe pot-au-feu? Dreaming of Paris?"

IN RETROSPECT, maybe I'd never forgiven Paris for the trauma of our first visit.

A couple of years into our American refugee life in Philadelphia, we finally got our "stateless" white vinyl passports. Mom was cleaning houses for $15 a day, but somehow she saved up for a trip to the city that had so thoroughly enthralled her from afar.

And Paris?

Paris greeted us with profound, crushing indifference: a stern unwelcoming finger-wagging abstraction of European civilization with its stony oppressive Haussmannism, its undreamy reality. The rain came down nonstop.

Mealtimes were the dreariest. We craned from outside the windows of Bofinger for glimpses of towering seafood plateaus we could never afford. We stared, from an intimidated distance, at the sidewalk savoir vivre at overpriced Flore. Our own dining in this kingdom of gastronomy mostly consisted of discounted Camembert shrill with ammonia, stale saucissons, and even staler moussaka from Latin Quarter Greek *menus touristiques*. My poor mom, besotted with her literary narratives of Paris. She did splurge on half a dozen Balzacian oysters, slimy revolting things to my thirteen-year-old palate—although not as traumatic as the rare tournedos with sauce béarnaise at a shabby bistro in honor of her beloved *Moveable Feast* of Hemingway. The garçon removed the uneaten boeuf with a *look*. In Philadelphia we'd been homesick, alienated, and destitute; but never humiliated. Paris could accomplish the latter with one imperious raise of an eyebrow. I still remember myself, a sulky émigré teen in polyester hand-me-down clothes, face glued to the chichi Samaritan window displays. How I wanted to twist the pert Parisian noses of mannequins modeling their ooh-la-la scarves—unaware at the time how the shaming of wide-eyed provincials was an enduring Parisian trope, part of the *national* narrative.

THERE IS SOMETHING called "Paris syndrome," so I'd learned on this visit from the young Japanese owner of a chic tiny coffee spot in the Marais. This affliction, *pari shōkōgun*, was the extreme shock suffered by dreamy Japanese visitors at the reality of Paris versus the myth. What traumatized *them* was that instead of Chanel-clad couples toting Louis Vuitton bags along cobblestone streets en route to romantic bistros, they encountered a scruffy globalized metropolis full of junk food and street trash and ugly scenes in the metro. My own feelings, however, were exactly the opposite—a reverse Paris syndrome. Gradually, day by day, my monthlong encounter with this *real* Paris liberated me from its tyrannical *narrative*, from my own projections and fears about the oppressive weight of its culture, its gastronomic ponderousness. And now with my pot-au-feu project behind me, I could feel something like happiness here *enfin*.

Mom was to depart the following afternoon for New York. Barry and I were headed on to Naples, then to Tokyo, Seville, Oaxaca, and Istanbul to probe their national food narratives. The task had seemed to me straightforward at first, but already appeared more complex and elusive—entangled with the paradoxes and fictions of history, and hinting at the surprising Möbius strip realities of globalization. For our last night in the City of Light, we raided the fridge with its *In Jackson Heights* poster for remnants of our "meal of the French." All that remained of our once-vast pot-au-feu was a quart of bouillon. For inspiration I scoured our hosts' packed cupboards. There, among jars of Fortnum & Mason piccalilli, Chinese chili pastes, and Moroccan harissa sat a plastic tub of instant Vietnamese pho cubes. I dropped a few in Carême's simmering amber bouillon, garnished our bowls with lime and cilantro, and we ate this improvised "pot-au-pho," our ersatz homage to French cuisine's postnational narrative, around our cramped kitchen table.

# NAPLES
## Pizza, Pasta, Pomodoro

❯❯❯ ❮❮❮

Within twenty-four hours of arriving in Naples later that year I'd made my very first pizza napoletana. It was the iconic pizza Margherita, of course—ablaze with the patriotic tricolore of the Italian flag and strictly codified: red San Marzano tomatoes, white mozzarella di bufala, buoyant green basil. According to legend, it was named to honor the blond queen of unified Italy from the Piedmontese House of Savoy, who so enjoyed it on a visit here to the South in 1889 that as a royal populist gesture she allowed it to be called after her.

I didn't come to Naples, though, to join the thin ranks of female pizzaiole. I came to this former capital of kingdoms—where Greeks, Romans, Arabs, Normans, Spanish, and French had ruled before the unification of Italy that was completed in 1871—to sound myths of *italianità* and, more specifically, *napoletanità*. To better understand pizza and pasta al pomodoro, the uncontested twin staples of the Neapolitan poor, which through migration spread "Italian" food culture worldwide—then became so relentlessly globalized they seemingly lost all connection to the teeming, histrionic city that spawned them.

Not that Neapolitans will ever let you forget the connection.

"The *croccante* [crisp] 'pizza' of Florence or Germany?"

Davide Bruno, my vigorous, athletic pizza instructor, was practically sneering. "The doughy focaccia that passes for pizza in New York? *Pathetic surrogates, all of them!*"

*Everything* was born out of Neapolitan pizza, insisted Davide—pronouncing "everything" (*tutto*) with an explosive force that suggested a cosmic Big Bang responsible for all life forms on the planet. And the father of Neapolitan pizza? "The Neapolitan genius of hunger." An early note of Naples's perpetual aria of self-mythology I'd be hearing a lot of.

At the time, Davide ran the Pizza Academy of La Notizia, a pizzeria owned by my friend Enzo Coccia, the greatest pizzaiolo of Naples. My debut Margherita was the culmination of a sweaty morning session with Davide and a gangly, blond fellow-student, Mo (short for Moritz), who had a pizza equipment business in Hamburg. Mo and I had spent the morning dutifully squeezing apple-sized balls called panetti from a big blob of slowly fermented dough, and then learning how to deftly use our fingertips to flatten the panetti. Then we struggled hopelessly to execute the virtuoso sideways flip for achieving perfectly round discs. In between bad-mouthing non-Neapolitan pizzas and Mo for tearing his dough, Davide expounded on the thermodynamics of the special domed Neapolitan oven. This 850°F inferno, resembling to me a fantastically white ash-covered grotto, is fueled by two woods: fast-burning beech teamed with slow-burning oak. The combo produces the three modes of heat—convection, conduction, irradiation—needed to bake the pizza in just ninety seconds.

My Margherita emerged from the glowing bowels of the oven slightly misshapen, its tomato sauce applied in nervous amateur splashes rather than suave circular sweeps. Trying to waggle it off the pizza paddle, I managed to slump it into the ash, so that now dark flecks disturbed the patriotic red, white, and green. Still. My first bite brought me somewhere close to elation. My Margherita tasted, well, it tasted like a true pizza napoletana, a terse modest essay in smoke, air, and acidity ringed by a textbook-perfect corni-cione, that crucial inch of raised border that rises up in a flash when you flatten the dough disc—somehow—just right.

"*Molta emozione, eh, la prima pizza?*" declared Davide. "*Un po' bruttina, ma tua.*" A little ugly, but yours. He took a cautious bite.

"*Almost* edible."

I planted a kiss on his sweat-seasoned cheek.

BARRY AND I HAD arrived in Naples the previous late afternoon, in classic Neapolitan style. Our airport taxi driver didn't grumble at our mountain of luggage. But he seemed agitated by where we wished to go: the sixteenth-century warren of lanes known as the Spanish Quarter. After much rocketing along, we got bogged down in a vast clog of construction near the port. Then suddenly we wrenched up into a maze of shadowy, tilted vicoli—the Quartieri Spagnoli. Turn followed absurdly tight turn; our driver grew more agitated, more bitterly operatic. Also, ominously, his meter was running, despite the list of set fares angled against the back of his seat. Up and up we wrenched, doubled back, doubled back again. Abruptly, we slammed to a halt.

We were at a small scrappy piazzetta out of a neorealist film. Blotched and peeling six-story buildings loomed overhead in the frazzled end-of-afternoon light; laundry sagged from humid balconies. Motorini wriggled up, buzzing and beeping like angry wasps, shot away. A group of mostly shaved-headed, heavily tattooed guys were milling around a betting shop; a soccer match was screening beside an enormous rampant visage of Diego Maradona, Naples's saint-devil of *calcio*. Two pit bulls roamed under him, unleashed. We took all this in chaotically while the cabbie unloaded our bags onto the grimy lava cobblestones. He announced the fare: double the listed price. Outraged, I protested in my standard Italian. Gesturing vehemently with clasped hands he counterprotested, crying *Molto bagaglio!* in an emotion-thickened Neapolitan accent. *Cheating!* I shouted back.

A crowd gathered at our time-honored spectacle: the Fleecing of the Tourist. A scooter with a burly woman, two kids, and a bulldog stopped to watch. Finally Barry yanked out his wallet and shoved some bills at the driver. Who took the money, gave a last outburst of hands and protests, slammed his taxi door, and drove off.

We'd arrived in Naples.

Our rental lay on the other side of the piazzetta. Top floor, no elevator. "The dwelling houses of Naples," Mark Twain exclaimed in 1869, craning his neck, "are the eighth wonder of the world . . . a good majority of them are a hundred feet high!" (Twain also complained of overcharging.) A pale imperious professoressa of Shakespeare awaited us, and our bagaglio, up at her vast apartment. She gave us a quick, preoccupied tour, handed over the keys, bade us arrivederci, and left.

We stood on her sprawling rooftop terrazza. Straight ahead in the distance a slope of Vesuvius rose like a shoulder of a stone Godzilla. Behind us, the landmark bulk of the Carthusian monastery complex of San Martino towered into the arching pink grapefruit sky. We'd arrived in Naples indeed.

The kitchen was barren save for a tightly sealed glass jar of blood-red tomatoes in an otherwise empty fridge, and three opened packs of spaghetti in a drawer. Too tired to go foraging in the piazzetta, I decided to improvise a spaghetti al pomodoro. It would be a salute to our first Neapolitan evening, *and* the start, plunging straight in, to the progressive monthlong "meal" I'd promised myself would consist of nothing but pizza and pasta—an epic carb-on-carb research overload. Quick-reduced in the last inch of the professoressa's nice olive oil, my pomodoro had an unexpected, almost urgent intensity, unadulterated by the missing garlic, basil, and cheese. Was it because the tomatoes were megaheirlooms, picked at the height of a Campanian summer and put up by the professoressa's wrinkled old nonna? Or were we just famished? I thought of those iconic nineteenth-century tourist images of the ravenous Neapolitan poor gulping spaghetti by hand. And how it was here in Naples where Italy's first pasta-tomato-sauce recipe—"vermicelli con le pommadore"—appeared in print in 1839 in a cookbook written in Neapolitan dialect by a gentleman called Ippolito Cavalcanti, Duke of Buonvicino.

Does food taste different when we imagine it embodies a genius loci—a spirit of place?

We pondered this at a rickety low table on the terrazza with some of the professoressa's sticky-sweet limoncello, which Barry had savagely chilled. From the piazzetta below, the preening schmaltz of a neomelodico song—the music of today's Neapolitan mean streets—was chorused by sudden angry barking, shouts, the harsh beeps and buzzing of mopeds. A bottle smashed loudly against a graffitied wall. And under the early stars, the slope of Vesuvius was a lingering cement-gray rosy-brown, an ancient, exhausted volup-tuousness, a monumental chunk of faded fresco.

This was Naples, a città doppia, the eternal duality of its splen-dor and urban squalor.

It was the mid-eighteenth-century discovery of Herculaneum's and Pompeii's ruins that fixed Naples and its beautiful and dreadful volcano as a highlight on the Grand Tour, launching a tradition of relentlessly stereotyping the city, by both outsiders and locals. And most every traveler since has remarked on the duality we were now experiencing. True, Goethe called Naples "a paradise." But opinion more inclined to the view long attributed (falsely) to Mary Shelley: "Naples is a paradise inhabited by devils." We went to bed and read some of Norman Lewis's *Naples '44*, his comic-appalling account of the bombed-out starving city right after liberation in World War II. Lewis was headquartered as a British intelligence officer a short walk from our Quartieri Spagnoli, in a palazzo down by the sea-front of Chiaia. He witnessed Vesuvius's latest eruption, in 1944. It was, he wrote, "the most majestic and terrible sight I have ever seen, or ever expect to see."

PIZZARIA LA NOTIZIA 53, the site of my Margherita debut, sits on a residential street in the Vomero district, part of the airy bourgeois Upper City. My taxi took me on a looping ascent along sweeping bay vistas that sent Grand Tourists into tizzies. On the horizon floated Ischia and Capri.

Enzo Coccia, La Notizia's fiftyish owner, was running late when I got there. Preservationist/ur-traditional baker, philosopher, author of a densely scientific treatise on pizza, Enzo has three very distinct pizzerias along this street. He also stars in documentaries on pizza, propounds on pizza to visiting dignitaries, jets around the world consulting on pizza. His regulars include the president of the Napoli soccer club and the city's top intellectuals. Il Pizzaiolo Illuminato—the Enlightened One—he's called.

Il Illuminato finally rushed in, a trim, ebullient figure with chic rimless glasses and a tomato-red pizzaiolo kerchief above a T-shirt emblazoned with the name "Ancel Keys," the American physiologist who coined the term "Mediterranean diet" in the 1950s.

"The status of a Neapolitan pizzaiolo," exclaimed the Enlightened One, kissing me ciao, "has changed! We were the lowest, dirtiest of artisans—brutal work, zero respect, *poco* money. And now?" He gave a derisive laugh. "Now these teenage pizzaioli, these shameless Instagrammers who barely know the tomato varieties—*they hire publicists!*"

"But Enzo," I pointed out, "*you* have a fancy Milan PR firm."

"I earned it!" quipped the Illuminato, showing me the scars on his hand—multiple carpal tunnel surgeries.

When I first ate pizza in Naples back in the late 1980s, pizzaioli were anti-Illuminati in wifebeaters and clunky gold chains. They dressed their pies to match, with unpedigreed canned tomatoes and cheap cow's milk fior di latte cheese, not today's fancy mozzarella di bufala. Achieving an authentic pizza apotheosis back then was pretty straightforward. Claim a worn marble table at an old-school dive, say Da Michele or Di Matteo, in the then-dangerous Spaccanapoli quarter. Order up a rigidly minimalist pie blistered and charred by the 800°F oven—so shockingly different from the doughy-gooey slices celebrated in New York's Little Italy. Over a chipped glass of bad wine, hearken to the pizzaiolo invoking *passione* and *sacrificio* and the holy pizza commandments outlined by the Associazione Verace Pizza Napoletana, an organization founded in 1984 to protect pizza's unique Neapolitanness at a time when safeguarding "cultural heritage" became a serious preoccupation in Europe, in response to globalization.

A *vera* (true) pizza napoletana, one learned, had to be the size of a plate, with slow-leavened dough kneaded and stretched out *by hand* (never rolled) before its brief stint on the floor of the forno. Puffy in spots with a blistered one-inch cornicione, la vera pizza was to be topped with no more than a smear of red marinara sauce and perhaps some mozzarella and basil for Margherita—*e basta*. "Fancy" pizza topping? *Contaminazione*.

"We scribbled down those Associazione commandments *by hand*, too!" Enzo was grinning merrily now. "In our first real attempt to codify what had been for centuries solely an oral Neapolitan tradition."

Until pizza went global post-WWII, the adjective *Neapolitan* wasn't added just for chauvinism or protectionism. In the Italian culinary lexicon, pizza simply means something crushed flat. From the Renaissance to the late 1800s, printed pizza recipes often involved sugar and almonds. What's more, as a *form*, Enzo noted, pizza is archaic, ur-universal—a flatbread related to Indian naan, Mexican tortilla, Arabic pita. "A form," I put in, "that followed function? A pre-utensil edible plate, perhaps, akin to the ancient Roman mensae and the medieval bread-plate called a trencher?" We both agreed that the ongoing debate over pizza's etymology— pinsere? picea? bizzo? pitta?—suggests its universality.

"So then, Enzo: What exactly made it *Neapolitan*?"

"Local *condimenti* [toppings]," he answered. More crucially still: the special Neapolitan forno—"the same kind of domed ovens found in Pompeii!" And baking techniques passed down through the generations since the mid-1700s.

A third-generation pizzaiolo himself, Enzo grew up in the harsh 1960s in a poor Lower City quarter near Naples's Stazione Centrale, where his family owned a trattoria cum pizzeria. When he was little his mother took him into the trattoria kitchen, to keep him off the dangerous streets; he watched his nonna, Fortuna, prepare fried baccalà, pasta e fagioli, pasta e patate, pasta lardiata with big hunks of lardo, and pasta al pomodoro—the Neapolitan cucina povera canon. Pizza? Those days pizza was more of a Saturday thing. Then in 1973 an outbreak of cholera—the shock return of one of the city's dreaded menaces—shut down many restaurants. New health regulations made serving fresh food such an ordeal, Enzo's father decided to keep just the pizzeria. There Enzo learned the craft.

At the cholera mention I shuddered. Nineteen seventy-three was the year that my mother and I were stranded by a cholera quarantine in Odesa, another cacophonous port city. The grimy specter of the disease had haunted me ever since.

When Enzo opened the first La Notizia in the Vomero in 1994, it showed how much the Italian foodscape was changing.

"But Italy's not France, eh?" he chuckled. "Forget lowly pizzaioli or pomodoro producers, in the past not even *chefs* got any respect!" But the 1980s boom economy gave birth to figures, Northern mostly, like Gualtiero Marchesi, the Michelin-starred chef who turned elegant minimalism into an all-Italian haute cuisine idiom.

The 1990s brought Slow Food, born likewise in the North, with its lofty mission to transform epicures into "ecological gastronomes," in the words of Carlo Petrini, the movement's founder. Artisanal foodstuffs achieved the status of, say, designer handbags, as Italy's gastronomic nostalgia marketing machine revved into high gear. Inspired by these developments, Enzo began to think of pizza as a canvas: for Alba truffles, for instance, or handcrafted Campanian cheeses. He created pizza still lifes with favas, asparagus, pungent pecorino from herb-fed Laticauda sheep.

In 2010 La Notizia became the first pizzeria—ever—to be cited in a Michelin guide. Meanwhile, following the 2008 financial crisis, Italy's sagging economy turned pizza all over the country from a Saturday thing to a *pasto completo*, a complete meal often eaten three times a week and now loaded with pedigreed toppings—but still costing under ten euros.

Which is how, Enzo cried gleefully, at the changes rung upon changes, "pizza has gone from being a dirty street whore to *la principessa glamour.*"

My first meal at La Notizia, shortly after it opened, changed how I thought about pizza. Twenty years later now, Enzo was ordering me a simple anchovy *"pizza mignon—per esaltare l'olio"* (a little pie—to exalt some esoteric olive oil). And once again I was mesmerized by that crust—that precise mathematical calibration of a mere trace of yeast, a ten- to fourteen-hour fermentation at room temperature (no fridges in the 1730s, when pizza was born, Enzo insisted), and extra-loose dough. The pie practically levitated onto the table, blistered to perfection and honeycombed with tiny air bubbles—as essential to pizza greatness as marbling is to Kobe beef. Eating it was an experience totally primal—bread and live fire. And yet completely aestheticized, I told Enzo.

"*Esatto!*" He nodded—exactly. But here was the thing: No matter how flashy the PR agent, a pizzaiolo would always remain an *artigiano*, an artisan. Never a maestro. A chef can *create* a dish wholesale. A pizzaiolo? *Boh.* "Okay, maybe he can vary the toppings," allowed Il Illuminato, "but pizza will always be pizza. Anchored by the impasto, the crust, which is a two-hundred-year-old craft . . . *and* a tradition." He sounded like a high priest of an ancient flame. "*And* a precise science," he added. "*And* a great Neapolitan patrimony. And *yet*"—his tone now a ranging philosopher's—"pizza evolves, eh? As a dialectic between *tradizione* (crust) and *evoluzione* (toppings) . . . within a single bite!"

Riding back down to the Quartieri Spagnoli, I recalled an aphorism of Enzo's friend Marino Niola, a local anthropologist and cultural critic who'd become my oracle of Neapolitanness. He'd put it more colloquially:

*The crust is the hardware, the topping is the software.*

IN THE MID-SIXTEENTH CENTURY, the harsh, construction-mad Spanish viceroy of Naples, Don Pedro de Toledo, decided to build quarters for his occupying troops in the area where we were now spending a month. So was born the Quartieri Spagnoli, the checkerboard of slanting lanes, alleys, and stairs footing the Vomero's heights, just west of Via Toledo, the pedestrianized and relentlessly globalized tourist thoroughfare of today. The Quartieri's original barracks were a story high. As Naples's population expanded, the buildings quickly towered upward; the vicoli became sunless swarming ravines where the teeming poor overcrowded into ground-floor windowless hovels called bassi, while the better-off occupied higher floors. This vertical mixing of the city's classes continues to today. It's something Neapolitans readily speak of with pride.

The Quartieri's density came into sharper focus on a stroll around our piazzetta the second evening. A small car wash was somehow wedged in between our building entry and the staircase into the church whose gray tower rose right over our terrazza. Just beyond, a short narrow passageway to a neighboring vicolo was commandeered as a parking space for various motorini—alongside a wall creche containing a religious family memorial, alongside laundry racks, alongside chairs and tables where residents of the bassi took the air and ate *their* pasta al pomodoro, alongside another table selling eggs.

We edged into the next lane. It was crammed with small shops— salumerie, alimentari, a pet shop with stuffed mini pit bulls and live rabbits, and two butchers. A tiny cubbyhole sold wine on tap—*vino sfuso*. It was also, to Barry's delight, a packed shrine to the Napoli soccer club and Maradona. "We're from New York; my boyfriend writes about soccer," I informed the gruff wine seller, who was stout, shaved-headed, and tattooed, and typically pale as a clam from lack of sunlight. "Tell him to write about *that*," he merely growled back, pointing without humor at a photoshopped poster of "Saint Diego" having his shoes shined by Lionel Messi. Across the lane—*Christ, mind the motorini!*—stood a little salumeria, whose proprietor, although not tattooed, was equally dour. Such was the Quartieri's masculine style. Later we learned from a resident sociologist that while the Camorra had been gone from the neighborhood for almost a decade, its codes of behavior— "aggressive machismo, reckless scooters, scary dogs, a particular use of Neapolitan slang"—linger as the Quartieri's "cultural capital." The same sociologist said that the Quartieri's population density—an astounding 23,000 per square kilometer—ranks just below Mumbai's.

DUTIFULLY RESEARCHING the four-euro pizzas in our vicinity, I found them mostly of the pre-Enzo variety: cheap canned tomatoes, seed oil, spongy-soft non-bufala cheese. But *always* with a deliciously fragrant "hardware"—a textbook impasto.

Still, it was a treat to be back at La Notizia 53 a few days later, to savor Enzo's rarefied Margherita with yellow pomodorini that practically burst with their concentrated Vesuvius origins. Even more of a treat was to share this yellow Vesuviusness with Antonio Mattozzi, author of *Inventing the Pizzeria*—the *only* book, according to Enzo, that didn't repeat "the same *bugie*, lies, about pizza!" An English translation had been published a few years before by a "*molto importante*" scholar at Harvard.

In his mideighties, slight and spry, the pink-cheeked Antonio suggested a trim, keen-eyed Maestro Geppetto. Towering beside him was Donatella, his lanky middle-aged daughter, a researcher of the Italian ottocento, the 1800s. Father and daughter made quite a twosome, she with her slightly wild cascade of dark curls and an excitable manner that often led her to interrupt her soft-spoken white-haired papa just when he was about to say something fascinating. For instance, how he researched his book in police archives— a notorious fire hazard, pizzerias had to be registered with the polizia—getting forever distracted by nineteenth-century knife fights, streetwalkers, crimes of passion, and larceny. "The research took four years," he confessed sheepishly.

The Mattozzis are Naples's most illustrious pizza dynasty—since the mid-1800s there have been twenty Mattozzi pizzaioli—and initially Antonio set out to write a family history. But as he combed the state archives, his project grew more ambitious: to cut through the sentimental froth of urban legend surrounding Neapolitan pizza, the "fictitious oral history often promulgated by the myth-spinning modern pizzaioli themselves, then repeated even in scholarly volumes," as he writes in his book. Sifting through decades of licenses, census statistics, and police records—"those nineteenth-century webcams"—Antonio, a rationalist in a city of bubble blowers, was able to construct a clear-eyed social history, not just of the pizzaiolo trade but of late-eighteenth- and nineteenth-century Naples itself.

"*La storia della pizza è la storia della città*," he began to expound . . .

Whereupon Donatella cut in to declare that the foreigners' accounts about Naples were more reliable than those of most Italians. In the 1840s, for instance, Alexandre Dumas père had the insight to call pizza "the gastronomic thermometer of the market." But Northern Italian visitors? She grimaced. "With their anti-South prejudice, Northerners showed no respect for Naples as the grand seat of the Kingdom of the Two Sicilies—a kingdom reduced by Unification to a mere provincia, stripped of its status and dignity. No, Northerners did nothing but denigrate our pizza!"

Donatella clearly was no fan of the Risorgimento, a sentiment long shared by many Neapolitans.

The most spectacularly disparaging pizza diss came from a famed Florentine, Carlo Collodi, Pinocchio's creator. "Do you want to know what pizza is?" he asked young readers in *Il Viaggio per l'Italia di Giannettino*, a late-nineteenth-century travel anthology for primary schools. "The blackened aspect of the toasted crust, the whitish sheen of garlic and anchovy, the greenish-yellow tint of the oil . . . and those red bits of tomato here and there give pizza the appearance of complicated filth that matches the dirt of the vendor."

"*Imagine that*," snorted Donatella, cutting a perfect triangle of Enzo's elegantly clean Margherita.

More important to the Mattozzis was a description of pizza by a renowned local writer, Matilde Serao, author of novels admired by Henry James and of a Zolaesque 1884 epic of reportage called *Il Ventre di Napoli*, The Bowels of Naples. Antonio liked quoting her at length. Cofounder of Naples's flagship newspaper, *Il Mattino*, Serao was fiercely proud of her city. But after first informing general readers that pizza was "a squashed round disc of dense dough"—because even in 1884, noted Antonio, the dish was still not widely understood outside Naples—Serao went on about how pizza "burned but did not cook"; how the pizzaiolo would bake his pies at night, cut them into slices worth a penny each, and give them to a boy to sell on a street corner.

"*The boy will stay there almost all day, while his pizza slices freeze in the cold, or turn yellow in the sun while the flies squat on them*," Antonio recited from memory.

I glanced down at the yellow pomodorini now congealing atop my pizza and felt slightly queasy. "Why such a turnoff?" I gulped.

"Squalor, urban density . . . *cholera*," the Mattozzis chimed in unison, "*that* was the vision of nineteenth-century Naples!"

Serao was in fact a crusader, desperate to bring attention to the appalling hygiene and overcrowding of Neapolitan Lower City slums—the fertile soil for the horrific cholera epidemic of 1884, which Serao so fervently chronicled. (And almost a century later, another outbreak of the dread disease would turn Enzo's family business, as I'd learned, into a full-time pizzeria.)

Antonio leaned forward. To truly understand pizza's origins, he insisted softly, one needed to appreciate this overwhelming fact: Nineteenth-century Naples was by far Italy's largest city, the third largest in Europe—with a population density *ten* times that of Victorian London. Almost half a million people, most of them destitute, were crammed into a mere eight square kilometers hemmed in by the bay, the backing hills, and Vesuvius. "A juxtaposition of stunning beauty and equally amazing decay and backwardness so extreme," Antonio wrote in his book, "as to be almost deliberately contrived!" High prices for even the most squalid Lower City real estate forced thousands to live on the streets; these were the legendary Neapolitan lazzaroni (after Saint Lazarus, the patron saint of lepers), the ragged, picturesque homeless who so fascinated Dumas and Goethe. Even those lucky enough to overcrowd into bassi, the same windowless hovels that we kept peering into in our Quartieri Spagnoli, didn't have cooking facilities.

"And that's where pizza came in!" exclaimed Antonio. A salvation. A dirt-cheap, palatable street food, flies or no flies, costing only a soldo and providing fairly decent nutrition for breakfast, lunch, dinner, snacks. *Il pronto soccorso dello stomaco*, Serao called pizza—first aid for the stomach.

"It fascinated Dumas," chimed in Donatella, "how our lazzaroni subsisted only on pizza and cocomero [watermelon]."

The pizzaioli, too, were victims of Naples's real estate squeeze, forced by high rents to work day and night for a minuscule profit. In 1807, there were fifty-four pizzerias recorded in the archives, Antonio found. A century later, the number had barely doubled.

"*La nostra pizza!* A product of the unique character of Naples," proclaimed Antonio.

"Of our topography, our hardships, our hunger," declared Donatella.

How indelible was pizza's connection to Naples? So indelible that Serao famously described a Naples entrepreneur opening a pizzeria in Rome to cater to its large colony of homesick Neapolitans. After an early flurry, the pizzeria faded away, like "an exotic flower" torn from its Neapolitan habitat. In the 1930s, Milan, for example, had only nine pizzerias. And today?

Today, across Italy, said Antonio, there were some fifty thousand.

There in the sleek air-conditioned cheer of La Notizia on its Vomero heights, I pondered how a scorned dish—the nutritional first aid of this squalid, stunning city of palazzi and tenements—had become the most globalized food in the world. How celebrity pizzaioli like Enzo were rebranding it, reclaiming its Neapolitanness through rarefied foodstuffs that never went anywhere near a pizza before, foodstuffs still out of reach for most basso residents of our Quartieri.

Antonio was quietly smiling at me. "Perhaps you're thinking pizza is so delicious, its worldwide success was inevitable? But it succeeded *against* all the odds."

"Yeah, succeeded to become *cazzato*, fucked over!" hollered Enzo, appearing with a bottle of Gragnano, a fizzy Campanian red, from a tiny local producer. "So now we Neapolitans have to rescue it from falsehoods and bastardization!"

Antonio chuckled into his white mustache. He was no fan of terroir fundamentalism, of that age-old urban legend, for instance, that Neapolitan water (the non-cholera-carrying version) was somehow essential to pizza. "Maybe pizza ultimately succeeded," he suggested—"*because* it's so easily globalized," put in Donatella, "as an adaptable container." "Whether for Hawaiian pineapple or Korean kimchi," concluded Antonio as Enzo presented his famous dessert calzone that exploded with a lava of molten dark chocolate.

DOWN AT THE FOOT of Via Toledo, just along from the Palazzo Reale, the vast Baroque seat of the Bourbons, stands the glass-roofed shopping arcade called Galleria Umberto. The Mattozzis dropped us off there after dinner. Modeled after London's Crystal Palace, this grandiose belle epoque structure was a showpiece of the Risanamento, Naples's Haussmannesque project of clearing and rebuilding the Lower City that began in 1889 in response to 1884's cholera outbreak. Risanamento means "restoring health," but it carried an uglier force. "We must disembowel Naples!" declared Italy's King Umberto and his then prime minister. According to Frank Snowden in his *Naples in the Time of Cholera*, the city was the only one in Europe where a single disease spurred such vast urban transformations.

At the edge of our Quartieri Spagnoli—which the Risanamento in fact left intact—we passed by tourists having sludgy pizzas on tables outside Pizzeria Brandi. Brandi's original owner, one Raffaele Esposito, famously delivered three pizzas to Italy's Queen Margherita when she visited in 1889, including the iconic tricolore I attempted on my first Neapolitan morning. Margherita loved it, supposedly, and Esposito named it after the Piedmontese queen. We stopped and ducked in.

On the wall behind the bar hung a yellow document dated June 11, 1889. It was signed by the "head of Mouth Services of the Royal household," and stated that the three qualities of pizza prepared for the queen by the pizzaiolo Raffaele Esposito were found to be excellent.

"Completely autentico," assured the manager. "We had it carbonated."

We thanked him and continued into the Quartieri's narrow confines. The motorini were out in maniacal force, mostly pizza deliveries at this hour. Smoking and gesticulating families sat outside their basso doorways, still windowless and shockingly overcrowded inside, but now with flat-screen TVs, cooking facilities, and floral bedspreads on tomb-like queen beds. Many housed new migrants. The sharp smell of curry and fenugreek wafted out of their kitchens and mingled with Neapolitan scents of fried garlic and basil. At our piazzetta we quietly hissed at the pit bulls and climbed to our apartment.

Despite it being midnight, there was an email already waiting from Donatella—the first installment of a research barrage to come. It was an article by Zachary Nowak, the "molto importante" academic from Harvard who'd translated Antonio's book.

Painstakingly and forensically, Nowak's article examined the pizza Margherita legend and its interpretation.

The basic facts and background, orthodox version: In 1889, Italy's King Umberto (from the House of Savoy of Piedmont) comes to Naples for the official launch of the Risanamento. A stolid, unprepossessing figure, Umberto has nevertheless won popular acclaim for his heroically compassionate visit during 1884's cholera outbreak. But Italy's Unification of the 1860s and its annexation of Naples have proved a disaster. This grand former seat of the Bourbons has lost its status and power; its economy has collapsed. Risorgimento, the creation of an all-Italian patria, is seen here as a project hatched by Piedmont at the expense of the South. The greater purpose of the 1889 royal visit, then, is an attempt to build rapprochement and support for the national idea.

Enter Margherita, Umberto's blond queen, charismatic as he is not. Tired of French food, she makes a populist gesture of inviting the celebrated pizzaiolo Esposito to prepare a tasting of the humble fare of the popolino at the royal palace at Capodimonte. She favors the patriotic tricolore pie that Esposito had especially custom-made. After naming the creation in Her Majesty's honor, Esposito asks for a letter of royal blessing on his pizzeria. There it hangs in honor down at Pizzeria Brandi.

This was the pizza Margherita story repeated with slight variations in every book, every website—every scholarly work. The latter tended to describe it as a masterstroke of House of Savoy propaganda. For John Dickie, author of *Delizia!*, an astute study of Italian food, the queen's gesture of bestowing royal approval on the poorest dish of the poorest city in Italy was a late-nineteenth-century equivalent of Princess Diana embracing an AIDS patient. "With pizza," wrote Dickie with nods to Serao, "Margherita took her own journey into the bowels of Naples." As an invented tradition, argued an academic tomato historian, pizza Margherita offered the perfect political cocktail—the populism of the new Savoy monarchy at the expense of the vanquished Bourbons mixed with the triumph of popular cooking over French cuisine mixed with "the Italianizing of a Neapolitan dish in the shadow of the Risorgimento." Pizza Margherita's creation became "an important detail in the narrative of Italian nationalism," added pizza scholar Carol Helstosky.

It all sounded pretty convincing. Until I read Nowak.

Other than the Pizzeria Brandi letter—which nowhere cites

"pizza Margherita" or its ingredients—Nowak found no documentation of a royal pie tasting in Capodimonte. Italy's state press agency of the time, which would have been raring to spread any morsel of unity propaganda, made no mention of either pizza sampling or naming. Esposito, for that matter, wasn't a "celebrated" pizzaiolo of the day. Plus his "custom-made" tricolore pie was already well-known in Naples. Not to mention Queen Margherita's famous obsession with hygiene. What were the chances, really, of her sampling the dish of the poor in a city associated with cholera and still suffering conditions of catastrophic unhealthiness?

And that yellowed testimonial on display at Pizzeria Brandi? A fake, Nowak concluded, after scrutinizing the "royal" seal and the handwriting. (The carbon-dating boast, I realized, would apply to a document's age, not authorship.) The first reference to the letter had appeared only in a 1930s newspaper article decades later. Most likely, Nowak judged, it was a marketing ploy by the pizzeria's then owners during Depression-era hard times.

So there it was. The legend of pizza Margherita wasn't just folklore, it was "fakelore," as Nowak put it. A fakelore that suited the dovetailing agendas of Northern Italy's promotion of unity, Naples's tattered pride—and Brandi's business.

The next morning, bleary-eyed, I called Donatella for comment.

"*Troppo complicato*," she commented.

For one thing, the royal visitors of 1889 weren't in fact "outsiders." Following their wedding in 1868, Umberto and Margherita *lived* in Naples for almost two years where their son, subsequent king Victor Emmanuel III, was born. Later Margherita would habitually visit the city in June. What's more, during her Neapolitan years, she savvily scored populist points by touring across Italy and honoring regional customs. All of which led credence to Donatella's own revisionist tweak of Nowak's fakelore revisionism: to wit, that Margherita at *some* point before 1889 definitely tasted the pizza that ultimately bore her name. Donatella in fact had the proof—"supersecret for now." But the Brandi/Esposito part was surely fake. And she agreed, the moniker "pizza Margherita" only first appeared in print in the 1930s—and only truly entered popular usage in 1989, when Brandi celebrated the (fakelore) "royal tasting" centenary just as the global popularity of pizza napoletana was about to explode.

And there was another bit of fakelore that greatly irked Donatella. It was the Associazione Verace Pizza Napoletana's commandment that marinara and Margherita were the only autentico, permissible pizza toppings. "*Pura invenzione!*" she huffed. Even Dumas had described pizza with strutto (lard), with pesciolino (small fish), with olive oil and oregano.

"Authenticity" . . . such a monster marketing tool, I reflected, as Donatella went on filling my telefonino with all the lies told about Neapolitan pizza. So was that it, then? Anxious to protect its edible artifact in the face of globalization, had Naples cooked up a phony foundational myth to historicize and canonize—commodify—a dish that until very recently was considered too base to even be included in any visual representations of the city? And wasn't it pura invenzione as well, I thought after Donatella rang off, our tourist poster vision of a blessed preindustrial Italy (of Campania, of Naples) steeped in some authentic mythical past where singing contadini plucked explosively delicious tomatoes from the organic soil and the urban poor delighted in hearty cucina povera pizzas and pastas while belting out "O Sole Mio"?

But then again . . . Urban legends and myths thrive off a purpose. They create imagined communities and perpetuate invented traditions. According to Nowak the sheer vitality of the Margherita story deserves its own sociological study.

But I was getting lost now in all the complications and layers. For instance, what did pizza Margherita's being exposed as fakelore mean for those academic narratives about the pie's "Italianization" in the service of the Risorgimento? Since pizza of *any* kind really didn't enter the national food canon until the mid-twentieth century?

MY HEAD SPINNING from Margherita *complicazioni*, I turned to the other reason for my visit to Naples. Pasta. Not the flimsy eggy Northern Italian pasta fresca, of course, but the protein-rich hard durum wheat pastasciutta, dried pasta—the economic engine of long-distance trade, the backbone of the modern Italian diet.

And for many years, a notorious Neapolitan street spectacle for Grand Tourists hungry for scenes of picturesque poverty. Braving one of the cheesy souvenir shops along Via Toledo, I perused some old nineteenth-century postcards and lithographs of local *mangiamaccheroni* (pasta eaters) in action. Here were the folklorically corpulent *maccaronari* (macaroni sellers; maccheroni being the old generic term for all pasta) presiding over their outdoor copper cauldrons of boiling water and mountains of grated *cacio* (cheese). Tourists' coins tossed, the ravenous indigent, the *lazzaroni* (beggars)

and tattered *scugnizzi* (urchins), had grabbed fistfuls of boiling, slithery spaghetti and were captured in the act of consuming
these in one single, uninterrupted, astounding gulp—eyes raised
heavenward.

Neapolitans were not Italy's original mangiamaccheroni, however; the Sicilians were. A twelfth-century Arab geographer, Mu-
hammad al-Idrisi, was first to report that people near Palermo were
making strings of dough called *itriyya*—from the Arabic? Greek?
Hebrew?—which they traded "by the shipload" to Calabria and
"other Christian lands." The Neapolitans? They were called *man-
giafoglie* (leaf eaters), or, more quaintly, *cacafoglie* (leaf shitters),
for their massive intake of dark leafy greens—a forerunner of the
Brooklyn dream diet. Pasta had been manufactured in Naples since
1295, but it was in no way a dominant food group. A pain to produce and a lot more expensive than bread, it was prepared by the
wealthy in fatty capon broth, *way* overcooked, and often served as
dessert with sugar or honey or cinnamon.

Yet by the mid-seventeenth century, dried pasta consumption in
Naples had exploded. Maccheroni had become a foodstuff of the
popolo. From here, it eventually spread northward.

This dietary transformation was brought to light and explored
in an influential essay, "Neapolitans from Leaf-Eaters to Macaroni-
Eaters," written in the 1950s by Emilio Sereni, a Jewish-Italian
communist, politician, and grand scholar of Italian agriculture.
Searching for causes, Sereni scrutinized the nutrition of the Neapolitan urban poor between the sixteenth and eighteenth centuries.
And what conditions drove the great foglie-to-pasta paradigm
shift—the momentous alteration of the "Italian alimentary grammar," per Massimo Montanari, a present-day Italian food scholar—
that was first ignited here in Naples?

As with pizza, the answer was again glaring at me as I read Sereni's analysis: *urban density.*

With the two-century-long Spanish rule commencing in 1503, the population of Naples skyrocketed—from 50,000 to four times that by century's end. Attracted by cheap bread and low taxes, the rural poor continued flooding in; by the mid-seventeenth century the population had doubled yet again. But the Spanish viceroyalty did a terrible job provisioning its spectacularly overcrowded metropolis. Corruption and mismanagement were rampant. Meat prices soared. The chaotically expanding city limits swallowed the leaf-producing agricultural plots. Rather than importing the perishable foglie from elsewhere, Sereni explains, Naples turned instead to durable dried pastasciutta—which by the seventeenth century was being produced far more cheaply and easily thanks to new production technologies. For Sereni, ever the Marxist, this dietary paradigm shift represented an example of the Neapolitan popolo's genius for survival and adaptation. Another genius move: adding extra protein via a little cacio for a complete nutritional package.

By the eighteenth century, the dietary shift was complete. Naples had become the world's pasta capital, lifting the mangiamaccheroni nickname from Sicily. "The macaroni . . . can be bought everywhere and in all the shops for very little money," Goethe observed in 1787. Within another half a century, its popularity would spread beyond Italy, so that Dumas in 1834 would note how today "macaroni . . . is an European dish, which has traveled like civilization." But its epicenter was here, along the destitute vicoli of the Lower City.

"As soon as he has two cents," wrote Matilde Serao in *The Bowels of Naples* in 1884, "the Neapolitan pleb buys a dish of macaroni . . . The portions are small, and the buyer fights with the owner because he wants a little more sauce, a little more cheese, and a little more macaroni."

FOREVER GETTING LOST in the dim, clamorous mazes of our Quartieri Spagnoli, I couldn't shake the feeling of inhabiting still *that* Naples—the swarming, harsh urban hive that turned pizza and pasta into survival imperatives. Whereas Europe's other historical quarters have long been gentrified and sanitized, the Spanish Quarter felt like a holdover from Serao's pages. Unemployment was still shockingly high. Our sidewalkless alleys were still thick with iron-lunged vendors of cocomero and, nowadays, Kleenex. Our senses were still being swamped—by graphic tripe at butchers' stalls, wall-side vitrines of lethal one-euro fritters, never-ending cheap pizza deliveries now via speeding motorini instead of *stufe*, the portable ovens of yore. Even that ubiquitous Quartieri business, the sports betting shop: Wasn't it a modern spin-off of the "true intoxicant of Naples" (Serao's phrase), the locals' long-fatal obsession with playing the lottery? Meanwhile the nonstop cacophonous theater of domestic living in front of the bassi brought to mind Walter Benjamin's 1928 tag for Naples as a "porous" city, where not only inside and outside, public and private, were constantly blurred, but spectacle and spectator were, too. "Balconies, courtyards, windows, entrance ways, staircases, roofs," wrote Benjamin, "all become stages and box seats."

Naples: always performing itself, ever observing itself.

For her part, novelist Shirley Hazzard, a longtime, more graciously situated resident, thought it a city of secrets. And so it was for us: after two weeks, our Quartieri hadn't grown any less inscrutable—or more welcoming. There was the sweet little kid in a sky-blue Napoli team shirt in our piazzetta who, when Barry grinned and waggled his fingers "ciao," simply glared back. There was the barber at the jaunty miniature barbershop who advertised cuts for only nine euros, only to add an extra four euros for what Barry supposed was a complimentary splash of overaromatic *lozione* (hair dressing). It was the perfumy version of our taxi chisel.

Desperately, I tried to imitate the slurry Neapolitan accent to win over *negozianti* (shopkeepers) who kept staring at me with indifference and charging different prices each day for the same eggplant caponata. Sometimes the caponata was spoiled. Ditto the porchetta from the dour-faced salumaio.

In the sixteenth century, back before the Spanish barracks went up, mulberry orchards stood here—fodder for silkworms. The orchards provided shelter as well for carousing and lovemaking. "Going to the mulberries," ran the idiom. With the barracks' and troops' arrival, the roistering prospered across the centuries. The Quartieri became the center of Naples's sex trade—*case di piacere* (legal brothels, finally closed in 1958), streetwalking (still legal), and transvestism (now dominated by Brazilian pros). Little did I know that the sex trade would lead to my pasta lesson.

One afternoon, coming along Vico Lungo del Gelso (Mulberry Lane), we smiled at a pair of older signoras sipping espressos inside their basso. *Ciao! Entra!* the sturdier, matronly one beckoned to us—actually *smiling*. Inside, two long tables stood surrounded by a veritable crèche of Neapolitan bric-a-brac; on the stove a pair of vast aluminum pots bubbled away. "Our space is devoted to preserving *vascio*"—Neapolitan for basso—"culture," Nunzia, our matronly hostess, explained. "Here we cook cucina povera meals, talk about our Quartieri, sing Neapolitan songs."

"Back in the days of *gli spagnoli*, this was a casa di piacere!" announced her striking companion, an elderly personaggio with a deep cleavage, bleached hair pulled into a topknot, chipmunk cheeks, and surgically prominent lips.

"Tarantina," introduced Nunzia. "Our Quartieri's most famous trans!"

"*Femminiello*," Tarantina corrected, in a low, diva voice. "Homosexual, transgender . . . such base, *vulgar* words." But femminiello (Neapolitan for third gender), *bello. Bellissimo!*

Naples, a city of ambivalences and contradictions—of secrets—was by legend founded by the siren maiden Parthenope, half-human, half-bird. With their own double identity, femminielli have been not just tolerated, but much romanticized—mythologized—here, thought to have access to special secrets and mysteries. It's why they draw the numbers for the lottery. Folklore also links them with Pulcinella, the archetypical Neapolitan commedia dell'arte hunchback who, besides his insatiable lust for maccheroni, possesses a truly amazing, double-sexed ability to give birth via his hump after impregnating *himself.* ("A very Neapolitan situation," observed Barry, still reeking of the barber's ghastly lozione.)

Our Tarantina turned out to be in her early eighties and indeed a celebrity, the subject of a documentary and author of a memoir. She came to the Quartieri after the war, escaping from her Apulian family, living as a scugnizzo (street urchin) and boy prostitute. "Then, on a whim," said Nunzia, "our Taranti headed to Rome and la dolce vita—where she started dressing as a woman!"

*Un*dressing, Tarantina corrected. "Federico!" she cried. "*Il grande*

Fellini! He saw me naked and said, 'A woman so perfect could *not* be a man!'"

IT FELT LIKE a massive breakthrough in my relations with the forbidding Quartieri when Nunzia invited me to come by the next day and watch her prepare three different pastas for one of her dinner performances. The pasta recipes were from her nonna—who had inherited them from *her* nonna.

While Tarantina smoked outside with her femminielli pals in geisha-like makeup, I sat with Nunzia, hand-breaking the long ziti for Genovese. Despite its name, Genovese is napoletanità in a bowl: an *importante* (big) pasta sauce of tough cuts of beef cooked over two days with masses of onions, an Arab-influenced pre-tomato precursor of ragù napoletano. Another fiercely local cucina povera classic on the dinner menu was pasta e patate, a carb-on-carb pileup of potatoes and smoked provola cheese that all sort of melt into *pasta mischiata—mmishkiata* in Nunzia's mushy Neapolitan dialect. In poorer days, Nunzia clarified, the mix of pasta shapes came from whatever dusty broken-up dried bits were left on hand. And now, I reflected, now it all came prettily packaged, a cheerful bag of neatly commodified former poverty. I noted that Nunzia's mix was produced by Garofalo, a five-century-old pastificio based in Gragnano, the famed pasta-producing hill town near Naples. Garofalo nostalgically advertises itself as *super-tradizionale* yet it's owned by the giant Spanish food-processing company Ebro.

Would Nunzia ever use pasta fresca? I asked. The eggy handmade fresh tagliatelle, for instance, favored by Northerners. She glared at me like I was mentally feeble. *Mai*, she snorted. Never. So much for the idea that pasta somehow unified Italy.

Reaching for cans of industrial-grade pre–Slow Food pelati (peeled tomatoes), Nunzia announced the next pasta. Puttanesca, a version of pasta al pomodoro, essentially, bolstered with olives and anchovies.

I gave a gasp.

*Puttanesca?*

Here it was: genius loci, the deepest spirit of place. Almost *too* authentic, really, comically so—to be cooking the pasta of whores in what was in fact a former brothel in the neighborhood known for centuries as Naples's epicenter of the sex trade. Incredible, too, how proud the sweet, churchgoing, grandmotherly Nunzia seemed of this heritage, nary a sniff of moral misgiving. With an archivist's zeal, she showed me the merry menus of casa di piacere prices for girls ("discount for US military"), which hung on a wall densely festooned with images of family nonnas, a haloed Saint Maradona, the bowler-hatted Totò (the Charlie Chaplin of Naples), and native son actor-playwright Eduardo De Filippo, along with a huge blowup of a tombola board (the Naples version of bingo, with dream images, la smorfia, assigned to the numbers)—and Jesus Christ looking rather reproachfully at photos of Tarantina striking Marilyn Monroe poses.

*Napoli . . . La nostra Napoli*, Nunzia murmured at her crammed self-mythologizing reliquary of Neapolitan archetypes. "Our Naples." For my part, I felt momentarily trapped inside a presepe, one of those claustrophobic Neapolitan nativity crèches.

The pungent smack of the puttanesca's sautéed anchovies, capers, and olives filled the former brothel. I remarked how my writer friend Amedeo, a bestselling connoisseur of napoletanità, insisted to me that prostitutes *never cooked*; that in Naples puttanesca was better known as pasta del cornuto, of cuckolds, the hasty sauce of unfaithful wives hurrying back from betraying their husbands.

*Bah.* Nunzia shrugged. *TARAAANTI!* she called.

"Sì, prostitutes barely cooked," Tarantina, a highly qualified eyewitness, attested, reeking of cigarette smoke. "*But* we got thirty percent of the client's food tabs *and* half of the bar." Pasta puttanesca? Named, she declared, for the red of the sauce and the red-light neighborhood. After the brothels were outlawed, puttanesca became a code word for a client seeking services; the pasta order was shouted, and the girl (or guy) hurried along to oblige.

I shook my head in amazement at these intimate details—facts, folklore, fakelore?—told at stoveside in this archival lair by two Neapolitan archetypes: a bighearted nonna and a third-gender celebrity. And if Tarantina was Pulcinella in the aging flesh, she was under the gaze, here, of two other grand Pulcinellas: Totò, who embodied his spirit in film, and Eduardo De Filippo, who famously interpreted him onstage. This Neapolitan fecundity of echoes and incarnations brought to mind an observation by Thomas Belmonte, author of *The Broken Fountain*, a great anthropological study of the Lower City. "If drama was originally invented as a metaphor for life," wrote Belmonte, "in Naples the metaphor has overwhelmed the referent, and society presents itself as a series of plays within plays."

Now in her own archival mode, Tarantina ran back to her basso to fetch some frayed photos. She was naked in all of them. Tarantina splayed atop a vintage car during a Quartieri street party for Maradona, Tarantina at some festa in Rome's Via Veneto, looking like a crude copy of Brigitte Bardot. ("I've met her.")

"Fellini, Pasolini, Alberto Moravia . . ." chanted Tarantina, invoking the grand figures she'd known.

But then La Dolce Vita was finita and Rome became boring. Naples was calling her back. "I Quartieri," she sighed, "i nostri favolosi Quartieri!" With its beautiful boys hawking contraband cigarettes and fetching espressos for whores. Where everything was sold *a voce*—by shouts—milk, watermelon, pizza, mineral water as *puzzolente* (stinky) as the inside of Vesuvius. Where thugs dressed up in suits and the puttane wore lipstick. "And the sailors, the American sailors!" Tarantina was lost now in nostalgic memories, memories that were probably myths, too, myths contrasting starkly with the harrowing accounts of Neapolitan poverty after the war. "A whole white sea of americani, fresh off the boat!" cooed Tarantina. "Here in our Quartieri, hungry for a girl and a 'pizza pie'!"

Nunzia nodded along with a beatific approval. "La nostra Napoli," she repeated. "A city of saints, whores, and pizza." The pizza of queens, I said to myself, and the pasta of prostitutes.

While the spaghetti was boiling, Tarantina listed the prices for the various services she had performed either as a man or a woman. All at once I noticed that Nunzia's small tubby grandchild had slipped in and was quietly playing with his phone at the other end of the table.

"Nunzia!" I whispered. "*Il bambino!* Should he really be hearing about . . . blow jobs?"

"Il bambino?" Nunzia hooted. She waved the kid over and smothered him with loud Neapolitan kisses. "Our bambini these days, they bring guns to school!"

Finally our vascio puttanesca was ready. No, it wasn't a sexy masterpiece out of a Mediterranean daydream. It didn't burst, à la Enzo, with organic pomodorini straight from the Vesuvian soil. True to its cucina povera roots, the pasta was a little gloppy and totally average, the kind one eats at a hundred unsung trattorias all over Naples. The flavor? Not good, not bad. But somehow inevitable, with the muted, melting, broken-down pomodoro sauce faintly pungent with anchovies, clinging inelegantly to the strands of spaghetti. If all else in the vascio was Neapolitan theater, the pasta was unnostalgic: it tasted of canned tomatoes and poverty. Perhaps archetypally so.

LA MISERIA . . . poverty.

The creation of a modernizing unified Italy from a clutter of duchies, kingdoms, and papal states was supposed to improve the welfare of a crushingly poor peninsula—two-thirds agrarian and three-fourths illiterate. Life expectancy in 1860, when Garibaldi entered Naples, was around thirty years. The wholesome grandmotherly cucina povera that Nunzia was cooing about? In rural parts of the country, it was a cruel joke of a "cuisine," mostly a sub-subsistence fodder of gruel and acquasale, or black bread in brine (outside Naples even pasta was still rare until the late nineteenth century). But even this wretched fare was threatened in the chaos of post-Unification. Southerners suffered particularly. The Bourbons' protective tariffs were abolished, destroying industries in Palermo and Naples. As Neapolitans love to repeat, the ascendant Northerners, the Savoys, looted the Bourbon treasury. Out in the countryside, peasants lost access to baronial lands. Worst were the taxes—on salt, sugar, flour, bread, macaroni, each bag of grain taken to a mill—squeezed from the poor to finance the military and the bureaucracy of the new state. By the end of the nineteenth century, Italy's taxation was the heaviest in Europe.

And so began one of the largest recorded emigrations in

history—and thanks to it, the globalizing of Italian culture and image, of Neapolitan pizza and pasta. As John Dickie, author of *Delizia!*, acerbically notes, "Exporting hungry peasants was a peculiar way for Italy to launch its food on the journey to worldwide popularity." France, meanwhile, exported professional chefs and their sauces.

Between 1880 and 1915, 13 million Italians sailed off, mostly to *le due Americhe* (the two Americas). Their mantra: *Mi emigro per mangar*, "I'm emigrating to eat." By the first decade of the twentieth century, one-sixth of Italy's population resided outside the peninsula—some 90 percent of them from the ex–Kingdom of the Two Sicilies and most of them rural, Neapolitans being the only major urban exception. The largest colonies were in the US, Argentina, and Brazil. The new Italian nation-state they fled was still an uneasy political construct united by nothing more than religion and hunger, in one historian's words. In 1870, the year that the last papal state was abolished, less than 10 percent of the population could speak the newly imposed (Florentine) standard Italian. Campanilismo, loyalty to one's local bell tower, still defined and divided the country (and still does, many would argue).

In the United States the new arrivals settled mostly along the Eastern Seaboard in tenements that packed together Calabrians, Sicilians, Neapolitans, and Abruzzese—strangers with not the slightest sense of any shared "Italian cuisine."

So what *did* they eat?

Certainly not the hearty regional recipes of their Calabrian or Neapolitan grandmothers that have now invaded popular myths. Italians emigrated, writes Dickie, precisely because they were excluded from Italy's civilization at table. On my first-ever trip to New York's Little Italy back in the seventies (myself a newly arrived stateless immigrant), I remember gawking at the crusty white bread, dusky salami, fatty pink mortadella, and golfball-sized meatballs smothered with blazing red sauce. Of course back then I had no idea that a century before in the old country, all this would have been a *cucina di sogni*, cuisine of dreams, a fairy tale for the Italian poor. However, as historian Hasia Diner points out in *Hungering for America*, her study of immigrant foodways, while the Italian peasants hardly *partook of* such fare, all over the peninsula "the poor made the food, saw it, knew how to assess its quality, but could only eat what those in power allotted." Over in the New World, the North and South American abbondanza of affordable white bread and red meat enabled famished dreams to become tasty realities. *In l'America every day is a festa*, the letters home crowed. *We eat meat three times a day, not three times a year.* Meanwhile, other Americans who encountered Italian immigrants marveled at how even unskilled workers feasted on imported pasta with Parmesan, on sausages, and on coffee and sweets.

And so was born the cucina italiana of American exile: a cooked-up fusion of New World plenty and yearning memories of wealthy tables back home. Mountains of spaghetti with meatballs, vast antipasto salads, veal chops "parmigiana," macaroni shells bulging with Polly-O ricotta? All Italo-American inventions, which to this day make the Italians back in Italy laugh.

Along with the old country's class hierarchies, regional distinctions, too, began to dissolve in immigrant kitchens and a unified food nation emerged, decades before such a thing happened at home—if it happened at all. Crammed together in Little Italies, whether of New York or Buenos Aires, paesani from disparate places smelled, sampled, and inevitably borrowed one another's dishes. In the US, social clubs and street festivals likewise served up pan-Italian menus: Neapolitan macaroni with a Northern ragù bolognese made with New World ground beef; Milanese veal scaloppine with Southern wild greens; a Sicilian spumoni ice cream to end. Emigration, Hasia Diner contends, caused Italians not only to raise their dining standards, but to do so patriotically—as *Italians*, their civic-regional identity now subsumed by a national one, at least in the kitchen.

Stoking this sense of italianità among the diaspora were the canny interventions of the Bel Paese itself. Dante Alighieri societies sponsored by the Italian government taught la lingua di Dante to children of parents who spoke only Calabrian or Neapolitan dialects. Chambers of Commerce promoted and protected the Made in Italy brand, turning immigrants into patriotic consumers. Citizenship was offered, no questions asked, to those who repatriated. Rather than let its diaspora assimilate, the new Italian state fostered a kind of transnational nationalism—a sense of belonging to *la più grande Italia*, or Greater Italy.

And so it went with pizza and maccheroni al pomodoro. From Neapolitan urban peculiarities (novelties to non-Napoletani when mass migration began), they've come to represent Italianness, first to immigrants, then eventually to the rest of the world. As symbolic dishes that eliminated regional differences, the eternal contrast between North and South, pasta and pizza, insists anthropologist Franco La Cecla, "became the banner flying over an entire nation . . . as the country's globalized image." What's more, they expressed the two natures of Italian eating. Maccheroni al pomodoro: a byword for Italian-American home cooking, la cucina di mamma, eventually igniting a North American boom in spaghetti joints and homey Italian trattorias. Pizza: the revolution of eating out on the cheap, an archetypal "carry-out" food carrying with it the irresistible cliché of Neapolitan (and now all Italian) public conviviality.

It helped that both were genius economic inventions, superbly adaptable, cheap, and, in time, mass-producible. It helped further, particularly in the case of pasta al pomodoro, that Italian emigration coincided with a small industrial revolution back home in the production and processing of pasta and canned tomatoes, which found a huge patriotic diaspora market in the Americas. When exports came to a halt, first with World War I, then with Mussolini's economic protectionism, American and Argentinean producers jumped in. In the end it wasn't so much the mom-and-pop eateries but big industrial manufacturers that were responsible for the popularity of Italian food in the New World—and beyond.

Chef Boyardee, anyone?

PIZZA AND PASTA, argues La Cecla, became global symbols of Italy "well before a parallel process took place in the homeland."

Okay, but what of the Bel Paese itself and its own *Italian* nation-building at table?

I went through the gardens of a former seventeenth-century convent just above the Quartieri, on into the small university office shared by Marino Niola and his wife, Elisabetta Moro, friends of Enzo and esteemed cultural anthropologists both, with a keen interest in food.

"Well, there was Mussolini, naturally!" answered Betta, who looks Germanic and comes from the Veneto region in the North. "Mussolini and his general cultural nation-building. *And* his patriotic food rhetoric—his autarky propaganda campaigns that particularly targeted women." (She meant the alimentary sovereignty Mussolini proclaimed after international sanctions were imposed in 1935 for Italy's invasion of Ethiopia.)

"But here in Napoli," chuckled Marino, who's Neapolitan, "Mussolini meant *niente*. All we remember is his stupid attempt to replace pasta, which needed imported wheat, with domestic rice."

"Which Neapolitans instantly saw as an anti-South bias!" cried Betta. She rolled her eyes. "Neapolitans, they see life as one long slur against them!"

"And then, of course," said Marino, "there was Artusi . . ."

Ah, Artusi. I was waiting to hear his name.

Born in 1820 in Romagna in central Italy, Pellegrino Artusi was a portly bachelor with muttonchop sideburns and a predilection for top hats. Patriot, bon vivant, amateur cook, Artusi, in 1891, age seventy-one and retired from banking, published a cookbook, *La Scienza in Cucina e l'Arte di Mangiar Bene*—Science in the Kitchen and the Art of Eating Well—now mostly known as L'Artusi.

L'Artusi is variously described as a landmark, not just of gastronomy but of Italian culture; as a foundational text of modern Italian *everything*; as a tome that helped forge a national consciousness. It did all this by consolidating the fiercely regional recipes from across the fledgling unified state, at a time when the Italian alta cucina of noble banquets was French, while cucina popolare was mostly an orally transmitted mishmash of diverse cooking traditions using disparate terms for the same fish or vegetable.

As the padre of cucina italiana, Artusi isn't just venerated in Italian food circles. He's deified. In 2011 the centenary of his death was celebrated together with the 150th anniversary of the Risorgimento and stole the thunder from the unpopular and divisive

Unification festivities. Artusi's genius? His understanding, perhaps, that the only way to bring a country together was through its stomach. Consequently, *La Scienza in Cucina e l'Arte di Mangiar Bene*, writes scholar Piero Camporesi in his introduction to the definitive 1970 edition, did more for national unification than Manzoni's *I Promessi Sposi* (The Betrothed)—another foundational text—at a historic moment when infinite regional peculiarities rendered any Italian unity "mythic and futuristic."

How Italians love their dear Artusi, their *grande unificatore*. The flowery compliments to lady readers, the frivolous banter ("Do not be alarmed if this dessert looks like some . . . giant leech," regarding strudel), the meatball recipe that "even a jackass knows how to make." And they adore L'Artusi's Cinderella success. Scorned by publishers, the author issued the first one thousand copies himself, dedicating the book to his cats. The initial 475 recipes reached 790 in the thirteenth edition of 1909. To date, the work has gone through 111 editions. Together with *Pinocchio* and the afore-mentioned *I Promessi Sposi*, L'Artusi is one of the most-read books in Italy.

It's celebrated as a linguistic achievement as well. Not only did Artusi purge Italian food talk of fancy French terms, but while the country was still a Babel of dialects, he wrote it in Tuscan, the new official literary language. The Romagnolo-speaking author had in fact moved to Florence in 1851 in order to better master the language of Dante, just as the Lombard-speaking Manzoni had done in 1827 for *I Promessi Sposi*.

Here, then, was an all-Italian cookbook written in Italian for Italians—at least for the new national bourgeoisie in search of common cuisine and domestic ideals (while the poor, mostly illiterate, were creating an alternative cucina italiana abroad).

"But for us there is a problem." Marino smiled, there in the office by a Neapolitan garden. "For Neapolitans Artusi is the *Cavour* of the Italian kitchen."

"Meaning," clarified Betta, "the Risorgimento is seen here as a project hatched by Cavour, the Piedmontese politician. Likewise Artusi's homogenization of the Italian kitchen! A Northern-hatched project, that, well, you can guess . . . *slighted the South*."

Ah, indeed. The Italy of L'Artusi is unified in a peculiar way: along a north-central axis—with a smattering of international recipes. Abruzzo, Apulia, Basilicata, Calabria? Barely mentioned. Sardinia simply doesn't exist; ditto hot peppers and other ingredients popular from Rome southward. Even when L'Artusi's later editions included tips and recipes from readers, the Mezzogiorno continued to suffer, with only a small handful of Neapolitan and Sicilian recipes.

I was eager to hear more about il grande unificatore's anti-South bias, but at this point a graduate student arrived to discuss the Camorra and mozzarella production in the Caserta region.

I left the anthropologists and their garden and headed downhill toward a large Feltrinelli bookstore near Galleria Umberto to continue my research. On the way I consulted some Neapolitan experts.

"Boh!" Nunzia blurted into her telefonino. "Never heard of *questo Artuzzi*. I only cook my nonna's recipes."

"Sure, I have L'Artusi," laughed Mela, a great local chef, "but honestly, his recipes suck."

"Artusi? *Ha ha!*" hollered Enzo. "Go check out his *pizza* recipe!"

As for Donatella, for a good twenty minutes she huffed how in his autobiography Artusi had dissed Neapolitan maccheroni al pomodoro. Apparently he tasted it on the street, complained about too much pepper and spicy cheese, went to a bourgeois restaurant and instead ordered—"Imagine!" cried Donatella. "He ordered spaghetti *con la balsamella*!" Spaghetti with béchamel!

"How's L'Artusi selling?" I asked a nice young clerk when I arrived at Feltrinelli.

"Artusi?" He squinted at his computer. "Of course in Napoli," he noted, "we have our own *importante* cookbooks, for example Cavalcanti's *Cucina Teorico-Pratica*, published in 1839 in dialetto napoletano and featuring Italy's first pasta with tomato sauce recipe—it's selling great, almost like Jamie Oliver!" All books on napoletanità were selling great here, in fact, he assured me. Maybe because Neapolitans no longer felt so bad about themselves and their city? "Artusi, Artusi . . ." he murmured, clicking through national sales figures. "In Naples, *niente particolare*, nothing special. Nothing like sales in Bologna!"

At the cookbook shelves I browsed the great tome again. It was the classic 1970 edition, with a vast, scholarly intro by Camporesi. A modern Italian cookbook, I reflected, it wasn't. Pastas, for instance—just some three dozen recipes among 790—were grouped under minestre, first courses, which were subdivided into dry and brothy minestre. Thirty years after Unification, dried pasta clearly hadn't been anywhere near the Italian edible life force it is today. Adulatory Italian scholars credit Artusi with spreading pasta al pomodoro across Italy. Given that his masterwork contained just two paltry maccheroni with tomato sauce recipes—one featuring *butter*—the claim seemed highly suspect. Following Enzo's suggestion, I looked up "pizza alla napoletana." There it was—a dessert. A delicious-sounding cake of ricotta, almonds, and sugar in a short pastry crust.

BACK AT HOME, I learned that the first savory Neapolitan pizza recipe appeared in Italy only in 1911, two years after L'Artusi. I also realized that I'd spent two whole days without pizza. Feeling sudden withdrawal pangs, I headed to the Spaccanapoli quarter, where most of the city's historic pizzerie and friggitorie (fry shops) are crowded along Via dei Tribunali.

Spaccanapoli means "Split Naples," a reference to its trio of ancient parallel streets that slice through the historic centro and are still known by their Roman name—the Decumani. For as long as I could remember, the quarter was operatically sinister: a dingy mesh of dark-cobbled streets, graffitied facades, spectacularly decaying palazzi, and churches with inscrutable opening hours. You'd visit its old-school pizzerie, like Da Michele, dreading the *scippatori*, the infamous Neapolitan drive-by purse-snatchers.

Now as I walked along Via dei Tribunali, I blinked hard trying to recognize something—anything—among the spiffed-up gelaterie and the salumerie touting Slow Food–sanctioned products. Unlike our Quartieri Spagnoli, Via dei Tribunali had been thoroughly gentrified; even the motorini were gone. Disoriented, I asked an old man in a wifebeater where to find Pizzeria Gino Sorbillo.

"Just follow the mobs," hooted the wifebeater, pointing. He wasn't kidding. A swarm of tourists and a moveable forest of raised selfie sticks ahead marked out the pizzeria's Neapolitan-blue-and-white awning.

Gino Sorbillo, charismatic forty-something scion of a famed pizza dynasty, greeted me in his sanctum on the second floor of a cramped old house adjacent to his pizzeria. He introduced the space as "La Casa della Pizza."

"*This* is where Gino Sorbillo goes," he announced, inexplicably speaking of himself in third person, "to collect his thoughts . . . to recharge . . . to escape the madness outside."

Gino Sorbillo planned to turn "this" into a museo della pizza, or perhaps a Sorbillo museum—a little redundant, I thought, since it already *was* a Gino Sorbillo museum. Every inch was crammed with menus, clippings, Sorbillo logos, knickknacks, and photos of the grinning, photogenic pizzaiolo with other celebrities. Lachrymose old Neapolitan songs lilted around us as the visage of Gino's aunt, Zia Esterina, a female pizzaiola, smiled saintlike from the wall.

I first met Gino Sorbillo in 1989, when he was still a teenager, with a boyish beautiful-handsome face out of a Bronzino painting, and a T-shirt that said "My nonna Carolina had 21 children, all pizzaioli"—apparently true. I'd asked him what he thought of the trendy pizzerias along the Lungomare; he replied with a contemptuous spit. Now Gino had a trendy pizzeria along the Lungomare, more pizzerias in Manhattan and Milan, a pizza fritta franchise called Zia Esterina in Naples—and upcoming projects in Miami and Tokyo. If Enzo was pizza's Illuminato philosopher, Gino was its Cristiano Ronaldo. He even had the furrowed pout of the soccer star.

"Bella Napoli," intoned Gino Sorbillo now, opening folders filled with vintage postcards of Naples of yore. But starting in the 1970s and '80s, his bella città, and Spaccanapoli especially, had suffered. Everyone who could fled the dirt, the Camorra. And then about five years ago pizza began to bring people back. "Now young pizzaoili look up to Gino Sorbillo," said the man himself. "Gino Sorbillo is like . . . their nonno [grandfather], a vero Napoletano, a hip-hop artist." I pondered being both grandpa *and* hip-hopper, while Gino answered a flurry of phone calls and text messages, periodically clasping his temples in operatic despair, murmuring, "*What* I am to do when everyone wants a piece of Gino Sorbillo?"

Without warning, he was on a phone interview with Radio Kiss Kiss Napoli. In between answers he shut his eyes and bit his lip, like a tenor before a difficult aria, or Ronaldo before a penalty kick.

"In front of pizza, everyone's equal," Gino Sorbillo told Radio Kiss Kiss. He continued the sound bites.

"Eat your pizza folded in four—*a portafoglio*—because one must never forget that pizza was born as cucina di strada. Pizza scugnizza—pizza the street urchin."

"A chef is simply a chef. A pizzaiolo is an artisan who touches people's lives."

"We've entered the golden age of organic Caputo flour."

"Via dei Tribunali converges with New York's Little Italy."

"There are more Neapolitan pizzerias in Brazil than there are in Naples."

"We are sending our history into the world, to teach it what it means to be Neapolitan."

And triumphantly: "Our hotels are bursting, our pizzerias are full, our pizza scugnizza has conquered the planet."

Over lunch in the basement VIP room of Pizzeria Sorbillo—"where Ben Stiller himself ate a Margherita"—my various reactions to the day gave way to just one. Tasting even the simplest marinara here was like experiencing a show-off but sublime Cristiano Ronaldo goal. Crisper and more robust than Enzo's ethereal pies, it was pulsating with flavor, a perfectly calibrated tour de force, the ultimate expression, I thought, of wheat, pomodoro, and olive oil.

Pizza devoured, Gino offered a tour of *his* Spaccanapoli—"the

lanes and the vicoli that spawned our Neapolitan pizza." We didn't
get very far. Every few meters grateful shopkeepers and street cleaners stopped us to testify how Gino Sorbillo and his pizza had
changed their lives and revitalized their downtrodden quartiere.
The proprietor of a baba au rhum shop, newly renovated, cried grazie for the spillover from Pizzeria Sorbillo. A sunburned quasi-
*lazzarone* informed us that he took Gino's pizza fritta to the beach
*every day*—even in winter. "If a pizza fritta can make a man
happy—I'm satisfied," said Gino magnanimously. There was a cop
who doubled as an Airbnb host—"Always full grazie to Gino."

A small crowd was now trailing behind us. Half, I realized, were
different incarnations of cops: stradale, comunale, carabinieri. All
pizza enthusiasts? Then I recalled hearing a few years ago that the
Camorra had burned down Gino's pizzeria—an incident he apparently preferred not to discuss. Was the police presence related?

*Ciao, Gino. Grazie, Gino. Gino il Grande. Gino il Generoso.*

The neighborhood chorus was like a scene from an opera buffa:
the fiery-eyed local hero greeted by grateful plebs (shockingly this
ancient Roman term is still much used in Naples). Except it was all
real, too real: the mile-long lines in front of every pizzeria on Tribunali, the sleekly renovated salumerie and pastry shops, the hordes of
global pizza pilgrims roaming the cobblestones, the fact that pizza
scugnizza, the one-soldo first aid of the stomach derided as "complicated filth" by Collodi, as "a piece of bread that has been taken
reeking out of the sewer" by Samuel Morse . . . that flatbread was
now a global industry worth, what? Something like $140 billion?

The "pizza effect." I thought of the term coined by the anthropologist and Hindu monk Agehananda Bharati to describe a situation
(in his case involving yoga) where a minor cultural phenomenon is
exported to another country, where its success causes its reevaluation

back home, where it then takes off as an original, long-standing tradition *but* now imbued with new meaning and status. Another anthropologist even added the notion of an "inverted pizza effect," whereby a cultural phenomenon becomes not just revived in such a way back home, but is reconfigured to satisfy the new expectations of foreign visitors—for authenticity, for tradition—forming a continuous loop of projections, expectations, and appropriations. And how *baroquely* ironic it was, I thought, how pizza was popularized and claimed as "Italian" by emigrants who'd crossed oceans to escape post-Unification chaos and poverty. A lowly dish exported, transformed and reimagined, then imported back to be celebrated and defended as a *national* icon of a unified Bel Paese—its global success a source of both pride and frustration to a city that still mostly regards Unification as a cosmic injustice.

I lost my train of thought on Via S. Gregorio Armeno, jam-packed with shops that make and sell presepi, the Neapolitan nativity crèches. Gino led us up to a second floor's crowded realm. It was the workshop of Marco Ferrigno, a fifth-generation presepe maker who is every bit Gino's equal as a telegenic celebrity artisan. Presepi have been a Neapolitan specialty since at least the 1100s, Marco explained as we threaded carefully through a florid terra-cotta multitude. "But they got really interesting in the late seventeenth century when the sacred started to mingle with the profane." I paused to watch a presepe crew fashioning miniature wooden arms and legs for Pulcinellas, shepherds, and beturbaned magi, as well as Maradonas and Totòs. Out on a half balcony sat a young apprentice from Bulgaria, meticulously hand-painting a tray of tiny crystal eyeballs—morbidly picturesque and creepy in a very Neapolitan way.

But it was the foods in the spectacularly cluttered historic vintage presepi that transfixed me. They were like secular reliquaries mirroring and narrating this teeming city—in miniature. A tiny monk carried a tiny pear-shaped provolone cheese; a teeny woman hawked ring-shaped rusks called friselle. In dollhouse-sized taverns, mini tables were set with insalata di rinforzo (cauliflower with anchovies), polpette (meatballs), and capitone (Christmas eel). At my side, Gino annotated the foods for me. The presepi, he said, "helped us discover—even preserve—the almost-vanished street food of Naples." Marco Ferrigno agreed, with a proviso. The crèches were a historical record—but an *aspirational* one, portraying an imaginary abbondanza in a city eternally plagued by disease and starvation.

"Which was why," Gino exclaimed solemnly, "until recently, as recently as the 1990s, pizza was considered too vulgar, too low to be even included in the presepe!"

"But now pizza is a cultural artifact," said Marco. "An old craft that just like presepe, like Naples itself, is once again flourishing!"

We stood gazing into this replica of the city on display, admiring the spectacle—just as Naples forever does with itself. "Autofolklorizzazione," I recalled Marino the anthropologist describing this Neapolitan syndrome. Self-mythologization. A narcissistic city, inventing and reinventing and beholding its historical identity. Always in the precious essentialist cause of napoletanità . . . the distinctive, superior condition that is Neapolitanness.

# TOKYO
## Ramen and Rice

I found myself mulling the pizza effect once more when Barry and I landed in Tokyo.

It was the very start of sakura season. The swollen buds on the cherry trees were just beginning to preview their upcoming Technicolor fantasias, but already the relentless Japanese engines of commodification and aestheticization were frothing out a floral-pink tide of themed merchandise, edibles in particular. Heading to the metro the morning after our arrival—to Ueno Park's expanses to catch the first petals—I noted that Sutaba (Starbucks) was pushing Sakura Blossom Cream Frappuccino with Crispy Swirl, while Makudo (McDonald's) enticed with sakura McFlurry cups, a soft serve studded with salt-pickled cherry leaves. Ducking into a 7-Eleven konbini (the generic term for Japan's omnipresent, indispensable convenience stores), I yielded to a quick scoop of Häagen-Dazs sakura mochi ice cream. It was laced with actual blossoms.

At Ueno Park, weekend revelers were impatiently massed on their festive picnic blankets and blue plastic mats, crowding under the spottily luscious pink and white boughs of the first-blossoming ume trees. Giggling Chinese tourists in rented polyester kimonos struck Instagram poses. We edged through, nodding hellos, declining an offer of hanamizake ("too early an hour for sake!") but accepting an onigiri (rice ball) to share. A pink one.

And the pizza effect? Partly this came to mind because in Aza-budai, the central neighborhood where we were staying by the landmark Tokyo Tower, you couldn't walk without inhaling the scent of charred dough and tomatoes from yet another wood-burning Neapolitan-style pizzeria (with mind-numbing Tokyo-style prices). And partly because the pizza effect was now being expressed as the ramen effect. Here again was an essential carb that started out as a disrespected source of cheap calories, became mass-produced in the industrial food era, then got internationalized, then transformed into a 1990s Slow Food artisanal darling while still costing under ten bucks—finally achieving apotheosis as a national treasure, tourist attraction, and soft power totem. And set on an endless global loop from the home country and back again.

But as in Naples, I was here to ingest-investigate not one but two iconic starches. The second was gohan—the cooked white japonica rice that accompanies most local meals and figures heavily in essentialist theories of Nihonjinron (Japaneseness, a kind of napole-tanità on nationalist steroids). Ramen and rice, rice and ramen. They made a curious dialectical binary: one a Chinese-origin hybrid that eventually relied on imported American wheat, the other a homegrown treasure imbued with a near-mystical aura as the "edible symbol" of the Japanese self. Fast versus slow, appropriation versus tradition. And yet both were part of the national food canon: rice, a hallowed cornerstone of washoku (a timeless and supposedly ancient ideal of an ur-Japanese meal); ramen, the "naturalized" modern star of kokuminshoku, inexpensive "people's cuisine," one that fueled Japan's post-WWII reconstruction and boom.

And there was another echo, a stupendous one, of our Neapolitan sojourn. The view! From our trim ninth-floor Tokyo pad in an apartment building called Oakwood, we beheld not Vesuvius but Tokyo Tower—from almost literally underneath it. The tower's mammoth latticed steel feet filled our main window; on the small balcony before bed we'd crane upward at its tapering monumentality, soaring away spotlit and blazing into the night. Here was another Japanese icon, borrowed and tweaked in typical Japanese fashion—a mid-twentieth-century simulacrum of Gustave Eiffel's Paris original, colored in cheery "aviation warning" orange-and-white—rising as an emblem of Japan's postwar prosperity and emergent global presence. And so, springtime Tokyo welcomed us with a looming faux-Parisian vista (whose construction labor had been fueled by ramen) while we could order in pizza officially approved by the Associazione Verace Pizza Napoletana and drink, say, a seasonal Asahi Cherry Blossom beer or a limited edition Sakura Pepsi. And for dessert, an equally seasonal Hello Kitty Sakura Sake KitKat.

"Nope, we're not in Naples anymore," announced Barry, a little redundantly.

I COMMENCED MY RAMEN research with our literary friends, an older generation mostly. Some of them, I discovered, were not wild ramen fans.

"Um, so greasy." Professor Motoyuki Shibata, Barry's fiction translator, hesitated delicately when I suggested gathering at a ramen-ya (ramen joint). And one didn't really *socialize* at a ramen-ya. Could he invite us for soba instead?

Others were amused by ramen's millennial celebrity. Highly amused, in much detail.

"I hear that Ippudo in New York charges $20 for a bowl—and has a maitre d' and a wine list!" hooted Kyoichi Tsuzuki, a cult chronicler of Japanese pop culture, as we sipped green tea in his crowded loft in Marunouchi near the Imperial Palace. Presiding over anti–Marie Kondo masses of art books, wacky posters, and kitschy-cool vintage collectibles, he resembled an amiable, mischievous Buddha in black T-shirt and wire-rim specs. Perhaps he was so tickled because in Japan the ramen chain Ippudo is akin to McDonald's.

"No, a *real* ramen-ya," Kyoichi elucidated, "should be a tattered place with week-old newspapers, *always* a TV screen playing a dumb quiz show, mangas scattered around—and folksy radio music, J-pop or enka maybe, that's our J-hillbilly style. Oh, and pimply customers," he giggled. "Lots of pimply customers!"

Because ramen wasn't *serious* food or even a *genre*, he insisted. In Tokyo simple shoyu (soy) or shio (salt) or miso ramen traditionally had been fast food grabbed from yatai (street carts) with their signature jingles played by Chinese charumera flutes. Like a hot dog, ramen was something you scarfed down at drunk midnights. But then suddenly—bam. The Japanese discovered regionality.

"Imagine a *regional* hot dog!" exclaimed Kyoichi.

I didn't point out that regional hot dogs were indeed a thing, elevated to a *serious* thing in the 1990s, just like regional ramen styles.

"And imagine how funny it was," he continued, "when suddenly everyone started talking about 'ramen originality' . . . about freedom and new ideas . . . for *ramen*! About 'collector's ramen' and 'ramen's holy grails'! When ramen shop owners even started publishing *philosophy books*. About a bowl of noodles!"

It was all delightfully absurd.

Going for a walk in the Harajuku district after seeing Kyoichi, Barry and I agreed that Tokyo didn't seem as exotic and sensationally bewildering as it did on our several previous visits. After the couple of weeks we'd just spent in frenetic Southeast Asian capitals, it seemed 1980s-quaint. Almost cozy. At Harajuku Bridge, where the cosplaying Goth-Lolitas and street-fashionistas used to preen, we found the outrageous couture mashups gone, washed away in the low-key globalized tides of Uniqlo and Muji.

From Harajuku, we went wandering among the massive evergreens of the Meiji Imperial Shinto Shrine nearby. Beyond its lofty torii gate, a display wall of vividly decorated straw sake barrels stood ranged along the pathway—annual shrine gifts from brewers. Sake, a favor from gods to humans, features in Shinto rites. To our surprise, there were other gift barrels, too—wooden ones boasting the grand Burgundy appellations of Corton-Charlemagne, Gevrey-Chambertin, and Beaune.

It turns out the late-nineteenth-century emperor Meiji, the embodiment of Japanese nationalism in whose name the modern state was established, was not only personally fond of French wine; this fondness was a tactic, I'd come to learn, of his nation-building.

Back at Kyoichi's loft I'd asked what he thought of the Meiji Restoration. "Honestly," he replied in his bemused way, "only hardcore nationalists think about it these days." And food historians, I wanted to add.

Me, I thought about the Meiji Restoration—a lot.

JAPAN BECAME A MODERN nation-state in the last third of the nine-teenth century, created, like Italy, from a hodgepodge of feudal domains without much of a national consciousness, and less of a national cuisine. Unlike Italy, Japan had long been a rigidly isolated archipelago, whose military dictators, the Tokugawa shoguns, had for over two centuries shut out foreigners, Westerners principally, and shut in inhabitants, in a policy later known as sakoku, "locked-up country" literally.

Then, in 1853, Commodore Perry's black American warships dropped anchor.

A woefully outmatched, backward country was forced to open up, bullied into a notoriously unequal trade treaty. The trauma and humiliation caused an existential crisis that in 1868 brought down the shogunate and brought in the revolutionizing Meiji period that was to last forty-four years. Indigenous Shintoism was made the state religion over Buddhism, with the emperor—then a teenager to be known as Meiji (Enlightened One)—as its new divine head. The capital was shifted to the shoguns' longtime stronghold, Edo, now renamed Tokyo, "Eastern Capital." Modernization on a Western model: that was to be the key for Japan to strengthen and claim its unique place among nations—paradoxically, all in the name of pro-tecting its "Indigenous" ancestral traditions and values, many of which were invented whole cloth. The emperor worship, for in-stance.

Italian unification was a decades-long chaos involving scant lifestyle or food reforms. In Japan, however, a new national char-acter was radically engineered from the top down. Traditionally emperors were not seen in public, sidelined as poetry-scribbling ornaments in ancient Kyoto. But the young emperor Meiji now became a national role model—a personal embodiment of the changes made in his name—swapping his kimono for a smart, braided European-style military uniform, bearded and mustached, his topknot shorn. Not only did he drink wine as well as sake, his 1873 New Year greeting included the taboo-shattering news that he ate beef and mutton—breaking a centuries-long Buddhist ban against consuming domesticated animals. Ten Buddhist hermits attacked the palace for this outrage; five were killed, the others arrested.

Meat eating figured significantly in the Meiji state's quasi-Darwinian efforts to socially engineer a better, stronger Japanese body to take on the West. Why were Japanese physiques puny? (Emperor Meiji's height: five feet, four inches.) Because of lack of animal protein, it was now widely believed. A first-time domestic cattle industry was encouraged, as Meiji ideologues waxed on about the merits of meat eating. The most influential of westernizers was Fukuzawa Yukichi, a public intellectual and educator (and ardent anti-Buddhist) whose short-haired portrait gazed somberly from the ten-thousand-yen note I'd taken from a konbini cash machine. An early traveler to Europe and America, Fukuzawa in 1870 wrote a famous treatise, *On Eating Meat*, which insisted that meat eating (along with science and technology, of course) was vital to the Meiji aspiration of *bunmei kaika* (civilization and enlightenment). "At this moment the absence of meat eating in our country," he warned, "will lead to poorer health and the numbers of our weak will only increase."

The policies of bunmei kaika "divided the life of the Japanese elite into two separate spheres," notes Katarzyna Cwiertka in her landmark study, *Modern Japanese Cuisine: Food, Power and National Identity*. The ideogram *wa* represented the traditional

Japanese sphere; the ideogram *yo*, the Western sphere. Just a decade after the Meiji takeover, *yōshoku* (Western-style food) served in a *yōima* (Western-style room) to diners dressed in *yōuku* (Western-style clothes) became all the rage among Japan's powerful. Thanks to its aspirational cachet, yōshoku then trickled down to the lower rungs of society. By the late 1880s, urban commoners were chowing down on "hamburg steak," kari raisu (curry rice), korokke (croquettes), and tonkatsu (breaded cutlets)—all to this day a vital part of the national canon—at democratically priced yōshoku-ya. While fancy hotel and diplomatic menus remained stodgily Gallic, yōshoku-ya eateries served a more accessible British-inspired hybrid cuisine, domesticated with soy sauce and side servings of gohan, cooked rice. By the start of the twentieth century, yōshuku had invaded the public catering sector and the army canteen—even the home kitchens.

Yet, it wasn't only yoshuku that had transformed the Japanese diet (we're getting closer to ramen).

By its later, imperialist interwar period, according to Cwiertka, Japanese cuisine had evolved into a Western-Japanese-Chinese hybrid "tripod"—even if it had taken several decades for the country to resume devouring the "Colonized East." For almost a thousand years Japan had borrowed heavily from China—tea and Buddhism, noodles and tofu, the written script, paper and textiles. But with the Meiji era, China was downgraded to a loser country status, unable to modernize like Japan, defeated first by Europe in the Opium Wars, and then by a now imperialist-minded Japan in the 1894 Sino-Japanese war. China's cuisine was accordingly neglected as the fodder of "stagnant Asia," explains historian Naomichi

Ishige—labeled "unsanitary" to boot. It wasn't until the end of the First World War that Chinese food began to be perceived as tasty and economical, and Shina ryōri-ya (Chinese restaurants) began sprouting in quantity in Japanese cities. Even less than a decade before, the scorn directed at these "sad and decrepit" places stinking of pig fat (according to one 1911 Tokyo food guide) echoed Northern Italy's contempt for Naples and pizza.

And yet. As Ishige contends, Western, and in time, Chinese cuisines became embraced largely because they provided what was missing in native Japanese fare: "meat, oils and fats, and spices." Ramen scholar George Solt meanwhile offers a geopolitical spin, noting how European imperialism caused Japan to adopt Western foodstuffs like wheat, meat, and dairy, while "Japanese imperialism in continental Asia accounts for the popularization of Chinese food in the interwar period."

Chinese cuisine spread through Japan from its treaty ports— Kobe, Nagasaki, and Yokohama—where the Chinese mostly worked for Western traders as servants, cooks, clerks, and handymen, as well as independent merchants and middlemen. Yokohama had the largest Chinese colony, a thriving Nankinmachi ("Nanjing town" a.k.a. Chinatown)—and it was here in the late 1880s, by all accounts, that a proto-ramen called Nankin soba made its appearance as a salty, fatty, pork-bone-based soup (no roast pork toppings yet), loaded with noodles laced with an alkaline liquid that made them stretchy.

The complicated story of how Nankin soba got reconfigured into ramen, the millennial darling and a $44 billion worldwide industry, was to occupy me for much of the rest of my Tokyo stay.

But for now, I urgently wanted to hang out with a ramen otaku.

I GOT LEADS ON a couple of ra-otas, as ramen otakus (obsessives)
are known. To my shock, both were Americans—ex–ramen colum-
nists for Japanese *Playboy* and bona fide celebs here in a land that
devours magazines, TV shows, and mangas devoted to ramen.

Abram Plaut, whom I reached out to first, suggested rendez-
vousing at a new-wave ramen-ya called Mensho, in the residential
Gokokuji district away from the city center. Before meeting him, I
stopped to admire St. Mary's Cathedral, a shining, up-swooping
showstopper of Japanese modernism designed by Kenzo Tange
around the time of the 1964 Olympics. Nearby, under elevated
railway tracks, trimly packed bags of possessions of the neighborhood homeless population sat poignantly undisturbed, awaiting
their owners' nighttime return.

Abram met me under Mensho's sign, which proclaimed in English: "A Bowl for Tomorrow." Tall, broad-shouldered, and pimple-
less in his midthirties, he wore a black Warriors basketball cap—he's
from the Bay Area—and black jeans extravagantly torn by a designer friend. His deeply semiotic sneakers were beyond my decoding. And I tried not to stare too hard at the lollipop-madness of his
big hands' painted fingernails. How would I even communicate
with such a forbiddingly out-there, hip-hop cool ra-ota? But Abram
just said, "Hey, let's go crush some bowls," put the requisite
thousand-yen coins into Mensho's ticket machine, and off we went
noodling.

Mensho is a branch of a boutique ramen chain that's the brain-
child of Tomoharu Shono, a hotshot young self-proclaimed "hyper-
ramen creator" who owns half a dozen Tokyo ramen parlors serving
outré foie gras tsukemen (brothless ramen) and chocolate-lamb

black ramen along with the more classic shio and shoyu. In 2016, Shono and Abram together opened a Mensho branch in San Francisco, where the tori paitan—ramen in white chicken bone broth available, if you please, in flavors like matcha—became an instant cult hit.

I could tell that Shono's was "a bowl for tomorrow" just by looking around. Behind a glass partition, white-coated young staff were grinding whole-wheat Hokkaido flour for noodles. Wall posters touted sundry locavore manifestos in English and Japanese and biochemical arcana, such as how ramen's dashi broth combines inosinic acid from katsuobushi (bonito flakes) with glutamic acid from kombu seaweed for some miraculously umami-enhancing effect. Or how Mensho's katsuobushi was hongare (the kind dusted with mold and aged for several months) from Makurazaki, a.k.a. "Katsuo town"—which I guess rendered the dashi both heritage-y *and* scientific.

"Super-legit farm-to-bowl stuff," approved Abram.

Shono-san's signature seafood ramen arrived. The wide rim of its oversize white bowl came scattered with shaved karasumi (bottarga) and alabaster nuggets of scallops crusted with carbonized negi (spring onion). Its noodles, at once toothsome and delicate, floated ethereally in a strong clear seafood broth topped with pink petals of (yelp!) chicken *sashimi*. "Even for Japan, a country of perfect eggs," Abram clucked, "*this* onsen egg in here is superquality." I nodded, amazed by the incandescent orange yolk of supernatural creaminess, by the sheer quality of this thousand-yen bowl.

"Shono's totally killing it here," Abram continued, "but hey, this is Tokyo, this isn't even the best ramen I've had *this month*." Apparently around three hundred ramen-ya open every year just in Tokyo. There was pineapple ramen, tequila and ice cream and pizza ramen; a famous place called Big Breast Ramen run by an adult video star; ramen-ya where customers wore themed outfits; secret pop-ups serving cricket ramen . . .

"Honestly," Abram confessed, on a note of exhaustion, "I can't even keep up with new places, let alone get back to the old ones."

Noodles as such arrived in Japan with Chinese Buddhist monks around the twelfth century. But it took another eight centuries for a dish recognizable as *ramen* (noodles + meaty savory broth + toppings) to emerge as a popular snack dispensed by yatai pushcarts and cheap Chinese restaurants. Possibly derived semantically from Mandarin Chinese *lamian*, or pulled noodles, the original Japanese term for it was the racist-imperialist Shina ("Chink") soba, or the more neutral *shuko* (Chinese) soba. Ramen joints began to break out of their Chinatown ghettos in the decades before the Second World War, but it was with Japan's post-WWII reconstruction that ramen took off as an indispensable "stamina food," supplying cheap calories made from overabundant American wheat imports (more on which later) to the labor force rebuilding the country's infrastructure—and later renovating Tokyo for the 1964 Olympics. Between 1955 and 1974 expenditure on ramen increased 250 percent.

By the 1980s ramen had made it into Japan's kokuminshoku ("national people's cuisine") pantheon—a romanticized symbol of daily life from the high-growth postwar era, as historian George Solt explains in his book, *The Untold Story of Ramen*. Then as Japan's bubble economy shifted from manufacture to service, the dish outgrew its cheap-fuel identity and began to attract the *Shinjinrui* ("New Breed") of urbanite yuppies with disposable incomes for whom *lifestyle* was more compelling than fond mementoes of their parents' toiling heroics. A gourmet boom fed the rise of food porn, of dining as spectacle—of floods of ramen TV shows, magazines, manga, and video games. There were ramen guidebooks to aid *ramen gyōretsu*, the new ramen tourists ready to drive miles to queue for that hyperdesirable slurp they saw on TV.

Ramen entered its new golden age (with another identity shift) when the nineties postbubble downturn brought a collective craving for comfort foods infused with nationalist symbolism *and* status ingredients, but light on the wallet (loud echoes of pizza's situation again). The emblem of hardworking industrial yesteryear was transformed yet again into a "slow-cooked object of handcrafted devotion," according to Solt, as part of a time when the country was embracing an image change from "Japan Inc. to J-cool," in the words of one anthropologist. So 1994 welcomed the folksy Ramen Museum of Shin-Yokohama, a theme park of regional ramen, followed by more such theme parks, with names like Ramen Philosophers Hall, and by designed-to-death (but still affordable) destination ramen-ya like Menya Musashi in Shinjuku, built like a theater—all the stuff that so amused our friend Kyoichi.

The eighties indie ramen shop owner might have been an escapee from a salaryman lifestyle. Shono's generation of hipster ramen auteurs, brought up in an ongoing recession with limited prospects, became, per Solt again, faces of Japan's readjusted identity— "redefining not only Japanese popular culture, but the idea of Japan itself—both at home and abroad."

And all that twisting, shifting history was what I was slurping at Shono's. Noisily finishing the last of my freshly milled noodles and carbonized negi, I broke a sweat just thinking about it.

. . .

Abram had his own take on ramen's popularity with millennial diners and chefs. For one, the "explosion" of ramen coincided with the explosion of the internet in Japan and the two "kind of fed off each other." But there was also ramen's promise of freedom—freedom from the codified straitjacket of Japanese genre cooking. "Sushi will always be sushi, kaiseki always kaiseki," he declared, adjusting his black cap with Day-Glo–tipped fingers. "Before ramen, the Japanese worshipped soba, which was refined and Zen-like and blah-blah, prepared by rules you just didn't fuck with." But ramen? Ramen was a "cheap slut" that you could mess with, opening a shop for the equivalent of $50,000 and making it totally "next level" and personal by playing with the endless permutations of broth, noodle, toppings, and *tare* (seasoning).

Which was pretty much Shono-san's story. Boyish and ramen rock-star *kawaii* (adorable), he joined us on a bench outside Mensho after we'd crushed our bowls and were reminded by Abram of the cardinal rule of a ramen-ya, "Eat it and beat it."

"I developed a ramen passion in high school," Shono-san began as Abram translated, "going around Chinese restaurants trying out different Shina soba [the old term for ramen]." His own experiments with cooking tonkotsu ramen—the cloudy-white hard-core pork broth style from Kyushu that sparked the millennial ramen craze—started after he befriended a croquette shop master who supplied him with leftover bones and scraps for his broth. "I threw ramen parties in college"—he grinned sweetly—"and thought myself totally genius."

In 2005, on a shoestring, he opened his first ramen-ya, a cheapo ten-seater serving only tonkotsu ramen. But soon, inspired by chef-y dishes he saw on the internet, he began dabbling in seasonal specials, going to French and Italian restaurants, traveling to China to learn about hand-pulled noodles. Eventually he realized that as long as there were noodles and broth, ramen could be almost *anything*. Opening more shops and crisscrossing Japan sourcing ingredients, he developed his farm-to-bowl concept—"the first in Japan!" Abram annotated again—and got to this point, where he now mills his own flour.

"Ramen in Japan was delicious fast food for poor people, *B-kyu gurume* [B-class gourmet]," Shono went on, using a Japanese term for lovable lowbrow comfort foods—edible B movies. But after being received like a culinary rock star abroad, he became convinced that ramen merited the same *kōkyū gurume* (high-grade gourmet) status as sushi. And the response astounded him. "Michelin chefs from all over the world!" he exclaimed. "They wanted to get to know *me*, a humble ramen guy!"

Shono's current dream was to go around the globe making farm-to-table ramen with foreign local ingredients. "'Cause Shono's that rare thing," Abram approved. "A locavore chef *and* a legit ramen master."

I wanted to ask about ramen and nationalism, but Abram didn't know how to exactly translate the question. So I asked if ramen was *Nihon* ryōri—*Japanese* food. "I respect its Chinese origins," Shono replied, tipping a polite little bow that seemed slightly ironic. "But it was us Japanese who transformed ramen, changed it and elevated it to the level of sushi." Did he patronize any old-school ramen shops? "Of course," he said. "At the start of each year I visit my favorite traditional ramen-ya. To apologize for breaking the rules." He wasn't joking.

I learned more about Abram as we repaired to a *famiresu* (family restaurant) with all-you-can-drink soft drinks across the street from Mensho. In 2003, as an exchange student near Tokyo, his mind was blown by an unsung ramen-ya out in the sticks. Next ramen-ya, different style dish, mind reblown. By his fifth ramen shop he had a wide-eyed epiphany: "Ramen is like snowflakes, each bowl is completely unique. And here I was," he said almost sheepishly, "in the ramen mecca, with ten thousand shops *just in Tokyo*."

Abram ended up staying on in Tokyo, teaching English, then dealing in rarified sneakers to "next-level" Air Jordan otakus on eBay—and building such a ramen database in his head that a Japanese *Playboy* editor he met one night cried, "Holy shit! You know more about ramen than most Japanese!" So Abram and a fellow Californian ramen otaku named Brian got a weekly column to dish on ramen shops. Their *gaijin* (foreigner) act was a hit. "Because we were so brutally honest," Abram explained, "trashing greasy pork shashu or 'cardboard noodles,'" to the scandalized delight of super-polite Japanese. Abram with his hip-hop style became an in-demand expert on ramen TV shows: "The Japanese fucking loved it!" Still, he mused, Japanese ra-otas made him look like a rookie. He showed me on Instagram a glitzy young dude stepping out of a white Lamborghini with a bowl of ramen.

"I eat two hundred bowls a year. That guy crushes at least two thousand bowls—between proper meals!" Abram shook his head in respect.

THE ODDS OF OTAKUS leaping from Lambos with a bowl of gohan, on the other hand, were exceedingly low. White rice has zero millennial-hipster glamour.

I pondered this fact as I made my way to the venerable Yanagihara

Cooking School, dedicated to preserving and renovating Edo-period recipes. Here I intended to absorb some gohan wisdom from its co-owner Naoyuki Yanagihara, the scion of a famed cooking family, author of many books, Japan's official cultural envoy for gastronomy, and a sometime TV star at that. So who knew, actually, maybe he did drive a Lamborghini.

The cooking school was a mile's walk from Oakwood, occupying its own three-story building with a roof garden—an astoundingly tasty morsel of central Tokyo real estate, tucked in under the glassy skyscrapers of Toranomon Hills. I was congratulating myself on finding my way in this megalopolis of inscrutable street addresses when an assistant approached to take my sneakers. Now I blushed at the state of my socks.

Maria, the assistant, young and dark haired—gaijin? half-Japanese?—led me into the state-of-the-art demo kitchen. "Ah . . . the smell of washoku," murmured Maria, her smile tinged with deep, hidden lore. Yes, that ur-Japanese umami scent: soy sauce, dashi broth, and slightly caramelized miso.

There was something ur-Japanese, too, about Maria herself, almost *exaggeratedly*, I thought, as I watched from my student chair. How deferentially she bowed to arriving pupils, how faithfully and soundlessly she padded after Yanagihara-sensei (the honorific meaning teacher or master), how slowly and contemplatively she arranged the demo kitchen utensils. She seemed nunlike, a perfect deshi (apprentice) attending the altar of Japanese culture. Yanagihara-sensei meanwhile hardly seemed typecast for his venerable role. In his early forties, he had princely good looks and a smile out of an elegant toothpaste ad. Nothing in his casual, low-key manner seemed to demand reverence. But later, he chuckled to admit that even an ancient octogenarian student addressed him as Sensei, which literally means "former-born."

Besides me, the class consisted of fifteen attractive young Japanese women and one middle-aged guy who looked like a retired corporate samurai. Sensei began by demonstrating a sashimi of fleetingly seasonal aji (horse mackerel). Maneuvering a huge gleaming knife with a jeweler's precision, he scaled, filleted, and sliced the whole aji into delicate petals. Decorated with tiny purple buds and adorable leek brushes, the sashimi was sent around the class on a shiso leaf. The students bowed in awe; I bowed along my gaijin best. Next, Sensei rendered a pork fillet into a painstaking heap of matchstick julienne. "For a foreign-origin soup," Maria explicated softly. "In Edo times, Japanese didn't eat pork." Sensei then prepared the requisite nimono (a simmered dish), a steamed heritage kabocha squash in a sauce of very minced chicken and his own signature dashi stock, made from shiitake mushrooms and kombu from a remote fishing village in eastern Hokkaido.

"*Ichiju sansai*, meaning, soup and three side dishes, plus gohan," summarized Maria.

This was the basic structure of *shojin ryōri* (Zen monastic cuisine) and of washoku, the traditional Japanese meal that Sensei strove to preserve and promote: Rice + Soup + Side Dishes = Japanese Meal.

By most accounts, Edo-period home cooking was awful. Household members swallowed down its austere monotony of rice/tofu/pickled everything at different times from individual trays. Then Meiji lifestyle reformers invested the family with new moral meaning. Eating became a shared activity around a low common table. The new Meiji woman was supposed to embody the Victorian-inspired ideal of *ryōsai kenbo*—"good wife, wise mother"—as a full-time up-to-date housewife (*shufu*), savvy in home economics and hygiene. She was expected to zest up the family meals with tasty new offerings gleaned from women's magazines. The rice + soup + side dishes grammar still held, but the side dishes became more plentiful, more varied and fusion-y: a Japanese-Western hybrid known as *wayo setchu ryōri*.

But nowadays? I mused, as Sensei's knife flashed with supernatural skill. Nowadays over 50 percent of Japanese women were working. Why would an exhausted OL (office lady) who slumped dozing in the metro on her crowded homeward commute spend time finely julienning pork or scaling a fish? All these little endless Zen-like ceremonies and protocols of ur-Japanese cooking . . . What *was* the point, when acres of ready-made gorgeousness awaited at supermarkets and depachika (department store food halls)—even at the better-class konbini?

Then again, my classmates here didn't strike me as part of the overworked 50 percent.

At last Sensei turned to the sacral event: the preparing of gohan. It was to be cooked in a traditional okama pot, an old-fashioned metal contraption shaped like a graduation hat, with a massive wooden lid to absorb excess moisture. But first the rice was washed in several changes of water. Then Sensei began swishing and massaging and lightly rubbing the grains between his palms. "*Togu*," whispered Maria, as if announcing an esoteric rite. "Cleansing rice of its bran."

"Listen . . . *listen deep to your rice*," intoned Sensei. "*Listen* to the *tch-tch-tch-sha-sha-sha* of the swishing . . . the *boku-boku-boku* of the bubbling water . . . the *pachi-pachi-pachi* of the water evaporating." The breadth of Japanese rice onomatopoeia was impressively rich.

After class I asked Sensei if his students really gutted and thin-sliced fish for sashimi in their own tiny home kitchens. "Our fish-cutting classes are the most in-demand," he replied in excellent English. "DIY sushi parties are massively fashionable, you see."

But why, I persisted, would Japanese students *pay* to learn how to cook rice, the national staple? It seemed as absurd as Italians having to be taught how to boil pasta. "You'd be amazed," he informed me, "how electric rice cookers completely took over our kitchens. When the Fukushima nuclear disaster shut down electricity, many people went hungry because they had no idea how to make gohan. By hand. In a pot."

For generations going back to the late Edo period, Sensei's family were cooks and restaurateurs specializing in Kinsaryu cuisine. This branch of chaseki—rice + soup + side dishes served during the tea ceremony—was a more humble version of kaiseki, the exclusive, elaborately ritualized, and massively costly multicourse meal. When Sensei was six, his granddad, who'd founded Yanagihara Cooking School in the fifties, presented him with a set of Japanese knives. Learning to cook from his parents, Sensei mastered the absurdly difficult technique of katsuramuki, slicing a vegetable thinner than paper. At university, though, he trained as a fermentation scientist, then worked for a big soy sauce company. In 2009, his life unexpectedly changed when he was summoned through his grandfather's arrangement to serve as an "inji," a person who prepares meals for Omizutori, a legendary two-week penance festival held at the eighth-century Todaiji Buddhist temple in the imperial city of Nara. During his three years affiliated with Todaiji, Sensei was also tasked with rewriting the monks' regular menus. He was stunned to discover how impoverished their diet was. The menus hadn't been updated since 1947, when Japan barely had anything to eat.

"But the monks resisted my food!" Sensei recounted, as we sat in an upstairs room in the cooking school where his mother gave flower-arranging lessons. "They treated me as an intruder!"

He was miserable at the temple. No alcohol, no meat, no going out. He lost eight kilos from stress. But immersing himself in Edo culinary texts while trying to modernize the monastic diet, he developed some fifty tofu recipes, including his hit with a musky black walnut sauce, his chichi Western-style avocado with wasabi dressing—previously the monks hardly ate salads—and his stunningly beautiful dish of tofu-stuffed yuba (tofu skins), which he showed me on his cell phone. "By the end," he declared, beaming, "the monks were really happy with me. Especially when I made tempura, everyone's favorite." And it was at Todaiji that Sensei learned how to cook gohan over live fire. To him it remained the most delicious thing in the world.

The cooking school building has been in the Sensei's family since the late Edo period, when geishas still roamed this Minato-ku neighborhood and rice consumption was about 270 kilos per person a year—some five cups a day. But now, Sensei lamented, now it had sunk to 50 kilos a year, half of what it was in the sixties. Bread sales had recently overtaken rice; beer was outselling sake. Japan had fallen to fiftieth place in the world in per capita rice consumption.

To Sensei this signified a deep spiritual crisis. Gohan, along with fermented seasonings such as mirin and soy, and dashi-based miso soup—for him they defined Japanese culture. "Dashi was usually the second liquid babies tasted after their mother's milk," he explained. "My son tasted it at just six weeks old. A breakfast of rice, pickles, and soup brought Japanese families together." And now? Now every street had fancy French and Italian bakeries—and who could resist croissants on the run? (Not me, I thought greedily,

remembering my breakfast earlier of konbini adzuki red bean croissants.) "All right," Sensei allowed, "to go with rice, our women can
buy side dishes at depachika, especially Western-style items. But the
moment we stop cooking dashi and gohan," he said, "we will no
longer be Japanese." He spoke calmly, without histrionics, but with
profound conviction.

Gohan is the Japanese word for *meal* as well as rice. In Japan the
round sticky domestic japonica rice had traditionally been a measure
of wealth, sometimes even currency, a form of taxation. Rice as
money was considered morally clean, whereas regular money was
regarded as a little dirty. Modern Japanese emperors—those semi-
divine descendants of Amaterasu, the Shinto sun goddess who created
the sacred rice-fields that fed the very first Japanese people—planted
rice seedlings on the grounds of the Imperial Palace to assure a good
harvest. Those mochi rice cakes and rice stalks offered at Shinto
shrines? They were for Inari, the beloved fox deity, protector of
rice crops.

The weight of rice in Japanese culture, I understood, was meta-
physical. I'd read *Rice as Self*, a slim but influential study by the
prominent structural anthropologist Emiko Ohnuki-Tierney, who
examined the long, loaded history of Japan's self-identification as
rice eaters and rice growers. Domestic japonica rice, argued Ohnuki-
Tierney, evolved into a central metaphor of Japanese collective
identity—the eternal essence of *Japaneseness* in essentialist Nihonjinron theories. It symbolized everything from uniquely Japanese
aesthetics (the ubiquitous artistic representations of rice paddies) to
agricultural policies to nation-building. Furthermore, contended
Ohnuki-Tierney, the Japanese rice-eating self was often constructed

in opposition to Others: to meat-eating Westerners, to the Chinese who ate a *different* (indica) rice, to the California rice lobby, which, in the mid-1990s when *Rice as Self* was written, was pushing its exports on Japan.

But rice was also an invented tradition.

The myth taught to Japanese schoolkids about how the grain nurtured Japanese people for two thousand years? Just that: a myth. While rice *had* been an important status symbol and tax crop, until rather recent history, the Japanese were "polygrain" eaters. Barley and beans were their basic diet elements. Before white rice became widely affordable in the early twentieth century, it was the food of urban elites. Commoners—including rice farmers themselves—consumed it only on special occasions. The auspicious rice-planting ritual at the Imperial Palace? Semi-invented by astute Meiji image-manipulators. Rice symbolism, according to Ohnuki-Tierney, became particularly potent during the Meiji era in the face of popular anxiety over Western technological and scientific superiority—and the government's radical, westernized modernizing. Meiji authorities turned to agrarian nostalgia, the farm village as the heart and soul of Japan, to unite the population—while simultaneously (Meiji policies were big on twists) industrializing and militarizing the newly conceived nation. Rice worship then took a very dark turn leading up to the Second World War, when the purity of white rice (*hakumai*) was evoked by the militaristic ultranationalist government as a quasi-sacred symbol of the "purity of the Japanese self"—unique among nations.

I didn't discuss any of this racist stuff with Sensei. He seemed way too cool to buy into the Nihonjinron myths about Japan as the most awesome country on earth. Instead we made plans to go shopping for kombu and katsu, and drink lots of sake at his favorite izakaya tavern. And he presented me with dried shiitake mushrooms and sun-dried Hokkaido kelp for the dashi stock—the first building block of washoku.

Before heading into the post-Edo afternoon, I couldn't help asking Maria-san for her story. She replied, diffidently and somewhat mysteriously, that she grew up in Quito—Ecuador!—devouring Japanese manga, wrote a thesis on sake at Italy's University of Gastronomic Sciences, then worked at a renowned Munich bar. She's been in Japan and at the cooking school since 1998, and planned to remain until she truly mastered washoku "the way it should be." And *that*, she said with an elegant bow, as she reunited me with my sneakers, took endless commitment and patience.

MY OWN COMMITMENT to washoku began to flag as I went looking for rice at a small supermarket on a tidily quaint modern shopping street near Tokyo Tower. Fake sakura branches bedecked the supermarket's entry; a Schumann piano sonata wafted from some hidden source. Schumann and sakura: there was something extremely Meiji about it. But only expensive five-pound bags of raw japonica rice were available, and what would a short-term gaijin planning on eating lots of ramen do with this load?

I returned to a konbini again, this time Family Mart, source of the perversely stupendous "pizza-man" (a steamed Chinese bun with cheesy tomatoey filling) and diaphanous raspberry-flavored "Fami-macaron" sticks for just 125 yen.

"*Irasshaimase!*" the konbini clerk cried, a Family Mart corporate smile sweeping over his face. *Welcome!*

His name tag said Akram. He was from Uzbekistan, part of a growing army of *konbini gaikokujin* ("convenience store foreigners"), students mostly, helping ease Japan's alarming labor shortage as its population aged. Formerly Soviet Uzbekistan! I tried to convey my rice dilemma in Russian. To my great relief, Akram understood. Japan's elderly are a hugely important konbini consumer sector. Hence the plethora of small-format items for "sad, live-alone pensioners," Akram explained as he and I went poking among the poignant, plastic-encased hard-boiled egg halves, the Lilliputian packets of mayo or miso dressing, the shrink-wrapped half sandwiches, the doll-sized jars of "marinara" for the 3.5-ounce boxes of imported Italian pasta. Finally we found it—a *small* portion of rice. Only it was already gohan—precooked and microwave ready. Akram's smile faded. "Japan, a sad country," he whispered in Uzbek-accented Russian. "When my mom makes her pilaf in our Samarkand garden, the entire mahalla [neighborhood] is invited!" Uzbek rice dishes, of course, were fragrant with cumin and lamb. Whereas plain Japanese gohan . . .

"Why would a rich country eat such a flavorless thing?" wondered Akram, his wide face full of great sympathy for the Japanese rice eater's sad lot.

Secretly, I shared Akram's feelings. Who *wouldn't* miss a cumin-laced Samarkand pilaf? But dutifully, I went tramping back to the minisupermarket and lugged home the five-pound bag of rice—a Koshihikari variety developed during the Meiji era—plus side dishes of miso-marinated salmon and microwavable gingery pork, and many small tubs of mysterious pickles.

While the rice cooked away mum in its electric cooker, and Tokyo Tower loomed domestically over my tiny but ergonomically perfect white kitchen, I hit Google Scholar. And learned that it wasn't just Sensei who worried about the decline of traditional Japanese home cooking. The government and its Ministry of Agriculture, Forestry and Fisheries worried, too. Their concern that Japan was losing pride in its unique identity along with its food was cited in the successful official petition in 2013 to get washoku onto UNESCO's Intangible Cultural Heritage list. And this concern linked to deeper, socioeconomic anxieties, according to Eric Rath, one of many Western scholars who've taken to busting and deconstructing the Japanese "national" diet. Since the start of the nineties postbubble recession, cascading problems have been battering Japan, including declining competitiveness in the global marketplace and an ominous level of food self-sufficiency, one of the lowest in the industrialized world.

The UNESCO petition made washoku—fuzzily defined as "the traditionally dietary cultures of the Japanese" and modeled on the equally fuzzy but successful "gastronomic meal of the French" application—sound ancient and timeless. In reality it dates to the Meiji era, when the deluge of Western culture and foods spurred a protective need to distinguish *wa* (Japanese Self) from *yo* (Western Other). But for most of the twentieth century, according to scholars, washoku wasn't a "thing"—maybe because yoshuku-style dishes (sukiyaki, tonkatsu, Hamburg steak, and the like) fused so quickly with the Japanese Self that untangling *wa* from *yo* seemed artificial and pointless. Mentions of washoku in the Japanese press did increase slightly during the late 1990s. Concerned about the drop in agricultural output and rice sales *and* the rise of cheap food imports, the government launched various "eat local" campaigns, while the educational ministry promoted the Japanese diet's cultural value through school lunches and shokuiko (food education).

But it was the UNESCO listing that produced a washoku explosion. A word only faintly known before to the Japanese public was now everywhere, celebrated in cookbooks, media articles, gastronomic guides, and scholarly studies. And the government—mixing *bunka gaikō* (cultural diplomacy) and Brand Japan building—promoted washoku abroad as the nation's ancient and healthy tradition. An *upscale* pizza effect swung into action. International recognition boosted washoku's domestic cachet, swelling the pride that Japanese home cooks now took, according to polls, in their own intangible food heritage.

Intangible indeed.

To scholar Eric Rath washoku was yet another invented national tradition—a "top-down attempt to guide the Japanese population into eating a certain way." Not that it was totally fake. But like white rice (or white pasta in Italy) it just wasn't *everyone's* diet. The rice + soup + side dishes structure mainly derived from chaseki, the tea ceremony touted as the aesthetic foundation of all Japanese cooking but in fact, historically, a male aristocratic pursuit. In reality, until the twentieth century, only urban elites had enough pots, pans, and fires to cook white rice *plus* side dishes (bland as those were until the Meiji era). Rural populations with their one hearth, one cauldron, dumped in together their grain (most often *not* rice), tubers, and miso for a porridge called *kate meshi*—which sounded remarkably like the stuff of trendy American grainbowls.

I was suddenly craving such kate meshi as I finally scooped the gohan from its cooker in my Oakwood test kitchen. It tasted . . . like plain boiled japonica rice. Pleasant enough, and a little mushy, perhaps because I couldn't decode the Japanese-only cooker setting instructions.

At which point Barry came in and sniffed the contents of the cooker. He shrugged. Then he turned his head and sniffed again. "Now *that*," he said, "smells *good*."

He was pointing to the saucepan of miso soup I'd made on the side.


That distinctive miso scent was what Sensei's assistant, Maria, had called, with reverence, *the* aroma of washoku.

Umami.

Darling of millennial eaters and chefs, umami is the "fifth taste," after sour, salty, sweet, and bitter. Identified in 1908 by Ki-kunae Ikeda, a Tokyo chemistry professor, it came to provide a kind of positivist scientific foundation for Japanese culinary exception-alism. The polite, bespectacled, German-trained Ikeda (from an ancient but impoverished samurai clan) had grown curious about what gave his wife's vegetarian dashi stock its deep, meaty savor. Analyzing the salty-savory crystals he derived by massively reduc-ing a mountain of kombu, a particular kelp used in stocks, he even-tually pegged the responsible agent as an amino acid called glutamic acid. Ikeda gave his discovery a cute name, umami, Japanese for "delicious." By mixing glutamic acid with sodium, he further cre-ated umami as a white soluble powder—monosodium glutamate, a.k.a. MSG—patenting and then marketing this flavor enhancer under the brand name Ajinomoto, "the essence of taste." After some initial stumbles, MSG spread throughout China and the rest of Asia. By midcentury it had been adopted by Western megabrands like Campbell's, Nestlé, and Oscar Mayer—as well as Chinese restaurants. Today Ajinomoto Co. is churning out $10 billion in sales a year across 130 countries.

But here's the thing: like washoku, the term umami as a *taste* description, at least, hardly figured for most of the twentieth century. When Ikeda created MSG in the late Meiji era, it offered "predictability, efficiency, convenience, and scientific guarantees of hygiene and nutrition" consistent with the Meiji program of civilization and enlightenment, as one historian wrote. Specifically, it appealed to the newly educated bourgeois Meiji housewives who were delighted with all that scientific cachet packaged in sleek shaker bottles. By the 1970s, however, its image had much changed. Worldwide crusades against food additives—remember the American "Chinese Restaurant syndrome" scandals that in the end turned out to be scientifically baseless and racist to boot?—had stirred Japanese eaters' distrust in corporate processed foods. Sales of Ikeda's white powder were slumping. And so in a wholesale corporate rebranding, Ajinomoto (and other MSG manufacturers) turned to Ikeda's original term: "umami seasoning." So harmonious and natural sounding. So Japanese.

MSG's rebranded rehabilitation gathered force thanks to efforts of the Umami Seasoning Promotion Association, the Umami Research Association, the Umami Information Center, and the like. Their promotional campaigns positioned umami as part of the "international language of food." Then in 2000, L-glutamate taste receptors were identified in humans by American scientists, so providing a fresh scientific boost to the idea of the exceptional and unique sensitivity of the Japanese taste bud, a taste bud that had recognized the "fifth taste" for so long. By the second decade of the new millennium, global cool-kid chefs from Dave Chang to Rene Redzepi of Noma went on an umami kick. And back in Japan, especially after the washoku UNESCO success, national broad-caster NHK TV aired hour-long programs touting umami as a national asset that Japanese chefs could teach foreign chefs.

AND YET FOR ALL of Japan's top-down manipulations, its brand-building and gastrodiplomacy, Japanese cooks were *still* turning away from their so-called traditional dietary cultures. Ramen sales had been steady since the mid-1990s, while rice was in big trouble, as I'd already learned from Sensei. Japan's food self-sufficiency ratio had now fallen *below* 40 percent. Younger eaters were eagerly embracing imported dining trends and ingredients.

Poll after poll showed Japanese cooks preferred Western-style side dishes.

I decided to do some spontaneous polling of my own one damp morning in Shinjuku, where the DoCoMo tower rises like a stripped-down Empire State Building in a neo-fifties remake of *Godzilla*. In the teeming basement food hall of Takashimaya department store, I accosted a stylish young shopper as a Japanese friend with me translated, her face flush with embarrassment. My pollee's signifiers suggested "parasite single," a Japanese term for unmarried young female consumers who live for themselves.

"Noodles (ramen, soba)—or pasta? Which do you prefer?"

The putative parasite single blinked in confusion. "Whatever I feel like eating that day!" she blurted, and then rushed off—to queue for freshly baked baumkuchen, a multilayered German cake all but forgotten in Germany but a hit in Japan.

My next respondent was a regal lady in Issey Miyake pleats,

contemplating an omiyage ("obligation gift")—a *square* water-melon costing $150.

"Wagashi [Japanese sweets] or French *shu* [Japanese for choux pastry]?"

She, too, looked very confused. "Isn't shu Japanese?"

My friend and I looked at each other.

I tried a revised line of polling in the drizzly countryside outside Tokyo while visiting a jovial sake *toji* (brewmaster) named Makato Ono.

"What food do you miss when traveling abroad?"

"Schnitzel and bratwurst!" came the reply.

So what, might I ask, did he think of the Meiji Restoration?

Ono-san was a fan. "Before Meiji, Japan was like North Korea, isolated and sad," he declared, pouring another round of his floral-nosed junmai. "But after we opened up, sake brewers could use Western technology."

Alas, that technology wasn't helping today's brewers of nihon-shu (literally "Japanese alcoholic drink"). Sales were a third of what they'd been in the seventies. Sake now accounted for a mere 6 percent of all booze consumed in Japan. So a few years ago Ono-san came up with a novelty: an ur-locavore sake brewed from rice he began growing right nearby (most sake relies on one or two "prestigious" standard national rice varieties). "We saw how the European concept of terroir was a huge hit with Japanese wine drinkers," he informed me. "This inspired us." Apparently nihonshu brewers were also fond of words like *domaine* and *cuvée*.

I flashed back to the Burgundy barrels at the Meiji shrine.

And I was reminded of an earlier conversation I'd had with Mr. Sano, the slender middle-aged owner of a celebrated Tokyo miso shop stocked with dozens of exotic varieties and boasting a miso soup café.

"Miso soup," mused Mr. Sano, "is an everyday thing, yes, but *also* a great national symbol that connects us to our homes, our roots, our heritage. All Japanese people carry with them," he added with feeling, "their deep childhood preference." And yet over the last several decades, the demand for miso had declined: from some 1,600 producers all over Japan, there were now only 900 left. *But!* Sono-san's grin took up half of his face. "In the last five years miso has become hot, a big trend, once again!"

For this, the industry had to thank the savvy Japanese Miso Promotion Board and its army of rigorously trained "miso somme-liers" educating the public. But more than anything, it was the global worldwide fermentation craze that helped the revival. Had I perhaps heard of such miso enthusiasts as Rene Redzepi in Den-mark, Mr. Sano inquired, and Dave Chang from America? "These days we're all once again crazy for koji mold!" he enthused. "And so, in my shop, I wanted our young Japanese generation to approach miso as they do fancy single-origin coffees!"

Nothing like some imported millennial locavore terroir fetishism to save national staples, I thought. *Wakon yosai* ("Japanese spirit, Western learning") . . . I recalled the famous Meiji period motto de-scribing essentially the native genius for adapting and appropriating—Japanizing and indigenizing—borrowed ideas. Of course before Meiji, the saying was *wakon kansai*, or "Japanese spirit, Chinese learning."

Next, I tried to assess Tokyo's breakfast preferences, mainly by loitering scientifically at a boxy fluorescent-lit 7-Eleven konbini. The data was muddled. Some sleepy OLs were grabbing onigiri or croissants or plastic-wrapped pieces of fruit to eat on the run. (But where? There was no eating in Japanese metros or while walking on the street.) Some salarymen stood bleary-eyed at the konbini's eating counters, dunking zaru soba into plastic condiment bowls or pouring hot water into foam cups of instant oatmeal.

I asked my Uzbek friend Akram what his Family Mart customers particularly enjoyed in the morning.

"*This!*" he cried.

It was chigiri-pan, literally "tear-off bread"—doughnut-shaped and glazed with a green matcha glaze. "*Zeleniy bublik!*" yelped Akram. Russian for "green bagel."

His accompanying facial expression suggested the end of civilization was near.

MEANWHILE, for ramen research purposes, I was trying to crush a bowl every couple days.

But even when exceedingly crowded and hip, a millennial ramen shop, that edible representation of the Cool Japan brand, gave out an oddly asocial vibe, no lingering post-slurping, and never, God forbid, any bowl-sharing.

No, my favorite places were tattered old stalwarts, the ones serving Tokyo-style shoyu (soy) ramen to Japanese septuagenarians misty for the good old postwar reconstruction years. Again and again, Barry and I went back for Chinese-style moyashimen noodles in a light broth laced with dried onions and crunchy bean sprouts at timeworn, overbright Kiraku in Shibuya. The place was a tip from our friend Kyoichi Tsuzuki, the pop-culture maven; appropriately, it was tucked away in a back warren of garish small love hotels—nowadays offering good cocktails, too, and family-friendly buffets as part of their own image makeover.

Then, just as general ramen-ya fatigue began to set in, there came a knock on the door. Our smartly garbed Polish Oakwood concierge had a vast, couriered box for us.

Inside: instant ramen.

I know I haven't mentioned it yet, the "just-add-water" fuel of American dorm rooms, the de facto currency of American prisons—the global industry of some 100 billion annual servings across eighty countries worldwide. As anathema to handcrafted-ramen heads as frozen pizza is to wood-fired Neapolitan pie fiends—*but* with an ever more massive following in its birthplace, Japan. Repeatedly the Japanese have voted it their country's most awesome invention, ahead of the Walkman (remember the Walkman?), the rocket-speed bullet train, karaoke, even the digital camera.

The box was from Hitomi Yoshio, a young academic we'd recently met at Barry's literary event with star novelist Mieko Kawakami at the International House of Japan with its voluptuously serene Japanese garden. During the postevent dinner at a faux-trattoria, Mieko, a fashion icon in Louboutin heels, boasted in her brash Osaka accent about her ramen obsession. Not the boutique stuff, arigato, but the hard-core proletarian bowls at commercial chains. "My generation is addicted to MSG!" cried Mieko. "Satisfying that Ajinomoto itch is our guilty pleasure!"

But it was Hitomi, one of Mieko's English translators, who turned out to be a real-life ramen princess. Her family produces a highly coveted healthy new-wave instant ramen brand called Yamadai New Touch (no MSG!).

A week followed now in an MSG-free blur at Oakwood. Barry

and I fought over each toothsome strand of New Touch as Hitomi
texted me translations and notations:

Seasonal leek miso ramen. (*soo good*)

Hakata-style tonkotsu ramen. (*trendy!*)

Kyoto ramen. (*Mieko loves!*)

Even my listless gohan came alive moistened with leftover New
Touch broth.

Suddenly, the ramen + rice "meal" that had begun to seem like
a contrived intellectual quest in my first weeks here made perfect
sense.

"I could eat like this forever," swooned Barry.


The world's first instant ramen went on sale in 1958, the same year
the Tokyo Tower looming out our window was completed, the
same year Japan's high-growth era officially began after all the
postwar hardships and humiliations. Only months earlier, a middle-
aged once-bankrupt Taiwan-born Japanese businessman named
Momofuku Ando (first name meaning: "tremendous fortune") had
at last created flash-fried *insutanto* noodles, able to be reconstituted in water. He achieved this feat by experimenting in his backyard hut near Osaka for an entire year, sleeping four hours a night,
no days off—a true model of a corporate superhero. Immediately
marketed in an iconic orange-hued package, Chikin Ramen, as it
was dubbed, became an edible symbol of Japan's emergent mass
consumerism. It was a "child of the times," in Ando's own words,
one that transformed its parent nation's diet and canonized its inventor as a national hero.

The hero kept on with his heroics. In 1971, Ando invented Cup

Noodle, packaged in individual peel-off-lid, pour-boiling-water containers. Half a century later, Nissin Foods, his company, sold 50 billion units of these Cup Noodles worldwide in a year. Ando's funeral in 2007 (a passionate golfer, he died aged ninety-four) was held at the national baseball stadium, where a Japanese astronaut sang the praises of the deceased's special ramen, consumable in space, while an earthbound former Japanese prime minister extolled "the creator of a culinary culture that postwar Japan can be proud of." (Naturally, no one mentioned Ando's prison stay for tax evasion.)

Instant ramen, in the words of ramen historian George Solt, fundamentally altered the relationship between the Japanese people and their sustenance. "Mankind is noodlekind!" Ando famously aphorized. But, contends Solt, the instant-noodling of Japan needs to be understood within Japan's postwar geopolitical situation—one that prominently featured American wheat.

"Ando's story," writes Solt, "illustrates the deep connections between U.S. wheat-flour imports during the Occupation, and the Japanese government's efforts to utilize the American flour."

The epic corporate narrative of Ando's invention begins in August 1945, the month Japan surrendered. Walking through his devastated adopted hometown of Osaka—where the population had shrunk from 3 million to 1 million, and survivors were starving—Ando famously saw a huge line by a dimly lit stall selling black market Shina soba, and thought (as he wrote in his autobiography), "People are willing to go through this much suffering for a bowl of ramen?" And so, goes the story, the seed was planted for an instant comfort food—one to cure not just Japan's hunger, but the world's, too.

American occupation officials, meanwhile, had their own

thoughts about hunger and postwar Japan. Initially reluctant to provide *any* emergency aid, they reconsidered out of Cold War fears that near-starvation could spark a political Red explosion. Cables from April 1946 show General Douglas MacArthur diverting surplus American wheat to Japan to undermine "leftist elements." The heavily discounted grain was also meant to help lean on the Japanese government to remilitarize and support the US against a potential Commie spread in East Asia. The obliged Japanese authorities ran campaigns encouraging people to eat the *meriken-ko* (American wheat flour). "Wheat flour contains 50% more protein than rice," one propaganda leaflet proclaimed. "America is spending $250 million for your food. Learn to use it properly . . ."

The occupation ended in 1952, but the Eisenhower administration continued shoving US agri-surpluses at Japan. Between 1954 and 1964, the country received $445 million in American "food aid"—much of it wheat, which US lobbyists pressured the Japanese Ministry of Health and Welfare to promote. The ministry, in turn, pressured nutritionists to compose treatises about the benefits of wheat over rice. "Parents who feed their children solely white rice are dooming them to a life of idiocy," warned one such treatise. Meanwhile US-sponsored "kitchen cars" roamed the countryside teaching housewives to prepare meals from bleached meriken-ko, American wheat, and canned American meat. US-sponsored school lunches for Japanese children featured American bread along with powdered milk and a meat-based stew. (Until the mid-1970s, according to Solt, Japanese school lunches included almost no rice.) The country's Agriculture and Forestry minister later lamented that "the shiploads of American foodstuffs coming to Japan to stamp out revolution produced in Japan another revolution: in eating habits." As historian Suzuki Takeo argues, the shift in Japanese dining habits in the two decades postoccupation was a top-down affair, cooked up and orchestrated by leaders in Washington and Tokyo. Shades of the Meiji Restoration, but with an almost perverse twist.

And Ando's instant ramen?

In his autobiography, the great inventor recalls how his contacts in Japan's postwar agriculture ministry urged him to develop a flour-based product. They even provided some funding. And yet Ando deemed himself a savior of the *Asian* diet—through noodles. Because otherwise, the Yanks would have hooked Japan on white bread. Ando's claims notwithstanding, early ads for his ramen featured Chibikko, a merry blond kid described in company literature as having a "wheat-flour colored complexion, a round nose, large eyes, and freckles, representing the image of health itself." Only in the late 1960s, writes Solt, when Japan's thriving economy relieved its inferiority complex about its place in the world, did Nissin ads start featuring "young kimono-clad men discussing the dish in relation to the uniqueness of Japanese culture."

Spreading this advertising across the land? The new technology of television, especially—broadcast, along with FM radio, from the tallest structure then in Japan: the new Tokyo Tower.

WHEN THE TWENTY-FOUR GIFT containers of Yamadai New Touch ramen were gone, I demanded to meet Hitomi's family.

"Gee, I've never even been here myself," Hitomi confessed, bringing us into Yamadai's Tokyo sales headquarters on a glum workaday street beside the cramped canal-like Kanda River. "I'm actually not into ramen."

In a sparse white conference room, we were welcomed by Hitomi's uncle, Keiichi-san, looking the part of a hard-drinking corporate boss, and her mom, Harumi-san, a vision of refined elegance in a beige designer twinset.

Yamadai, we learned from Uncle Keiichi, was started in 1948 by Hitomi's maternal granddad, Shuzaburo-san, who came from a big rice-farming, land-owning family in Ibaraki Prefecture just northeast of Tokyo. He began with udon, then "jumped on the instant ramen bandwagon." But eventually, instant ramen developed an image problem. Ando's original method relied on flash-frying, which left the noodles with *20 percent* fat. And so in the aughts, Yamadai embraced the nifty steam-boil-dry technique—no frying involved. A healthier product! The noodles, dubbed Sugomen (or Super-Noodle) even approximated the supple chew of the artisanal ramen-ya item.

Uncle Keiichi now scribbled stats on a blackboard. "Currently Japan consumes over five billion portions of instant ramen a year . . . Nissin controls some forty percent of that business . . ."

"In comparison we are just two-point-five percent," Hitomi's mom put in modestly.

"Which is *not* tiny," boomed Uncle Keiichi, "our sales are ten billion yen."

With consistent top spots on TV blind-tasting instant ramen shows, Yamadai pretty much controlled the very high end of the instant ramen market. And as Japan's graying population was getting more health- and quality-conscious, that sector was growing.

"Yeah," whispered Hitomi, "the competition for our country's elderly taste buds is fierce."

"Pardon," I whispered back, "but could we, um, maybe have a little tasting, possibly?"

It was now lunchtime. The display stand of vibrant New Touch tubs was like a bell choir for a Pavlov dog.

"Oh—" said Hitomi.

Five minutes of scrambling later, Barry and I were crushing, for starters, bowls of light Kyoto-style shoyu ramen with sliced pork and a very special "Kujo" leek from Kyoto. Reconstituted in broth, it had an amazing lifelike leeky deliciousness. "It's Yamadai's top seller among our seventy different noodle types," noted Keiichi-san, looking on as we slurped away. "The idea of a region contained in a bowl is big!" What's more, for all the talk of the older slurpers of graying Japan, instant ramen sales were still strongest with youths: "They love having instant ramen parties, unique, strong, standout tastes!" Case in point, a ferociously spicy, extremely chewy brothless tantanmen (a Japanese take on Sichuan dan dan mian noodles) that made me think yet again, as we crushed it into ob-livion, that bland white gohan was doomed.

In search of new potential bestsellers, the Yamadai team scoured the country, taste-testing, focus-grouping, consulting with super-markets. "But at the end, ha ha," Hitomi put in, "our master taster is Grandma! She's the one who chose the package we sent you!" Apparently at ninety-two, Grandma had a supernatural ability to divine trends. This ramen sibyl's own current favorite? The newly launched Nagasaki-style seafood Sugomen, "an instant bestseller!"

"But to be honest," mom Harumi-san confided, "my mother and dad, our whole family, we prefer udon or soba. Dad, in his late nineties, still makes soba by hand each year for our family New Year party in Ibaraki, where my parents live by a rice field. Ah, soba!" She gave a fond smile. "So healthy, such perfect nutrition, so Japanese."

. . .

We left the Yamadai headquarters now and were ferried by a glossy Mercedes to Harumi-san's favorite retail playground, the blindingly sleek acreage of Ginza Six shopping mall. Past a sausage stand advertising "Aging Beef Dog" and displays of Mexican-inspired paletas (ice pops) in flavors like Okinawa mango-pine, we ascended to Tsujiri, a dessert café owned by a legendary green tea brand from Kyoto. Here, over a fantastical parfait featuring emerald layers of matcha jelly, matcha ice cream, and matcha chiffon cake, Harumi-san told us her story.

A foodie who jets to Lyon or Hokkaido to taste local specialties, Harumi-san grew up on the edge of the family's Ibaraki rice farm, eating gohan and miso and pickles—"with no tasty Western food, not even an Italian restaurant for miles." Having now learned to appreciate "our washoku," she breakfasts every day on rice and miso soup. But in her childhood this diet seemed depressing and unrelieved, and she felt like a bumpkin, even if it *was* fun to watch Japanese pop stars in her family's ramen TV commercials.

To give her a ladylike upbringing, her noodle baron dad bought her a huge house in Tokyo, where she lived alone with six staff and a nanny. She took classes in tea ceremony and flower arrangement, and attended an elite school where many classmates came from actual royalty. Perhaps I'd heard of Princess Mikasa, granddaughter of Emperor Taisho? The one who married the hereditary grand master of the most important tea ceremony school in Japan? At school Harumi-san was embarrassed by her Ibaraki accent, her family's ramen business, and her bento box lunches that smelled of the grilled fish packed by her peasant maid. Her classmates' exquisite bentos were composed by professional chefs.

"But the princesses all wanted the real country food from *my* bento!" she laughed, shaking her head. "And now after all these years, Japanese people are proud of their regional food."

Gohan, miso soup, soba and udon noodles . . . *this* was *Japanese* food, she murmured, softly rattling her pearls as I spooned up my last emerald bits of parfait.

"But Harumi-san," I asked, "what about ramen?"

She pursed her lips slightly. "Ramen, if I could be perfectly honest, is junk food, *never* washoku. Though we really do hope our healthy New Touch Sugomen has elevated its image somewhat."

Back at Oakwood, under the by-now cozy presence of the orange copycat Eiffel Tower, I had a shock. Contrary to popular lore and official accounts, I learned that Momofuku Ando, celebrated inventor of that source of Japanese national pride and sustenance, was born Wu Bai-fu in Taiwan (then under Japanese colonial rule). His parents were Chinese. He moved to Japan in 1933, aged twenty-three; he didn't become a citizen until 1948.

As if this wasn't enough of a twist to a Möbius strip of identities and histories, there was evidence he'd been beaten to the punch with his invention—by another Taiwanese, also in Osaka, named Zhang Guowen. Zhang produced and applied to patent a type of instant ramen (called "longevity noodles") right before Nissin's debuted. He sold his patent rights to Ando in 1961 (for a good sum). And with that, Zhang disappeared from the great national narrative.

BUT HERE IN MODERN Tokyo, how did one even *begin* to define a "national" food narrative?

The pink of sakura had given way to the magenta of azaleas, then the purple of irises. Almost four weeks now in Japan, and I was still waiting for some moment of epiphany. Sitting under a ginkgo tree in late-Meiji-era Hibiya Park, munching a bestselling 7-Eleven cookie—the one featuring "chicken cream" and chocolate chips—with a panorama of glossy skyscrapers rising over the greenery, I reflected that Japanese cuisine could be represented as a very large and elaborately compartmentalized bento box. The local love of designations, of branding and nomenclature, divided the compartments into washoku and yoshuku: here, elite A-gourmet subgenres of Nihon ryōri (Japanese cuisine) such as kaiseki and sushi; there, B-gourmet comfort foods such as ramen and other mostly Asian hybrids such as curry rice. Further compartments held *esunikku* ("ethnic") cuisines encompassing mostly Southeast Asian dishes; Shina ryōri (straightforward Chinese cuisine); and various cuisines of Europe (French and Italian, principally) and the Americas, either unadulterated or glocalized.

In *reality*, however, eating in this megalopolis of assimilative everythingness was like consuming a vast multicultural bowl of blithely mishmashed familiar categories, rendering the idea of taxonomy meaningless. The fetishistically traditional and outrageously outré were combined in ways that were sometimes strained and contrived, but more often than not, just wondrously casual.

What did it mean for any national food habits?

I put the question to my friend Hiroko Sasaki, a prominent Tokyo food journalist, at her favorite soba-ya, a woody minimalist spot that resembled Tokyo—by way of Berlin.

"Breakfast gohan versus croissant, udon versus spaghetti, it's all just a minor consumer choice." Hiroko shrugged, dipping her green tea soba into a newfangled walnut sauce. "It says *nothing* about who we are. Anya, truly, people just don't *care*. Many of them think McDonald's is Japanese!" She rolled her eyes. "As soon as a foreign food trend takes root, we completely forget about provenance." Some decades ago when crepes entered Japan, creperies quickly mushroomed in Harajuku district, then spread to the rest of Japan— as "Harajuku cuisine."

What's more, most people were turning away from fully Japanese restaurants. Kaiseki places especially were perceived as expensive, rigid, and boring.

"Actually," said Hiroko, digging her spoon into crema catalana, this soba-ya's signature sweet, "young Japanese don't even *know* what kaiseki is."

In her forties, serious and slightly formal, Hiroko was, like Sensei, a crusader. Her cause embraced a traditional diet, rice, and especially local fish sustainability, which was apparently in dire shape "despite all the supposed Japanese worship of nature." She was someone who stopped to inhale the aroma of gohan from her okama pot every morning.

One day, Hiroko suggested we go visit a rice geek.

"A rice otaku!" I yelped. "Please!"

I'd been searching for one such for almost a month. Maybe he could help me finally to that elusive epiphany?


Masaki Funakubo, the rice geek, was in his forties as well, with a youthful sweep of dark hair and an intense bespectacled gaze to go with the big craggy hands of a farmer. From his website I'd learned he was "5-star Rice Meister," a "Rice Sommelier"—ah, that Japanese cult of connoisseurship and credentials—and a "Ministry of Agriculture, Forestry and Fisheries Award Winner." He was also,

I'd learn, a rice supplier to some of the most exclusive sushi temples in Tokyo.

He received us in his small third-floor office in Koto ward, in an old commercial area known for its granary trade before World War II. Papers, boxes, and a clunky old fax machine crowded the place. It was stiflingly humid. Down on the ground floor sat our geek's boutique rice shop, Funakubo Shoten, and a modest onigiri café. Right below us buzzed a rice-hulling facility, which smelled sweetly and then some of bran—"amazingly rich in amino acids," the rice otaku enthused.

As Hiroko struggled to translate his fervent perorations, Funakubo-san described how he grew up eating his mother's gohan without particular zeal. In his twenties he worked as a French cuisine chef, which involved zero rice. Then his father, who manufactured wagashi—sweets often based on glutinous rice—died suddenly, and Funakubo inherited his rice-selling license. At age twenty-five, Funa (for short) bought his first rice crop. "As a chef I'd often visit producers," he exclaimed, "yet this farmer seemed shocked by my visit!" To his own shock, he discovered that retailers and chefs hardly ever had actual contact with rice growers.

"And they say rice is our sacred crop," he muttered disdainfully.

Yet the entire country consumed just a few standard varieties. The national bestseller was (and remains) Koshihikari, the one I cooked in my rice cooker.

"Koshihikari is pretty, large grained, and reheats well," interjected Hiroko.

"And is utterly *flavorless*," came the retort.

As he continued visiting farmers, Funakubo grew more depressed. Since the Meiji period the government had been investing in rice-growing technology, while heavily subsidizing its rice farmers—who eventually formed a crucial political voting bloc for the ruling conservative Liberal Democratic Party, in power since 1955 with only short interruptions. "Rice," proclaimed one prominent LDP politician, "is the core of our spiritual civilization." Rice production became one of Japan's most protected sectors, with the aforementioned subsidies, prices set artificially high (counting on consumer patriotism), and until very recently, draconian tariffs on imports. But, as I knew from Sensei, after a peak in the sixties, consumption of rice has been steadily falling. Kept on life support by the government and entangled in endless bureaucracies created by the all-powerful farming cooperatives, most rice farmers, Funa discovered, simply had no motivation.

"How I wished such farmers would just disappear!" he growled.

The situation has only gotten worse. Over 80 percent of Japanese rice farmers are now way past retirement age. "Their knowledge will die with them," said Funakubo. What's more, 90 percent of them do other farming, and over half work office jobs or the like. "And if you earn money from other sources"—the rice geek was now in fulminating flood—"where is the incentive to grow better rice? It takes thousands of people to consume one rice field's worth! And who eats rice these days?"

The questions hung in the humid, bran-sweet air.

Eventually Funa did find some committed and passionate rice growers, though he often had to buy their entire crop to keep the motivation going. With their unique special rices, he began to approach sushi masters. But yet again, frustration: haughty and entrenched in their ways, sushi masters just weren't interested.

"They talked about their secret seasoning vinegar, their shari (rice ball) shaping techniques—even the water. But *rice*?" He snorted. "Most swore by some standard so-called prestigious variety, because that's what *their* master had taught them. Because that's how it's *always* been done!"

His eventual first client, Masahiro Yoshitake in Ginza, was savvy, however. He understood that the brutal competition between elite Ginza sushi masters made it virtually impossible to compete in the fish game. But with rice, he could distinguish himself.

"Sometimes it takes a whole year to work with a sushi master on perfecting their shari," said Funa. "Because there's so much they don't know about rice." But Yoshitake listened, chose well, and recalibrated. "And now he has three Michelin stars!"

With his next client, Sugita (currently one of the hardest reservations in Tokyo), Funa went further, trying to tailor not just the rice variety but the degree of milling and polishing to particular seasonal fish. Fatty and rich fish needed a rice with lots of umami; for leaner, more delicate species, 3 percent more milling achieved the perfect harmony.

It was *consumers*, however, proclaimed the rice geek, who needed the most education. His eyes took on a kind of valiant but bleak zeal. It was a look that suddenly and weirdly put me in mind of Momofuku Ando, perhaps at his lowest point in his backyard hut. Funa wasn't any "geek," I realized. He was a fervid, embattled crusader—a more fiery, yet saturnine, variant of Sensei and Hiroko. A gloomy rice samurai, flying the heroic true flag into dire odds.

We went downstairs to the narrow blond shop. Photos of farmers in conical hats toiling in their bucolic paddies hung above crates of their rice—each crate as unique as its grower.

"When clients come I first ask how rice will be used, and advise them accordingly," said Funa. "Onigiri? Gohan? Kids' bento boxes? Cool, hot?"

He shifted to the onigiri café section to prepare a rice ball with the Japanese "national" filling—tuna and mayo—for an elderly customer. But it was a losing battle, he fumed as he draped the onigiri with a shiny rectangle of nori. The kitchen wisdom was lost; most rice was eaten *outside* homes, and people judged the quality of gohan or onigiri or donburi bento boxes not from the memory of their grandmothers' cooking. No—from konbini chains and chain restaurants.

"*This!*" he exclaimed, holding aloft his rough-hewn, sumptuous rice ball while the customer patiently waited with his two hundred yen. "Cold rice has its own character! It took me months to locate perfect onigiri rice, at a small family farm in Niigata Prefecture—and another *nine years* to persuade the farmer to work with me . . ."

As for konbini onigiri? Funa seemed ready to spit. The stuff Barry and I found so delectable was apparently made from rice that was basically some wretched industrial leftover.

"Onigiri is among Japan's most ancient food!" cried Funa, hefting his rice ball like a sacred chalice cum weapon. "Onigiri was what our samurai took to battle! Onigiri was what our moms packed for our school lunches, each ball unique because it had the imprint of *her* hand. Onigiri is Japan's most familial, most intimate snack!"

Was onigiri in fact *the* national dish? I suddenly wondered.

"And those *konbini versions*?" The rice crusader was red in the face. "Pressed so hard by machines they have no air, no human imprint, zero umami!"

In the Edo period, he finale'd, as we made ready to leave, when rice was off, people would spit it out. And now? "Now they don't even know how to judge!"

"Which is what I was saying about kaiseki," said Hiroko.

. . .

Not about to spit on any konbini onigiri myself, I let Hiroko rush home to cook a virtuous washoku meal for her family, and made a beeline into the nearest Lawson.

It was Tuesday, the day most convenience chains introduce new products. Lawson's clerks in their spiffy blue and white stripes practically erupted with welcoming cheer. I surveyed the fantastical onigiri display. Yes, Funa was probably right, but the konbini—the konbini were so savvy. Here was healthy brown rice mixed with bright green edamame. A wholesomely rusticated ball of barley and seaweed. Adorable sekihan—pink balls of rice steamed with adzuki beans. Something called "Black Ramen Onigiri" that riffed on a Toyama Prefecture regional delicacy, its rice cooked in a ramen-style chicken bone broth colored with eco-friendly bamboo charcoal. And as part of Lawson's exclusive line with Niigata Koshihikari rice: limited edition treats with seasonal and regional fillings like chirimen (baby fish) and roasted Hokkaido salmon belly.

All this in a convenience store.

The original Japanese konbini—then called konbiniensu— debuted in the late 1960s on the American franchised convenience store model. They sold decidedly down-market onigiri and bento boxes to young salarymen and commuters; classy people were embarrassed to eat from them. But now, numbering around sixty thousand Japan-wide—with 80 percent of the trade controlled by the fiercely competitive troika of 7-Eleven, Family Mart, and Lawson—konbini with their lightning-fast product turnover represented the cutting (and cutthroat) edge of Japanese taste. The Lawson's onigiri before me mimicked every newfangled current artisanal trend, every homegrown desire.

I picked up half a dozen varieties, then stopped by a 7-Eleven for green matcha tea parfait (as pretty as any Ginza Six item) and a container of instant tantanmen, a spicy collaboration between Ando's Nissin and the Michelin-starred ramen-ya Nakiryu. At home I found Barry luxuriating on the couch, unwrapping a nifty Lawson's egg sandwich four-pack—yes, the cult one featuring tamago-taki (fried egg), a creamy egg salad combo, *and* a sliced soft-boiled egg that boasted a brilliant orange cross-section of yolk. He'd also picked up more konbini "hangover potion." Liver Plus, it was called, an extract of animal liver, $B_{12}$, and turmeric in minuscule bottles whose labels depicted the organ in question—human version? animal?—as a kawaii pink triangle. We swallowed the stuff religiously before hitting izakayas and bars.

They say a human body is 60 percent water, a fact that impressed me deeply as a schoolgirl back in Russia. After four weeks in Tokyo, Barry and I were a more impressive 90 percent konbini.

My session with Funakubo had brought to a head what had been a creeping suspicion, but resolved now into a conviction. The current actual "national cuisine" of the Japanese was, gulp, a konbini creation. There were hard stats. A staggering 1.5 billion people pass through these stores every month. A new one opens in Japan approximately every six hours; at 47 million visitors daily, the konbini footfall is equivalent to over one-third of Japan's population.

What's more, konbini proudly stay open a grueling twenty-four/ seven—year-round for the most part.

And what's more again, in their tracking and adapting to consumer demands and gathering marketing data, with some three

thousand products crammed into extremely limited shelf space—
konbini are clinical. One day when no one was looking, my Family
Mart Uzbek friend, Akram, showed me their "secret weapon": the
POS (point of sale) system. As he scanned a product barcode, the
POS terminal recorded the details of "when, what, where, how
many." Before giving out change, Akram had to input the customer's
gender and approximate age. (The last part drove him mad. "How
am I supposed to tell if a Japanese person is forty or sixty?") All this
data was transmitted in real time to the chain HQ *and* to the manu-
facturer of this onigiri or that kari-pan (curry bun), so they could
fine-tune product development and distribution to a location and
demographic—to both react to and anticipate customers' preferences. Even the weather forecast apparently figured in somehow.

One morning I shared my konbini-as-national-diet thoughts with
Sensei over a delicately crisp breakfast tempura.

*Konbini* . . . Sensei widened his eyes in mock horror, but I noticed a twinkle. Interesting, he noted, because fast food and takeout
had been the culinary idiom of premodern Edo. And it was Edo that
ultimately set the *national* diet. In the mid-nineteenth century, there
were apparently three males to every two females here, half of them
single, making for a city of takeout and street snacks. "Carts with
nigiri sushi, soba, tempura, those elite Japanese foods that enjoy
high-class status today—all were Edo-period konbini equivalents!"

Did *he* have a secret konbini habit? I asked.

"Japanese people think that Lawson's karaage fried chicken is
delicious," Sensei answered elusively. "*Very* delicious."

I shied, tactfully, from bringing up onigiri rice.

I inquired of Hitomi's family if they sold their Sugomen ramen at konbini.

"No way," replied Harumi-san by text through Hitomi. "The competition for shelf space, too brutal. We're not about flash trends."

"I'm afraid, Anya, you're totally right," lamented Hiroko. "The *konbinization* of our national diet is an unstoppable process." And whereas even supermarket chains had different regional produce in, say, Nagasaki or Okinawa, konbini all featured nationwide standards. Uncanny, Hiroko continued, how konbini both reflect and mold trends and our needs, our appetites. "Take my in-laws," she sighed. "Educated middle-class people. Initially konbini-resisters who now live in the countryside too far from a supermarket and have a konbini lunch every day. It's convenient, yes, and it gives human contact. *Konbinization* . . ." she murmured. "Not just our diet, but our lifestyle. Our society."

Because it wasn't only the food. Barry and I hadn't been lonely in Tokyo, or alienated *Lost in Translation*–style, not for a second. Almost every night we'd gone drinking at smoky izakayas or tachinomi-ya (literally, standing-drinking bars; our favorites were in office building basements) with Barry's literary friends or my food colleagues. And yet konbini became my refuges, my clean, well-lighted places, my emotional and practical anchors.

In the 1980s konbini began to branch out from food into services when the government allowed them to sell postage stamps—a godsend for anyone struggling with the Japanese post office bureaucracy. They've evolved since into *seikatsu infura*, life infrastructure. In the endless pursuit of brand loyalty, chains keep unfurling extra features. Family Mart was launching twenty-four-hour Fit & Go gyms. 7-Eleven was rolling out new mobile payment apps (indispensable in this cumbersome cash-focused economy) through its Seven Bank. Lawson, a leader in green healthy living, could recycle your confidential documents into eco-cool toilet paper. And in Osaka Prefecture—which leads this country, with the world's most aging population, in elderly-related afflictions—konbini employees were being trained to help the dementia-stricken.

At least three times a day I popped in, if not for the onigiri or corn dogs, then for the cash machines or nifty sanitizer dispensers in bathrooms, or the cell recharge stations. Konbini were strange paradoxes, I reflected: de-ideologized, de-territorialized and anonymous, a-national, demanding almost nothing but chain distinction and brand loyalty—brand as fluorescent-lit nation-state of this hyperconsumerist society—and yet creating not just brand communities but hubs of actual physical interaction. In our own district, so dark and quiet at night, teens still loitered outside konbini smoking and drinking beers late; the elderly would drop in to relieve loneliness. As scholar Gavin Whitelaw argues, while konbini play into the image of consumer capitalism's "incessant march towards global uniformity," they actually represent not just the standardization of postindustrial Japan, but its individualities and differences as well.

Quite often I'd stop by just to chat in Russian with Akram or English with Farhad, who was a handsome, ambitious engineering student from Pakistan clerking at our nearest 7-Eleven. Farhad was as awed by konbini as Akram was skeptical. "Konbini are the future of world's civilization!" he'd repeat over and over. Indeed. One prominent Japanese scholar, in fact, has written about the unstoppable rise of *konbini bunka*—konbini civilization.

Even the Japanese language was getting konbinized, I learned from Akram.

*Keigo.* That elaborately honorific hierarchical speech that Japanese youth didn't bother to master? It lived on as *konbini keigo*, a superpolite but rapid-fire "high-turnover" konbini jargon taught by employee manuals. "This language," Akram lamented, "I have no idea what half the sentences mean! I have to memorize them by rote." I had a feeling he *really* couldn't wait to return to his mother's pilaf in Uzbekistan.


Barry and I, on the other hand, lingered, and lingered some more, extending departure dates. We just couldn't bear to leave our trim Oakwood aerie under its blazing orange colossus.

But at last came our final day in Tokyo.

And I gave in to what my taste buds had been craving in the land of umami. Just a five-minute walk down our avenue brought me to the chamber of my grail, boldly announced in red neon: "PST—Pizza Studio Tamaki."

Tsubasa Tamaki, its hotshot young pizzaoiolo, had begun as an apprentice at a celebrated nearby pizzeria, Savoy, where he was not even allowed to *touch* dough for three years. Finally, he broke free and in 2018 opened cult-favorite PST. Here the oven was fueled with ur-Japanese cherrywood and nara (oak), and the toppings came fetishistically sourced. And here Tamaki devised his now famous technique of pinching the pizza dough to create air bubbles and baking his marinara dangerously close to the flame while feeding the fire with sugi (Japanese cedar) chips.

Through Craig Mod, an expat pizza otaku and writer who came along, I asked Tamaki how he got into pizza. After pondering a moment, he confessed to the "pizza toast" of his childhood break-fasts: a slab of ketchup-smeared Japanese milk bread topped with tomatoes, green peppers, and sliced American cheese, heated up in a toaster oven. "A postwar comfort classic," Craig, a great scholar of pizza toast, noted. "Popular at kissaten, old-school Japanese cafeterias."

"To me pizza toast was as washoku as rice," Tamaki-san went on. "Because it couldn't be anywhere else but Japan."

Pizza toast as washoku . . . Just another twist to the culinary Möbius strip.

And had he been to Naples? I asked.

"No interest!" came the cool, cocky reply. At least not for pizza. Tamaki-san was happy doing his own take right here in Tokyo, finding Japanese heritage toppings, working with farmers on the tastiest basil and garlic. "Marinara and Margherita," he said, "perfect vehicles for our otaku obsessions. And it's our otakuness that makes for a purely *Japanese* pizza!"

"Wakon yosai." I recalled the Meiji-era motto once again. "Western learning, Japanese spirit."

Still, Tamaki-san allowed, one day he *would* like to see Naples. "Gorgeous, passionate women, funny men who don't work, romantic beautiful scenery."

My marinara arrived. It was tiny, and extremely light—unlike Neapolitans, Japanese don't appreciate chewiness. Big swollen bitter-burnt blisters (from pinching?) disrupted the Japanese (Neapolitan?) harmony. I didn't dare tell Tamaki-san that maybe he *should* go to Naples for the pizza.

Instead I forked over $22 in yen and headed to Family Mart, where I said goodbye to Akram and stocked up on umeboshi plum onigiri, instant ramen (not New Touch, alas), and raspberry macaron sticks for the long flight back to New York the next day.

# SEVILLE
## Tapas: Spain's Moveable Feast

In Seville, my symbolic national meal would involve no labors by me in the kitchen at all—and nada extracted from dismal Spanish convenience stores.

No, the plan for Seville was to jostle along from one packed bar to the next, lubricating our jamon, chorizo, croquetas, more jamon, montaditos, cazuelitas, yet more jamon, with cañas (small beers), dry fino sherries, and tannic tintos de casa. This is the tapeo, the route of grazing and browsing tapas, the small bites utterly central to the Spanish national food narrative *and* its frenetically sociable lifestyle. So central, in fact, that the Spanish government has been lobbying to promote tapas onto the UNESCO intangible heritage list as "one of the most representative elements of the Spanish cultural identity"—crucial to Marca España, the national brand.

And so here we were in Spain's southwestern corner, to assess this edible essential of Spanish alma in the heart of Andalusia, tapas' supposed birthplace. And in the process, to probe the all-important issue of regionalism.

. . .

Except our very first Seville tapeo was beginning to mushroom alarmingly into an ominous flashback of our last visit a decade before. When, on assignment for a magazine story, we'd found ourselves desperately gulping weapons-grade aguardiente one afternoon *para bajar la comida*, "to push down the food." Food meaning our clinical excess of midday gluttony, three lunches' worth.

"*Claro*." Our current host, Patxi, grinned when we recounted this. "A very Sevillian situation."

Patxi, who lives here but hails from La Rioja in the north, had gone squeezing through the mob at our first stop, Manolo Cateca, to shout our opening drink orders. "Should *always* be cañas," pronounced Rafa, Patxi's pal he'd brought along. "To 'open the pores.'"

Tucked away in an alley off the hubbub of Calle Sierpes, the pedestrian high street, Cateca was a taberna out of Spanish central casting, with its azulejos (decorative tiles) on the walls, dark sherry barrels, and paper-napkin-strewn floor. "*Except* for its unusual and geeky three-hundred-label sherry list," exclaimed Patxi, gleefully burying his post-caña nose in a glass of an opulent yet dry oloroso opulently called Sangre y Trabajadero, Blood and the Worker.

"Hazelnuts . . . with a hint of the sea," appraised Rafa. "*Estupendo* with mojama!" He waggled a petal of the dusky cured mullet roe—"jamon of the sea."

A platter of glistening purple-red paleta Iberico, the *real* jamon, materialized next, its fatty umami nuttiness matched by a rare amontillado en rama (meaning unfiltered). Then came lomito (cured pork loin), then chorizo, then blood sausage, then melt-in-the-mouth paprika-crusted slices of pork belly known as chicharrones de Cádiz.

Woozily, I noted that we'd already ingested a month's load of pork fat, which gave a fair sense of how central the pig is to the Spanish appetite, and indeed to the whole culture.

And Patxi, mind you, wasn't ordering *tapas* portions. Perhaps because our introduction was by our mutual pal, Alberto, a legendary Madrid food personality, he'd squeeze back out from Cateca with *raciones* (big expensive servings), which we balanced precariously on somebody's motorcycle in the alley outside. Inside, the crowd was nine deep: *la hora del aperitivo.*

"I joke that this place is my office," said Patxi.

Tall, suavely going gray, Patxi was a self-proclaimed *amante de la gastronomía* with a happy day-job as a distributor of boutique sherries and wines. Rafa, who was fiftyish and suggested a genial crew-cut kid brother of Sancho Panza in a gray cashmere vest, declared himself an amante *también*. And when Patxi left town on a trip, Rafa became our Seville Virgil. *His* day job, it turned out, was coleading a nationally popular local music group, Siempre Así.

"Siempre Así are kind of like an Andalusian ABBA," said Patxi, thumbing up a cell-phone clip of the group's sold-out concert at Barcelona's Teatre del Liceu.

We were now at our tapeo stop two, a seafood taberna called La Moneda, diminishing a bottle of Manzanilla Pastrana. "Single-vineyard, from a prized albariza chalk dune near Sanlúcar," explicated Patxi. Sanlúcar de Barrameda being the sea-breezy port at the mouth of the Guadalquivir River that flows through Seville, from whence Columbus sailed off on his third voyage and Magellan set off on his 1519 global circumnavigation. The Age of Discovery has long since passed into history, of course, ditto Spain's status as a vast global empire, and nowadays Sanlúcar is best known for its manzanilla, the briny-fresh sherry variety best enjoyed with sub-limely succulent langoustines the size of a baby's arm.

We took care of a ración of these, courtesy of La Moneda's San-luqueño owners.

And then we took care—somehow—of the sopa de galeras, a slightly archaic mantis shrimp soup thickened with bread.

And then we even found space—somewhere—for the lacy-crisp Sanlúcar-style tortillitas laminated with tiny shrimp in their shells.

"*Joder*, shit!" cried Rafa all at once, checking the time over a forkful of "definitive" papas aliñás, another ur-Andalusian tapa of yellow potatoes in a lake of robust olive oil. "They're waiting for us at Mercado de Triana for lunch."

It was four p.m., the languorous Andalusian lunchtime.

WE'D ARRIVED IN SEVILLE the previous day. To my immense relief, the city still seemed much like the Spain I'd fallen for back in the post-Franco 1980s. That timelessness, that profundo intensity of "*España de pandereta*"—tambourine Spain. The phrase was from an ironically critical line by the great early-twentieth-century Sevil-lian poet Antonio Machado: "The Spain of street bands and tam-bourines, of enclosures and sacristies, devoted to Frascuelo and Virgin Mary . . ." (Frascuelo being a famous torero).

In the depths of Triana, where our Airbnb was located, in the old gypsy barrio across a short bridge from Seville's centro histórico, oldsters in woolen cardigans plodded past ferreterías (hardware stores) piled with paella pans and electric kettles and cheap earth-enware casseroles. Clothing shops displayed old-lady corsets and dowdy, astonishingly pricey fringed shawls for Feria (Fair of Seville) outings (whoever bought the shawls?) and baby flamenco outfits. Even the non-flamenco outfits had a sea of ruffles and fringes and red fabric roses fit for a retirement home production of *Carmen*. It was all a frayed cliché, the Spain of polka dots, the Spain from late-Franco-era posters with their famous slogan, *"españa es diferente"*: Spain Is Different.

The country's molecular-cuisine revolution, that head-spinning transformational leap spearheaded by Ferran Adrià, which I had gleefully chronicled in magazine pieces and a cookbook called *The New Spanish Table*—it had mostly left Seville on the sidelines. In Triana and elsewhere, the bars still appeared as crammed baroque reliquaries of Virgins, toreros, and soccer stars, all rubbing shoulders above the free olives. A vendor of caracoles stood on Triana's chaotic main street with a basket of slow-twitching snails and a bigger variety called cabrillas—a favorite tapa at a worn, popular bar right by us, Casa Ruperto, which specialized in quail (codorniz) as well. Snails and quails. In Madrid and Barcelona, such places were being gentrified away or taken over by the tattooed generation, who updated classic tapas with ironic quotation marks and heirloom ingredients. But here in Seville, the cocina still "reeked of garlic and religious preoccupations," a much-repeated aphorism by early-twentieth-century writer Julio Camba, the Spanish Brillat-Savarin. Garlic wafted from every floor of our prefab sixties building—*ajo* frying in olive oil.

And as for religious preoccupations, there was no getting away. Semana Santa was looming, the stupendous, crushingly crowded Holy Week of penitential processions by Seville's hermandades (lay confraternities of neighborhood churches). Every shop window

in town featured cloyingly cute baby mannequins in ominous
capirotes, the Ku Klux Klan–like peaked hoods derived from the
Inquisition.

DID WE KNOW, inquired Rafa, that the Inquisition had its main
fifteenth-century HQ at the Castillo de San Jorge, a hundred meters from *here*?

"Here" was a long wooden table in Mercado de Triana on the
Guadalquivir's west bank, stop number three (a.k.a. lunch) of our
first day's tapeo. Immediately around us, the market stalls over-
flowed with artichokes and luminous leeks; grandmas trudged by
toting hauls of jade-green fava beans and alabaster slabs of salt cod.

We were a large, merry group now, devouring guiso de chocos,
a squid stew, and a refreshing octopus salad, all supplied by the gregarious David, owner of several mercado tapas spots.

"Tapas! Spain's great gift to the world!" rumbled a macho-
looking gent named Alberto as he dipped bread into the profoundly
fruity olive oil he produced himself from olives grown on his finca.

"*Aceitunas*, still the best tapas!" added Borja, the dandyish
owner of a nearby olive stall that served vermouth on tap.

"*Perdóname*, but jamon is king!" countered Israel, vendor of
Iberico hams from a stall cum aperitivo bar on the other side.
"Jamon," he insisted, slapping the table, "is the symbol of Spain!"

Now Rafa rose to extemporize a flamenco-like ditty to Israel's
ham, as one does, I suppose, after all the manzanilla, oloroso,
amontillado, very strong fancy Rueda, white vermouth in big glasses,
mini gin and tonics. And palo cortado, the maverick type of sherry
we were now all enjoying.

Then, what with Semana Santa approaching, the disputations turned to another Seville obsession, as Israel kissed the anchor embroidered on his polo shirt, the emblem of the nearby Capilla de los Marineros.

"*Our* church, of *our* Triana," Israel growled in his lisping Andaluz Spanish. "*Our* barrio of mariners, gypsies, and ceramicists—*and our patron*"—he yanked out his cell, planted a cherishing smooch on an image—"Esperanza de Triana! *Our* Virgin!"

"Bueno, I'm a Trianero también," snorted Rafa. "I adore Esperanza, okay. But La Macarena *es una virgen diferente*"—he mimed a swoon—"*Pura elegancia!* She gives me goose bumps!" A husky arm was displayed.

"But Esperanza is a *mujer*, a real woman!" retorted Israel. "A *gitana*, a gypsy, dark skinned, one of us!" He zoomed in on his Virgin's prominent dark brows and incredibly long curly eyelashes. He displayed *his* goose bumps.

Seville: where two grown, burly guys will lock horns, *con* goose bumps, over which holy statue of the young Virgin is best.

BASÍLICA DE LA MACARENA rises as the neo-Baroque yellow-trimmed landmark of what used to be one of Seville's folksiest barrios, just within the Moorish twelfth-century city walls. We were taking a long stroll there now, in the Andalusian twilight scented with orange blossoms, to pay respects to Seville's most iconic Virgin—named for her barrio—and walk off some of our tapeo excesses. Along the way I reflected on what a naïve La Macarena junkie I've long been myself, lugging home posters and fridge magnets over the years.

Inside the basilica, gazing up once more at María Santísima de la Esperanza Macarena, Virgin of Hope, patroness of gypsies and bullfighters, I felt overcome yet again. A strange mix of dazzle at her celebrity glamour, tender thrill at her sorrowful beauty, and something else . . . something close to spiritual awe in my Jewish atheist heart.

A museum-quality polychrome work in wood by an anonymous seventeenth-century Baroque master, La Macarena was looking especially stunning for her pre–Holy Week red-carpet showcasing, when Seville's Marian mania builds to a fever pitch as churches display their prized Virgins in full processional splendor, and online polling ranks which Mary is looking *más guapa*, "most beautiful." La Macarena was out on her throne-like silver *paso* (float), its gold-brocaded, tasseled *palio* (canopy) supported by slender poles hedged round by a magic forest of tall candles, silver candelabras, and white floral bouquets.

"She looks like a grieving 1950s Italian movie starlet," murmured Barry. "In a fairy-tale prison."

From behind, I gaped at the Virgin's famous processional *manto* (cape). It was a flooding waterfall of green velvet and raised silk and gold-embroidered fruits and cherubs, all under a gossamer netting of gold mesh—hence the cape's nickname, "Camaronero," as in shrimp-fishing nets.

"Like William Morris wallpaper—on Baroque steroids," said Barry.

Indeed. The nineteenth-century English Arts and Crafts movement influenced this revolutionary 1900 tour-de-force cape by master bordador (embroiderer) Juan Manuel Rodríguez Ojeda. Ojeda's dazzling flamboyance—for costumery, for free-moving swagged canopies, for general stagecraft—transformed not only La Macarena but the whole previously dour Semana Santa aesthetic, single-handedly turning a dwindling festivity, one getting unpopular even with locals, into Spain's most emblematic attraction.

Another prime example of reinvented tradition?

I stood there a while still, transfixed by the five green-jeweled brooches glittering among the cascades of white lace on La Macarena's breast. These mariquillas (ladybugs) were a gift brought from Paris in 1913 by the young superstar "prince of bullfighters" Joselito, El Gallo. When Joselito was gored to death horribly, aged twenty-five, Rodríguez Ojeda dressed La Macarena in widow's black. The clerical authorities were scandalized by this melodrama between matador and Mary, and she never wore black again.

VOLUPTUOUS VIRGINS AND BULLFIGHTERS, fiestas and siestas, sherry, sangria, tiled patios, cooling gazpachos, Moorish palaces, whitewashed villages, polka dots, red roses in hair, gypsies, the haunting wail of the flamenco *cante* . . . All these sultry clichés of Machado's "tambourine Spain"—they all spring from a single region: Andalusia. It's Spain's largest, and one of its very poorest. The clichés and their abiding power were part of why I came here instead of the better-fed País Vasco or Catalonia, with their Michelin stars, modern bourgeois lifestyles, and cosmopolitan tapas.

How is it that a region comes to represent an entire country, I wanted to learn. How has the tapas bar endured and thrived as a vital expression of a place that "has occupied a twilight zone," as one scholar wrote, "in which it is at once the essence of Spanishness and its orientalist other"?

Andalusia also embodies a political paradox. As the spiritual heir to fabled Al-Andalus—medieval Muslim Iberia, conquered in 711 by invading Arabs and Berbers—it's the heart of the modern, liberal Spanish foundational myth of convivencia, the harmonious and supposedly creative coexistence of Christians, Muslims, and Jews. At the same time, as the final scene in the Christian Reconquest of Al-Andalus—the 1492 taking of Granada—Andalusia is simultaneously the symbolic heart of La Reconquista, the foundational myth of royalists, right-wing Catholics, fascist Falangists, and Francoists. And more recently, of Vox, the far-right Islamophobic political party that's been rising alarmingly.

Franco's relationship with Andalusia? It was, shall we say, *complicado*. The Generalissimo hated its anarchist spirit, harassed its gypsies, and executed its intellectuals, such as García Lorca and the celebrated regionalist theorist Blas Infante. But as historian José Luis Venegas notes in his excellent book, *The Sublime South*: "Franco's regime silenced liberal views on regional and national identity, while promoting the old notion that Andalusia is where you can find Spain at its most intense." Particularly in the post–Civil War *años del hambre* (hunger years), recounts Venegas, "Andalusian Spanish was the idiom of film musicals featuring a benighted folklore realm of bandits, bullfighters, and *bailaoras*, or exotic gypsy dancers in polka-dot dresses." Auto-exoticism, as Venegas puts it tartly, had "great propagandistic value."

The cash value of this auto-exoticism shot up in the mid-twentieth century as El Caudillo's currency-starved, backward, inward-facing regime decided to open itself up to the world and court emerging mass tourism. And what did foreign visitors want? Lamented one *turismo* minister: "Flamenco, singing, Gypsies . . . Seville, Córdoba, Granada . . . We must resign ourselves, where tourism is concerned, to being a country of pandereta." Tambourine Spain.

And so was launched Franco's famous "Spain Is Different" tourist campaign: a swirling fiesta of ruffles and polka dots—*and* one of the last century's most epic image makeovers. Those who claim that the country's great rebranding came post-Franco, with Joan Miró's cosmopolitan sun logo and Barcelona's sleek 1992 Olympics, forget that between 1955 and 1964, tourism here soared by an astounding 334 percent, bringing economic and even political stabilization at home, and transforming Franco's pariah Spain into cheap package holiday paradise.

In the decade after 1959, two-thirds of Spain's trade deficit was covered by "pandereta" tourism. Flamenco clubs sprouted on the Costa Brava up in Catalonia (its flamenco history, zero). And Andalusian sangria flowed freely to wash down omnipresent mushy paellas—that Valencian specialty now rebranded as national beach food—from the newly introduced *menús turísticos*, a hit with vacationers *and* Spain's own rising consumer classes.

"OF COURSE FRANCO didn't *invent* Andalusian stereotypes," declared Alberto Troyano. "Though he manipulated them savvily."

Still woozy from my debut tapeo's excesses, I was discussing regional identity with this esteemed elderly cultural critic at a bar under the Setas, or Mushrooms—the flamboyant giant 2011 architectural parasol that gave self-exoticizing Seville a shot of a Bilbao-style urban regeneration.

Among Alberto's oeuvre on Andalusian stereotypes was a study of the "myth of Seville" as expressed in operas like *Don Juan*, *Carmen*, and *The Marriage of Figaro*, set here but all written by foreigners. And it was foreigners, insisted Alberto, Romantics such as

Byron, Washington Irving, Mérimée, Gautier, the English travel writer Richard Ford, who created and perpetuated stock images of Andalusia.

"Which until the late eighteenth century didn't even possess any kind of separate regional consciousness!"

*Andalusia . . . fabrication . . . foreign gaze . . .* I dutifully wrote the words in my notebook.

"But didn't the Romantics treat *all* Spain as Europe's orientalist 'Other,'" I wondered. "Didn't the French say Africa begins at the Pyrenees?"

*Claro, claro,* Alberto agreed, sipping mineral water—he had a boozy reunion in Cádiz upcoming that evening. "But which opera, tell me, is set up north in Barcelona? In Bilbao? And disgraceful," he went on in a huff, "that they even played *Carmen* at the Seville 1992 Expo, which was meant to show off our newfound post-Franco *modernity*!"

Incidentally, the term "orientalism" first appeared in the French Academy dictionary in 1838. "Exoticism" appeared in 1845, the same year that Prosper Mérimée published *Carmen*, his brutal novella about the murder of a femme fatale gypsy, on which Bizet based his opera. In mid-nineteenth-century Paris, the fan and the mantilla shawl—products of Spain's colonization of the Philippines, actually—were the dernier cri of fashion accessories. And Spanish dance was so hot, certain performers at the Paris Opera lied that they were Spanish gypsies.

But the most enthusiastic consumers of Andalusian stereotypes?

"The Andalusians themselves," chuckled Alberto.

"From the Romantic times on, we've loved the applause from abroad, loved the limelight, eventually developing this foreigners' vision of us into our own *identidad desbordada*, overflowing identity. Our motley altarpiece of tropes and clichés."

Self-orientalization.

Immediately I recalled Marino, the Neapolitan anthropologist, talking about his city's *auto-folklorizzazione*. Marino had spent time in Seville, noting its kinships to Naples—both histrionic poor southlands, basking in the foreigner's gaze. But a crucial difference existed between the cities: Naples (once part of Spain's empire, in fact) was never considered "of Italy" until Unification, whereas Andalusia has always been regarded as the very cradle of Spanishness.

"The Catalans and the Basques," Alberto continued on, "industrialized, developed their self-stereotypes as hardworking and clever. Never mind that their industrial workforce was Andalusian migrants. Whereas here . . ." He squinted unhappily at a group of Asian girls in flamenco outfits posing for selfies. "Here we didn't industrialize; we still fan ourselves, we wear mantillas, we have the country's lowest GDP. And we cling on to our Semana Santa and Virgins, our toreros and fiestas and tapas bars."

But was it so wrong, I wondered, to have such an overflowing festive identity?

Alberto shook his head glumly. "Spain's post-Franco decentralization granted Andalusia greater autonomy in 1981. Our regional government could have promoted *different* stereotypes—improved our economic conditions. We have Spain's richest and most complex history. Surely there's another alternative besides fiestas and tambourines or pretending we're these dour, 'hardworking' fake Catalans."

He pronounced *catalanes* with the usual Andalusian sneer.

I nodded, mulling the contortions of regional consciousness as we sipped our mineral waters together—until suddenly I remembered my original purpose in meeting Alberto.

To talk about Andalusian taverns—and tapas.

"Ah, yes, tabernas!" Alberto's face brightened. "Around the 1880s tabernas became a hub of particularly Andalusian social identity: a mix of lowlifes, flamenco artists, gitanos, toreros—and *señoritos*, indolent rich party boys, another classic Andalusian stereotype, who were important early flamenco patrons and audience members. Alcohol erases social distinctions, eh? You became a *parroquiano*, a parishioner literally, of your taberna."

What about tapas, the food?

Alberto regarded me blankly. "*What* food?"

Tabernas didn't have food licenses, it turns out. Most were wine stores that drew vinos generosos (sherry wines) from barrels, accompanied by an anchovy or an olive at most. There were still places like that in Cádiz, said Alberto. His tone turned almost dreamy; he loved the Havana-like Andalusian seaport. In the eighteenth century after the Guadalquivir silted up, all the New World trade moved from Seville to Cádiz. The latter became Spain's most cosmopolitan city. It was where La Pepa (the nickname for Spain's 1812 liberal constitution) was drafted.

"And believe me," Alberto chuckled, "the manzanilla of Cádiz definitely fueled our national foundational document."

TAPA IS SPANISH for "lid," and one of its legends involves King Alfonso XIII, known as "El Africano" for his 1920 incursion into Morocco with Primo de Rivera, the pre-Franco Falangist dictator. Alfonso, so goes the story, went to Ventorrillo El Chato in Cádiz, a fabulous restaurant still in existence, situated on a sand dune. Cádiz being Chicago-class windy, the bartender covered the royal wineglass with a slice of jamon to keep out the sand (though some less appetizing accounts feature cockroaches or flies). Alfonso liked this "tapa" so much he ordered another. The "cover" theory appeared in the first gastronomic definition of tapas in the Spanish Royal Academy dictionary:

"A slice of ham or sausage placed on top of chato [squat glass] or caña [small slender glass] at colmados [grocery stores] or tabernas."

The date of the dictionary's edition: 1936.

Tapas, that edible representation of Spain, hasn't been around long at all. The initial recorded mentions of such edible glass "covers" only trace back to early-twentieth-century Andalusia. And the social institution of tapas is even more recent. Many older Sevillanos I questioned came of age at a time when tapeo—the modern bar-to-bar shuffle—didn't exist. Because besides panderetas and polka dots, poverty was Spain's longtime defining national feature, especially hereabouts in the south. Regular folk hardly went out. Foreign Romantics might have waxed on about femme fatale gypsies, but their reviews of local—and tapas-less—cuisine are summed up by Théophile Gautier's famous lip curl, that not even a French dog would sully its nose with gazpacho.


Tapas? Definitely *not* poor man's food."

University of Seville anthropologist Isabel González Turmo was quietly setting me straight.

"The term crops up on early-twentieth-century menus," she noted, "usually at fairly classy establishments."

I was back on my tapeo trail, in the company of this author of a definitive book on Sevillian cuisine. We were quaffing Cruzcampo cañas at the weathered 1940s zinc counter of a populist bar called La Flor de Toranzo, which boasted a ceramic mural of beautiful orange trees, and a perversely delicious signature tapa of freshly baked Antequera rolls mounted with anchovies under squiggles of condensed milk.

To the scholarly, reserved Isabel, tapas had less to do with Andalusia's racy flamenco tabernas than the latter-nineteenth-century vogue for an imported drink—beer. The original local cervecerías and beer depots were mostly owned by Germans and Brits, she explained; the Andalusian bourgeoisie thought it "muy chic" to accompany an imported cerveza with some Teutonic sausages. Come the early twentieth century, Cruzcampo, a Sevillian brewery (now multinational) began to monopolize trade.

"Our thirst for icy beer became truly unquenchable," said Isabel. "It's our torrid climate, perhaps?"

Then in the late 1920s, a vogue for little hors d'oeuvres and aperitivos arrived from Madrid. In Seville, the first establishment known as a "bar" was registered around then as well. "And so it was from *that*," said Isabel, "that tapas as we know them began to evolve."

I sipped my Cruzcampo with a renewed appreciation: a small, crucial detail about how foreign import fueled the most iconically Spanish tradition. With Franco's autarky, continued Isabel, Spain became closed to imported beers and salamis. The post–Civil War years of scarcity, poverty, and inferior food were of course terrible for the dining industry—but that benefited tapas, ironically, as bars began selling tiny cheap portions of the impoverished restaurant food. There were cazuelitas of stewy things, scant on protein, big on sauce—sangre encebollada, for example, a blood stew still found on some menus—and wedges of tortilla sacromonte, an omelet with brains.

And the tapeo as we know it? The manically sociable bar hop?

That began with the 1970s late-Franco economic normalization, said Isabel. "But it really took off with the post-Franco Movida, when going out became a symbol of our new freedom."

Of course, she added, it suited "our Mediterranean lifestyle, our hot climate, our love of street life and fiestas."

"Identidad desbordada?" I yelped. The overflowing identity?

I bid Isabel adiós and wondered where to continue my tapeo while Barry was off "anthropologically souveniring," as he called his trinket collecting, nosing around Maestranza, the world's oldest bullring, and its museum.

Flor de Toranzo was kitchenless, hewing close to the early-twentieth-century proto-tapas bars that served only small premeal aperitivos. Just up the street I could reexamine Enrique Becerra, a fairly serious restaurant with a downstairs bar turning out neotraditional tidbits, often tinged with sweet-spicy Moorish accents that became fashionable post-Franco, as local chefs here began to explore long-ignored Al-Andalus recipes. Or I could order artful nibbles of tuna tataki at nearby La Azotea, a chichi postmolecular gastrobar, which is to say that by the twenty-first century, tapas even in staunchly old-fashioned Seville have evolved into something truly protean. After the 2008 crisis, when high-end restaurants pretty much crashed, tapas bars flourished in Spain. Small shareable plates were by then a global phenomenon—Asian tapas, Mexican tapas—undermining the tyranny of the French-style sit-down menu.

So was the tapeo a kind of anarchical anti-meal, tailor-made for our distracted noncommittal twenty-first century? Did Spain's status as a mecca and model of progressive cuisine stem from liberated Spaniards' readiness, and eagerness, to engage with new tastes—to try anything once, as long as it's small? Weren't the fantastical tidbits dished up by Ferran Adrià at El Bulli essentially a form of tapas?

With all these questions crowding my head, in the end I grabbed the last empty stool in the lunchtime pandemonium at Bodeguita Romero, a serious *eating* bar a short walk away. Amid the manic clanking of plates and iron-lunged countermen rasping out their pregones (tapas recitations), I tried to mentally extract some kind of "national" meal from the exhaustive menu of classics here.

Spain isn't Portugal, the other Iberian seafaring giant that folded foods of its former colonies—Goan samosas, African piri-piri sauce—into its own canon. But here in Andalusia, ruled by Visigoths, Romans, and Muslims long before the Age of Exploration launched in this very city, cuisine had already been shaped by invaders, colonizers, and trade. Here on Bodeguita Romero's menu were salazones (salt-cured fish) and vinegary aliños (pickles)—all loved in Roman Hispania. As was jamon. Roman, too, were the origins of gazpacho and salmorejo, its bread-thickened cousin. Both were totally white until the arrival of the tomato, which made one of its earliest recorded appearances in the 1608 accounting books of the charitable Hospital de la Sangre near La Macarena's basilica (it's now the site of the Andalusian parliament). Mediterranean aristocracy began growing tomatoes in fancy gardens as a botanical curio; here in Seville the curious fruit was being served to the indigent—in a modern-sounding salad with cucumbers.

I continued down the menu. Albóndigas, meatballs, the Spanish collective obsession—named from Arabic *al-bunduq* (hazelnut), they featured heavily in the seminal thirteenth-century Al-Andalus cookbook *Kitab al-Tabikh*. The omnipresent croquetas, fried breaded béchamel balls—originating from the days of French domination by the Bourbons post-1700, but *españolized* in the late nineteenth century when culinary patriotism became de rigueur.

And around me, I saw everyone ordering the sine qua non of Sevillian tapas, montadito de pringá, which is to say paprika-stained mashed-up meats from potaje (boiled dinner) pressed into sandwiches. Potaje, cocido, and other pig-centric one-pot stews loaded with chickpeas and sausages all derived from olla podrida, or rotten pot. To Spaniards, olla podrida constitutes a hallowed quasi-mythical dish, celebrated by such Golden Age grandees as Lope de Vega, Calderón, and Cervantes and then elevated into a national symbol in the aforementioned patriotic late nineteenth century.

So tapas, I mused, were like little road signs or historical plaques, couched in the language of the plate, marking the long epic national narratives of power and politics . . .

"Y? *Qué te pongo?*"

The counterman's impatient growl for my order goosed me out of my reverie.

I went for the season's first tomato gazpacho and a wedge of tortilla de patatas, the thick potato omelet so adored as a national comfort food. It was one of the dishes featured at Spain's very self-orientalizing pavilion at the 1867 Paris World Expo—and then promoted under Franco as a *plato nacional*, along with paella and cocido.

Sipping the smooth cooling gazpacho amid the lunchtime din, I pondered more about Seville itself. The so-called Columbian

Exchange, with its unprecedented globalization of agriculture and foodstuffs—and all its terrible cascading consequences, from ecological destruction to slavery—was launched right here, in this buoyantly insular city, so seemingly immune to current globalized ways. Instead of today's tapeo decodings, I could have braved the teeming afternoon to contemplate the shady small patio adjacent to the tourist-mobbed Almohad palace, the Alcazar. The patio used to belong to Casa de Contratación, the House of Trade with the Indies, established in 1503 by Queen Isabella to centralize the Crown's administration of the New World. (In 1508 Amerigo Vespucci was appointed its Chief Navigator.) With a tightly controlled monopoly on exports and imports and communications, Seville, thanks to its strategic position, became a *puerto y puerta de Indias*, port and gateway—the starting and ending point for *all* crops and vessels, all precious metals, seeds, cuisines and cultures, diseases and weapons moving back and forth across the Atlantic. By 1600, this city on the Guadalquivir was the empire's de facto capital, an urbanistic and cultural prototype for emerging colonial capitals like Mexico City.

*Quien no ha visto a Sevilla, no ha visto a maravilla*, went the popular saying: *He who hasn't seen Seville hasn't seen marvels.*

And then the Guadalquivir silted up.

IN THE DAYS that followed, my tapas research mainly involved socializing at the Mercado de Triana with Rafa, who lived nearby. There'd be not much purpose, really, but a great deal of pleasure. Which sort of was the point. After the frenzy of Tokyo, I was slacking off in a city that elevated slacking off to an art form, an existential MO. Rafa proclaimed Seville's pride in being *ociosa*

(hedonistic)—also *exótica, espontánea, voluptuosa y sensual*—a city that constantly self-mythologized its party spirit and indolence. (The early-twentieth-century philosopher Ortega y Gasset, a man of the north, wrote how visitors here got treated to a "presentation of a magnificent ballet called Sevilla"—which he ascribed to Andalusia's "astonishing case of collective narcissism.") Nothing was premeditated or planned. I'd finish my mercado shopping around hora del aperitivo, Barry would meet me, and there was Rafa, perched at a counter or table. Amigos passed by, joined. Sometimes we'd be off after a couple of copas. Or a late-morning tot would balloon into a tapas crawl *en pandilla*—going out "with a gang"— ending at two a.m. with our long ramble homeward from deep in the centro, across the Triana Bridge and the sleeping Guadalquivir. My pleasure at this spontaneous, voluptuous social life lived out at tapas bars—Seville's famous *gracia*—was always tinged with re- gret: the regret that I lived in the wrong part of the world. In Na- ples, it seemed the Camorra had ravaged such a sense of neighborhood texture. In New York, you had to make an appointment to see close friends. In Tokyo, poor old people sought human contact at fluor- escent 7-Elevens. It felt like a deep privilege, almost extinct now in the world, to walk out of your house and into a bar, and find an easy sense of belonging—of *community*.

The great communal magnet of Mercado de Triana was the *puesto* (stall) of our voluble ham vendor, Israel, with its several stools and decent red wine. Here, burly Israel spent eight hours a day meticu- lously slicing jamon into long elegant pieces called lonchas and pro- fessing to love every minute, even if his kidneys hurt from the labor. Munching his jamon montaditos while gazing at acorn-fattened pata negra hams hanging from the rafters like swollen Christmas stockings, I kept flashing back to Almodóvar's dark, campy early masterpiece, *What Have I Done to Deserve This?* It's the one where a glue-sniffing Carmen Maura bashes her husband to death with a jamon bone. Not quite so uncanny, perhaps, given the country's ratio of 50 million pigs to 46.5 million humans. On a sunnier note, jamon is Spain's great common denominator delicacy, as Rafa and Israel chorused, a shared cultural totem, even if an expensive one. "Jamon is the *original* tapa!" insisted Israel. "Without it, half the country's bars would instantly go out of business!"

But the current Spanish jamon brand adulation was bullshit, he also insisted. As long as acorn-fed Iberico purebred pigs were the source, *all* jamon tasted divine. Meaning I could do my research right there at his stall—no need to get so excited by the invitation I'd received from Cinco Jotas, Spain's most prestigious marca, to visit its black-hoofed porkers out in their natural habitat, followed by a tasting of $200-a-pound cured flesh.

"*Hombre, muchísimas gracias*, let me think about that," I lied.

And so a cool, cloudless morning found Barry and me heading excitedly into the Sierra de Aracena, the uplands an hour away in Huelva Province. I was dying to see its dehesa, the southwestern Spanish savanna-like ecosystem rich in the oaks whose acorns lend Iberico hams their preternatural sweet, unctuous nuttiness.

Last time I saw Aracena, the main town, many years before, it seemed like another dusty whitewashed Andalusian nowhere, dominated by a ghostly Gothic-Mudejar thirteenth-century castle. Now meeting Maria, our host, at a new chichi ex-convent hotel, I goggled at the effects of jamon-centric tourism: the restored houses, the adorable locavore food shops. A trained biologist and sometimes Cinco Jotas PR person, Maria presented an immensely attractive

vision of young liberal Spain: vigorously friendly, smart, environ-
mentally conscious, not self-orientalizing at all. She had moved to
the region from Seville and now lived a self-sufficient green life in a
solar-heated house, pressing her own olive oil, growing all she ate.
At the same time, she was on a first-name basis with the world's
great chefs; she had recently hung out with Wolfgang Puck at the
Oscars ball, where 5J porcine producto was a huge hit, she told us,
with *estrellas de Hollywood*.

We drove along the dehesa's edge, with its soft Mediterranean
hillsides and meadows dotted with curly-leafed oaks. "Though it's
getting a bit absurd," Maria was laughing, "how fetishistic the
Spanish are about jamon. We go to a wedding, then spend a week
dissecting not the bride's dress but the ham!"

We parked and walked up the gravelly road to behold the black-
footed, ridge-backed Iberico pigs, the fruits of ancient interbreed-
ing, they say, between regular hogs and wild Mediterranean boars.
Already during the Roman rule of Hispania, their salt-cured legs
were a prized commodity, praised by Pliny the Elder and even featured on some Roman coins during the reign of Augustus. Pretty
much ever since, the pig has been an essential part of Spanish cultural identity. Even during Islamic Al-Andalus, pig husbandry
somehow continued.

"They're so smart, social, inquisitive," Maria cooed as one social specimen came charging over, oinking demonically, and snuf-
fling at my boot. "So clean, they don't even stink. Go ahead, touch
him." I thought of English writer Richard Ford's description of
Spanish pigs "like a legion possessed by devils," and passed. "Yeesh,
they give me the creeps," muttered Barry. "So gray and *hairless*, like
ambulatory rhino-skin sausages."

The athletic pigs roam many miles daily, burning off calories

looking for food, which is why their meat is so red. Spring and summer they graze on whatever they can find across the dehesa. October
through March brings *montanera*, the months of acorn-dropping,
when bellotas carpet the ground, and the cerdos (pigs) sniff out the
fattest and sweetest—holm oak is a favorite—to put on 40 percent
of their weight, most of it heart-healthy fat so rich in oleic acid that
Ibericos are known as "four-legged olive trees."

Suddenly a porker broke off from the group and scampered off
into the hills. "*Escapistas*, the shepherds call them," said Maria,
"the ones who run away to frolic with wild boars, but come back."
A pig who refuses to behave, exercise, and put on the required
weight? A "Judas"—a traitor, a waste of investment.

Of nearly 50 million jamones produced each year in Spain, less
than 10 percent are Iberico; the rest are classified as serrano (meaning
"of the sierra"), which still tastes like the best prosciutto of Italy.
Until recently the Spanish government tolerated crossbreeding and
indoor grain-feeding for the Iberico rating, but laws now are more
stringent. Cinco Jotas, though, has always used Iberico purebreeds
only, because the unique silky mouthfeel of "purebred ham," Maria
explained, was all in genetics. The fat *infiltrates* the cells, producing such fine internal marbling that though the flesh might look
meaty-red, on the tongue—"Oh, on the tongue it feels like butter or
oil!" What's more, pure Ibericos are certified to have consumed
only bellotas for ninety days before reaching their kill weight of
about 160 kilos, at which point they're stunned with $CO_2$, and
slaughtered.

"They've spent the world's most charmed lives!" you regularly
hear insisted in Spain, about these acorn-munching cerdos. The
same gets said about toros bravos, the fighting bulls put to the
sword in the corrida, bullfights.

Around us now the dehesa possessed a soft luminosity, so unlike the usual parched Spanish landscape. In the late-morning light the gnarled oaks shimmered gently; the air smelled of wild thyme and rosemary. To Spaniards dehesa conjures up picnic idylls amid green hillsides and frolicking piglets. But Spain being Spain, the dark undertow of the Reconquista is never too far away, if you probe. As an institution dehesa, from the Latin for "defense," dates to the times when pastureland seized by the reconquering Catholic Crown was awarded to Christian hidalgos, to fence off and protect.

"The fact that the cultivation of Iberian ham," opines one scholar, "is tied to . . . the triumph of Christianity over Islam renders it a powerful signifier of Spanish Catholicism."

I mused again about Almodóvar's jamon bone as murder weapon. About how hereabouts they never use the word "slaughter" but *sacrificar*, sacrifice, for the pig's death. A religious ritual of a sacral Christian dehesa?

Cinco Jotas was founded in the small Huelva town of Jabugo in 1879 by a local entrepreneur named Rafael Sanchez Romero. Since the early 1980s, it's been owned by the international sherry giant Osborne. Now on the brand's premises in Jabugo—whose main square is Plaza del Jamon, and most of whose two-thousand-plus residents work in the industry—we ambled with Maria around two vast whitewashed courtyards. Here the butchering, salting, and curing were done in days past. Climate change, however, has made outdoor drying so unpredictable that the curing now happens indoors; the "technology," though, still amounts essentially to opening and closing windows, and adjusting humidity by sprinkling water on the dirt floor. Nevertheless, Maria grinned, the company chairman consulted Ferrari engineers on "optimal jamon-curing aerodynamics."

Donning hard hats and white coats, we entered the curing cellars. Above us, as advised by Ferrari experts, the violin-shaped, yellow-grease-coated symbols of Spanish national psyche dangled, air-curing for up to five years. The cave smelled profoundly of Spain: dusky, gamy, macho, fatty, a little harsh. I thought of Cervantes, of potbellied Sancho Panza crowing about his own seven finger-widths of "old Christian's fat."

How many hams did 5J produce a year? I wondered.

"It, um, depends . . ." answered Maria, obscurely. "Well, um, it's a *secret*, actually. We're a small company—and what if the Chinese want *all* our ham? They're insatiable!"

Apparently there was much alarm in Jabugo these days over China's ravenous new appetite for iconic Spanish pig flesh.


Eating curls of exalted-quality jamon has the mildly intoxicating effect of a slow-release endorphin bomb, as its delicate dewy fat coats your mouth—gradually. Pure pleasure, especially with the thirty-year-old Osborne maverick palo cortado we now sipped upstairs at 5J's sleek tasting room. Seve, the top master carver, was fashioning glistening lascas (squares) and lonchas (long slices) the hue of an El Greco cardinal's robe. Of 5J's sixty resident carvers—who hand-cut all its packaged jamon—the gregarious Seve, with his picturesque sideburns and cashmere sweater, was the chosen one for occasions like King Felipe's coronation. His cutting technique, I noticed, was smooth and suave, unlike Israel's more fitful slicing.

So why *was* jamon such a perfect national symbol of Spain?

"Because as a country we appreciate the culture and craftsman-ship behind each jamon," Seve answered immediately. "The years of hanging, of opening and closing the damn curing-room win-dows." But there was something else. He paused over his stainless steel carving cradle. "Look, I'm from here, Jabugo," he finally said. "Fifty years ago nobody considered jamon any 'healthy sustainable luxury.' Nobody went on about omega six or seven or eight—like Maria can for hours and hours. The cerdo? It was family susten-ance *puro y duro* [clear and simple]. My parents were ganaderos [ranchers]. In November we 'sacrificed' pigs to eat the rest of the year. It was for our survival."

From survival to status, I thought, popping another glistening loncha into my mouth. The current way of the world.

"Jamon, it's *muy nuestro*," Maria summarized. "So ours, *our* fiesta."

Which, of course, was begging my usual question.

HOW *DOES* ONE connect a food to identity?

Well, the Spanish Inquisition—originally headquartered near our Triana market—knew all about this.

With the capture of Seville in 1248, the centuries-long Christian Reconquest of Al-Andalus was almost complete. Only Granada ob-durately held out. Finally, in 1492, two and a half centuries later, Isabella of Castille and Ferdinand of Aragon, the Catholic Mon-archs, marched into the Alhambra, Granada's ethereal Nasrid palace. The defeated sultan, Boabdil, handed over the keys to his city with the words, "These are the keys to this paradise." Then he rode into exile, pausing for a last, tearful look back, as his stern mother harangued, "You do well, my son, to cry like a woman for what you couldn't defend like a man."

The "Moor's last sigh," romanticized by foreigners from Washington Irving to Salman Rushdie, is another one of Andalusia's great orientalist myths.

Later that fateful year of 1492, Columbus would depart Seville and then Sanlúcar, on a voyage that forever altered the world's food ecosystem and led to so much wealth and so much catastrophe. Spanish Jews, meanwhile, would be given four months to convert or be expelled.

Jews had been hitherto tolerated in Spain, if often uneasily. A century before, there'd been bloody pogroms in Seville, which at the time possessed the world's largest urban Jewish population. Then in 1481, after Isabella requested special leave from Pope Sixtus IV to appoint inquisitors to investigate the genuine faith of Christian converts, Seville staged its first auto-da-fé, on a plaza near all our favorite tapas bars. Dozens of prominent converted formerly Jewish families were burned at the stake. Over the next five years some seven hundred executions took place, along with countless imprisonments. The pontiff was shocked, claiming not to have realized the cruel scope of Isabella's intentions.

In its drive for a Spain "united by one true faith," the Catholic Crown next gave Muslims the same ultimatum it had given Jews— reneging on the Treaty of Granada's assurance about their religious rights. By the mid-sixteenth century, the only minorities remaining in Spain were its populations of conversos (former Jews) and Moriscos (former Muslims). All under the Inquisition's baleful eye.

But how to force a single, common identity onto a previously hybrid society with a seven-century history of social and devotional pluralism? Who *was* a Spaniard and a "true" Christian now? How exactly could a conversion's sincerity be measured? How to unmask a Crypto-Jew or Crypto-Muslim?

Complicating the issue were the infamous statutes of limpieza de sangre, the blood purity doctrine—likely one origin of the modern concept of race—which privileged Old Christians over New Christians, with their "tainted" blood and possibly insincere beliefs corrupting the body politic. Spanish identity, then: Was it biological, religious, or cultural?

Or was it the food?

In this paranoid environment, *you are what you eat* acquired a grave, existential dimension. Eating habits revealed one's true faith, the Inquisition insisted. Particularly, the inquisitors were "obsessed with the pig," scholar Anna Foa writes, as a telltale giveaway of secret Muslims and Jews, for whom pork was taboo. Popular inquisitorial guides prescribed the serving of "forbidden" foods to converts to assess their religious veracity. Or an inspector might drop in at mealtime to examine cooking pots. A single subtle gesture of disgust or acceptance turned pig's flesh into a lie detector. The public eating of pork, the hanging of jamons and chorizos over the stove, were seen as proof of one's Christianity.

We know much about this weaponizing of pig flesh from the chillingly detailed records of Inquisition proceedings. These are eerie documents, sinister, poignant, oddly banal—about how an empanada filling or the exact composition of sausage could get you waterboarded. Or worse. So in sixteenth-century Spain, someone brings bacon, *tocino*, to a neighbor to add to her stockpot. "When she saw the bacon," the accuser testifies, "she turned the pot over so that the bacon fell on the bench, and filled it with water again." Another woman is suspected after refusing a piece of wild boar, since how could anyone refuse such a delicacy? Yet another, for covering her nose when a maid threw a piece of pork into the fire. Yet another, for walking away when someone was rendering lard. In one village, Almazán, north of Madrid, according to historian Christopher Kissane, there were over forty Inquisition documents of the early 1500s involving the ubiquitous bacon.

And so it would go on for decades, leading eventually to what another historian, María Menocal, calls "a Spanish society obsessed with the public and ritualized eating of ham as a display of Christian authenticity."

BUT WHOSE SPAIN was it now? Whose Andalusia?

With Franco's passing, the Christian Reconquista, foundational narrative of his Catholic nationalism, gave way to the more hopeful myth of convivencia. Meaning literally "living together," the concept was formulated by Américo Castro, a liberal cultural historian exiled by Franco in 1938. In a seminal book published abroad in 1948, Castro celebrated the creative cultural interaction of Christians, Arabs, Berbers, and Jews in Al-Andalus. Scholars since have hotly debated whether Al-Andalus was, in fact, such a harmonious paradise, or if this "living together" business was more of an uneasy and constantly shifting balancing act constructed from political and economic necessities. What's important, however, is that Spain, searching for a new image post-Franco, adapted the convivencia trope as a symbolic model for a democratic, tolerant, and multiculturalist future—while conveniently brushing under the table the violently divisive memories of the Spanish Civil War (still unresolved to this day). Postdictatorial Andalusia embraced convivencia with particular vigor. As historian José Venegas writes in his

*Sublime South*: "The intercultural, transcendental myth of Al-Andalus . . . became an identity-marker and a trademark: both an essential building block of regional political autonomy and a tourist attraction."

And right now?

Fucking Reconquista," muttered our Airbnb host, Alejandro, a soft-spoken leftie journalist. "It's back!"

The day after our puerco excursion, Alejandro was giving a lunch party on the terrace of his own, sprawling Triana apartment. Across the Guadalquivir, La Giralda, the Moorish brickwork masterpiece converted into an iconic Catholic bell tower, thrust into the blue sky beyond the white and mustard-yellow of the Maestranza bullring. The anxious talk of Alejandro's journalist guests concerned the shocking rise of the neofascist Vox party, whose macho Islamophobic leader, Santiago Abascal, had posted a video of himself triumphantly riding a horse through the Andalusian landscape to the soundtrack from *The Lord of the Rings*. "The Reconquest begins in Andalusian lands," reads the video caption.

"*Fucking* Reconquista," repeated Alejandro.

"Fucking *catalanes*," somebody else muttered down the table. Not what you'd expect to hear in such liberal company—except that, along with the rest of the country, here, too, the blame was on Catalonia's separatist mess for fueling Abascal's "Spaniards First" rhetoric, for handing him toxic political leverage.

"But so when exactly *did* Spain become a nation?" I broke in brightly. "You know, in the modern sense."

Foreigners' standard knowledge of Spanish history leaps from the Age of Discovery and Catholic Monarchs to the Golden Age of

Cervantes, then straight to Franco, with maybe a brief, fuzzy detour into Peninsular War and Trafalgar and Goya. But how did *Spanish* people view their own history?

"A nation? *Perdón?* How do you mean?" asked Alejandro, a slice of jamon poised midair in his fingers.

"You know, some sort of transformative, nineteenth-century nation-building event," I tried to explain.

An odd pause took over the table. Everyone chewed their jamon or their queso manchego or roasted peppers from the panregional spread anchored by a gigantic Galician-style tortilla de patatas brought by a woman called Reyes.

"La Pepa?" one journalist offered, meaning the liberal 1812 constitution. He didn't sound very sure.

More tablewide munching and head-scratching. And I scratched my head, too. In amazement. I'd been asking people all over the world, as a running gag almost, to comment on their foundational nation-establishing moments: Meiji Restoration in Japan, Unification in Italy, the French Revolution. The answers had often been surprising, irreverent, cynical.

But this silence?

"*Nation . . . national*—those were tainted words after Franco," Reyes began to explain. A thoughtful blond radio journalist who hailed from Ferrol, the Generalissimo's birthplace, Reyes grew up with Franco as God and socialists as devils brandishing tridents. "I didn't hear that Spain was a *dictatorship* until I was eighteen," she confessed.

"Maybe we just had a particularly fucked-up nineteenth century?" suggested a middle-aged writer called Boni (for Bonifacio). "While other countries built nations, ours went *ppffftt*."

Boni was right, even if Spain's decline as a powerful global empire had already started at least two centuries prior. The woeful nineteenth began with the catastrophic 1808 Napoleonic invasion and the Peninsular War—renamed the War of Independence in Spain and sparking, in fact, something akin to a national sentiment. The century concluded with El Desastre, the 1898 loss of Cuba, Puerto Rico, and the Philippines in the ten-day-long Spanish-American War, which massively wounded the national ego. In between there'd been losses of all the other American colonies, multiple abdications, two regencies, interventions by the military, pronunciamientos (coups), two civil wars—and several constitutions succeeding La Pepa. By the end of the accursed nineteenth, Britain's prime minister Lord Salisbury famously rated Spain a dying nation. Some historians claim that the Spain of the day did possess a liberal state and some nationalist sentiment, but was too broke and disorganized to establish the infrastructures, agencies, and standardized education needed to nationalize the masses (something that Third Republic France pulled off so successfully). Why, Spain even sucked at invented traditions, lacking an uncontested flag and national anthem. Meanwhile, the ultraconservative Catholic Church acted almost as a parallel state.

"Regional nationalism erupted instead," said Alejandro, spooning dark caramel over his flan. "País Vasco . . . Catalunya . . ."

"Actually, maybe Spain did begin *as a country* with the Reyes Católicos," suggested a striking Almodóvaresque brunette named Pilar.

She had a point. After the fifteenth-century unification of Castile and Aragon under the Catholic Monarchs, Isabella and Ferdinand, Spain unbelievably maintained its borders, historic identity, and its staunch Catholicism for almost half a millennium.

Nevertheless, our entire table erupted: "Stop, Pilar, stop! You sound just like Vox!!"

"The Vox that's literally promising the return of fucking *Isabel la Católica*," Alejandro huffed bitterly. And suddenly it occurred to me that just a few hundred yards from his table, the dungeons of the Inquisition once lay.

DESPITE SPAIN'S SUBPAR POLITICAL nation-building, its culturati worked hard to "write the nation into existence," as one scholar put it, to create an imagined community through national literature, historicist public art, and revisionist historiographies. And defending a distinctively Spanish culture at table was part of that effort. It was about time, too, given that most of Spain's nineteenth-century cookbooks were translations from French, and upper-class restaurants served third-rate veal *noisettes chasseur* and *goujons de sole frites*. As the great twentieth-century historian Manuel Martínez Llopis lamented: Spanish food culture had been almost lost to *el ridículo afrancesamiento*. "Ridiculous Frenchification."

This state of affairs was addressed for the first time in the 1870s by a pair of Andalusian-born, Madrid-based men of letters: José Castro y Serrano (pen name: His Majesty's Chef) and Mariano Pardo de Figueroa (pen name: Dr. Thebussem). In a spirited epistolary exchange later published as a book, *La Mesa Moderna*, they concede that a national cuisine might not exist—*yet*—but since every Spanish city has its own "princely specialties," they propose that an inventory of native "illustrious delicacies" *must* be created. They also suggest that Spanish court menus be written in "the Language of Cervantes" instead of mistake-ridden French, *and* that olla podrida—"a dish that fed Don Quixote of La Mancha"—be present, as it was once, at the king's table. King Alfonso XII, a great fan of Cervantes, obliged.

Spain's most interesting gastronationalist, though, was also one of its most prominent realist novelists: Emilia Pardo Bazán, a countess, scholar, and women's rights activist whose fiery speeches implored women to nationalize all their domestic activities, from childcare to home decoration, but especially cooking. In her pair of cookbooks *La Cocina Española Antigua* (1913) and *La Cocina Española Moderna* (1914), part of her Women's Library series, the countess lays out her own crucial inventory of "cocina española," from gazpachos to frituras to one-pot stews (*ollas*). Bazán praises Spain's "strong and simple" flavors, free from the "ambiguity of sauces and dressings." (Oh, how I agree with the countess.) Writing in chatty, colloquial Spanish, Doña Emilia declares Spanish sopa a la marinera as "better and more logical" than the "mushy" French bouillabaisse; extols the succulence of Spanish croquetas while dissing the French original as "massive" and "graceless." Cuisine to her is a precious part of the Spanish national patrimony. "There are dishes of our national cuisine" proposes the countess, "that are no less worthy of attention nor less historical than a medal, a weapon or a tomb" (those masculine symbols)—in effect inviting women to participate in forging a nation through cooking.

Though Bazán, born in Galicia, mentions the "picturesque variety" of Spain's regional foodways, her vision is ultimately Castilian-nationalist (with an occasional xenophobic tinge, I might add). The first gastronome to address regional cooking in any actual depth was Dionisio Pérez (pen name: Post-Thebussem). In 1929—a great year for regionalist food guides all over Europe—Pérez published his now-iconic *Guía del Buen Comer Español*: a gushing foodie

travelogue through *"las gloriosas cocinas de las regiones españolas."*
His most excellent journey was state-sponsored, in fact. It was commissioned by Spain's Patronato de Turismo, newly founded by the
pre-Franco dictator Primo de Rivera (nickname: the "Iron Sur-
geon") to stimulate local and international tourism and promote
domestic ingredients.

The fact that the patronato "would have considered it important
enough to provide detailed information about Spanish cuisine," historian Lara Anderson writes, "was no doubt due to the incredibly
bad press Spanish food received from foreign travelers." Ouch.

Pretty much ever since, every scholarly text and every cookbook
has defined Spain's cuisine as a "patchwork of regional traditions
and tastes as different . . . as Galician bagpipe tunes are from the
plaintive wails of flamenco"—to quote my own magazine article
about different regional tapas.

But when I met again with Isabel González Turmo, the food anthropologist, at our favorite spot, Flor de Toranzo, her words almost
made me drop my anchovy canapé.

"Actually, regional Spanish cuisine is an invention of Francoism."

Academics, they do relish their revisionist pyrotechnics. But this
seemed so counterintuitive, on *so* many levels.

And yet Isabel came to her controversial conclusion via exhaustive research for a book called *200 Años de Cocina*, in which
she charted the evolution of Spanish cuisine across two centuries,
from 1776 to 1975. Examining some four thousand recipes in handwritten family cookbooks, she was startled to discover a common
centralized heritage where she expected nothing but regional differences. This heritage was drawn from widely circulated printed

eighteenth-century cookbooks, and the migrations—people, ingredients, food, fashions—across the Iberian Peninsula.

"Aside from super-local variations in names for some mushroom or fish," she said in her slightly stern way, "the *recetarios* were all pretty similar across the country. *Curioso, no?* Take butifarra, for instance. Such a *Catalan* sausage, you say? But, Anya, I swear I was actually shocked at how much it featured in *Andalusian* manuscripts. And equally at how often our Andalusian gazpacho appeared in Catalan texts."

I thought of Cajun andouille sausage turning up, say, in Seattle recipes or New England chowder in Savannah family cookbooks.

"And talking of gazpacho," said Isabel, "its mentions are scant even in Andalusian manuscripts until the late nineteenth century, when this dish of shepherds and farm laborers jumped onto bourgeois tables, to be served with the now-usual chopped veggie garnishes. And the first recipe of it using tomatoes? In a text from Madrid!"

Not that Isabel was saying people cooked identically from Galicia to Andalusia. Yet the differences could be more striking, she found, within the same village or town, where they were determined by class and access to foodstuffs. The geographic adjectives that we now take for granted—Asturiano, Granadino, Gallego—didn't feature in old family cookbooks, because naming foods in this fashion was historically recent all over Europe.

"Spain's geographical food designations," she declared, "only got institutionalized and codified with Franco."

I was completely bewildered now. "But didn't Franco brutally *squash* regional differences in his push for a unified Spain?"

"*Politically*, yes," Isabel agreed.

But cooking, like crafts and folklore, was an *asunto menor*—a lesser affair entrusted to La Sección Femenina, the women's branch of the Falange, Spain's fascist movement. Cofounded by Pilar Primo de Rivera, the dictator's daughter, La Sección Femenina was charged with molding what one historian called "true Catholic Woman-hood." Its 1950 cookbook, *Manual de Cocina*, a generalized Falangist *Joy of Cooking*, sold over a million copies and was still much loved by some oldsters.

But for La Sección's follow-up book, *Cocinas Regionales*, published three years later, female teams were sent out to different parts of the country to select and assign names to regional recipes. And that was how a formerly shared cuisine became carved up into cocina andaluza, cocina valenciana, cocina riojana, and so on. The same happened to crafts, costumes, and dance. La Sección Femenina was *the* institution promoting and celebrating a sanitized, politically acceptable form of cultural diversity—under the banner of unity.

"*Interesante*," I muttered, savoring the revisionism along with the last bite of my fat, buttery anchovies. "*Feminization* as the engine of Spanish regionalism."

"Yes, something like that," Isabel allowed. "In fact, when the Spanish constitution of 1978 created seventeen autonomous regions, Franco's food map served as a convenient blueprint for distinct regional identities, for promoting food patrimonies. Because, after language," she mused, "isn't cuisine the most effective weapon of chauvinisms—nationalist or regionalist?"

"So you're saying—you're saying cocina andaluza—"

"Yes, it's a *construct*." That dreaded word again. "Just like Basque cooking or Catalan cooking. But there's this difference: Catalans and Basques throw lots of euros behind their celebrity chefs and cookbooks and food conferences. But Andalusia? We're

poor and split between eight competing provincias whose governments fight about who'll finance which cookbook or food fair.

"The kitchen as engine for fragmentation," sighed Isabel. "All
this regionalism. In reality food is fluid, vital, adaptive. Ephemeral.
It bubbles like foam . . . it seeps through like oil."

I walked out of Flor de Toranzo into the fierce Andalusian sun-
shine. Aperitivo drinkers were beginning to gather at the bars on
narrow Calle Gamazo, a great tapas-central. Isabel's last words
were some of the wisest I've heard from a scholar. And yet our conversation left me feeling oddly deflated. At this point in my overall
journey, the academic critiques were starting to sound oh-so-very
familiar: the notion of a "national (regional?) cuisine" as a construct;
the top-down manipulations of image-creation and marketing forces
of corporations and governments; the peculiar selectivity of a national food canon that often ignored poor people's gruels as not
worthy of a "cuisine." All along my travels, I had a sense of two
parallel roads that never quite joined. One, where scholars called
bars "ethnographic arenas" and a shared meal "commensality" as
they deconstructed and busted up myths, trying to prove that even
tap water was some sort of "social construction." The other, where
actual people ate and drank and bonded and celebrated together,
internalizing, perpetuating, and yes, embodying the myths and invented traditions that were so engrained they felt totally natural—
indisputable truths.

Mulling the issue, I headed up Calle Sierpes, to meet Barry at
the Cervantes statue by the former site of the Royal Prison. The
father of the modern novel had done time there in his years in Seville; it's where *Don Quixote* was supposedly hatched. A text came

now from Barry. "Running late. Fyi, our fave bars in centro—inaccessible once Semana Santa starts, no?"

Why, of course. Immediately I turned around and went hustling back to Calle Gamazo, telling Barry to meet me at Casa Moreno, in order to resample its Andalusian-identity overflow while it was still possible to get near a bar counter.

You enter Casa Moreno through a 1940s Ali Baba cave of comestibles, every inch packed tight with multicolored jars, cans, bottles, sacks, and bins under the meaty stalactites of chorizos and jamones. It's one of Seville's last remaining ultramarinos ("beyond the sea," literally), petite grocery stores originally specializing in colonial products—Colombian coffee, Venezuelan chocolate. Half hidden away at the very back of the store stands a bar that's a narrow, congested shrine of taurino and Catholic iconography. I ordered a fino and took in again the great-horned bull's head jutting over glossy depictions of a suffering Christ and a weeping, gorgeous Virgin, all facing a tattered cabinet of rare sherries and wines curated by Emilio, the barman at the counter, who is one of Seville's most beloved taberneros. A single beat-up toaster oven churned out warm montaditos. It was thickly flanked by postcards and family photos, by colorful cookie tins and sheaves of old lottery tickets, the whole dominated by a gallery of toreros, interspersed with yet more beautiful sorrowful Virgins—and white paper stickers of handwritten aphorisms famously composed by Emilio himself: "Joy makes us invulnerable." "Haste destroys all tenderness." The son of a well-known football journalist, Emilio wanted to write himself but ended up pouring his creativity into these bar-counter wisdoms—and into entertaining his parroquianos, his regulars. A barrio bar, he liked to repeat, is the city's kitchen, its living room, its confession booth. And a good tabernero is both priest and psychologist.

The parroquianos around me were discussing the current celeb matador Morante de la Puebla, whose autographed photo hung above us, puffing a fat Montecristo. Recently Morante had caused an international scandal, Emilio annotated, by wiping a dying bull's face with a handkerchief. The gesture—stunt?—went viral.

"Fuck the animal rights activists!" growled a hefty señor, sunglasses up in his dyed hair, who turned out to be a ganadero, a bull breeder.

"I watch the video of it and cry every time, it's so beautiful," confessed a frail grandma in a tweed jacket who was sharing an aperitivo with her elderly girlfriend. The old ladies then switched to another hot but eternal topic, what with Semana Santa about to arrive and the local soccer derby kicking off the next afternoon. La Macarena: Was she Sevillista or Betica? Meaning, which of the city's rival soccer clubs, Sevilla FC or Real Betis (Betis, the city's Roman name), could claim her as patron?

"A loaded question," agreed the sagacious Emilio, an ardent Sevillista and devotee of a different Virgin, Estrella.

"La Macarena's cape is of course *green*, Betis's colors," the ganadero chimed in.

"Claro," seconded the Betica grandma, "my grandson even sleeps in green underwear."

"*But* La Macarena's accessories are always Sevillista *red*," insisted Emilio.

"Exactly!" cackled the other granny, a Sevillista, adding that green was not even *allowed* in her house. "I haven't eaten even a salad for decades," she boasted—literally, not figuratively—and ordered another manzanilla.

I chewed on my pork-laden pringá montadito, which Emilio slid across the counter on wax paper, and thought of Almodóvar's

Spanish everyday absurdities; of what Alberto the historian had said about tabernas as spaces of Andalusian convivencia, that peculiar confluence of street and home, public and private, an important part of local mythology; of how now-iconic tapas bars took on the function of presenting and preserving the overflowing local identity.

Where all the clichés of "Spanishness" were unabashedly embraced and on display.

The following day our pal Rafa, an ardent Sevillista, helped us score impossible tickets for the actual Derbi Sevillano—one of the most fervent soccer clashes in Spain—held at Sevilla FC's stadium. La Macarena didn't make an appearance, no. But the vast fan-made banner covering part of the stands starred a colossal heavy-metalized Virgin in Sevilla's red colors with the words "LA PASIÓN."

*Con la pasión* Sevilla won, 3–2.

THE DAY SO FEVERISHLY anticipated by me and the entire city was finally here.

Lunes Santo, the Holy Monday of my first Semana Santa.

Over the course of the week, sixty-one hermandades, brotherhoods, were to crisscross the city with their backbreaking floats, many of them centuries-old Baroque treasures.

Rafa, a self-proclaimed Semana Santa experto, now took us in hand. "Nine important confraternities are all in action today," he announced, snaking us past the centro's police cordons via mysterious shortcuts while waving hola to his musical fans among the cops. Somehow we edged our way into jam-packed Plaza del Duque, the main processional crossroads. A phone number was hastily thumbed. A besuited amigo from Banco Santander squirmed along to bring us to a second-floor viewing party.

That was whom we'd be witnessing the Passion of Christ with, I realized. Moneylenders.

Dusk descended. The room filled with women in smart cocktail dresses and caballeros with *pijo* (preppy) sweaters draped over striped shirts. We'd been boozing and eating since prelunch aperitivos at Triana market, but nevertheless I made an assessing beeline for the bankers' tapas buffet table. Tuna empanadas from a special bakery inside El Corte Inglés department store, grand reserve jamon and chorizo Iberico, albóndigas, croquetas, crumbly ivory triangles of aged queso manchego, squares of a particularly fluffy tortilla de patatas. How eternal they seemed, these national nibbles. The Iberian canon, the bite-size feast that seems to move with you wherever you are in Spain.

I turned to the dessert table and its load of Semana Santa torrijas, a kind of Spanish French toast rife with Catholic meaning, its stale bread revitalized as a luscious dessert symbolizing Christ's death and rebirth. Here I chatted up a famous liberal essayist, and wondered aloud to him how Andalusia could reconcile its three decades of socialist government with all its religious obsessions and extravagances. The writer chortled and gave a wondering shrug, too. He'd come to Seville from Castille in the north in the early seventies, during Franco. And seeing the same zealous socialists who furtively handed out lefty leaflets going on about Semana Santa and torreros and Virgins, he asked himself, "*Where have I landed?*"

Trying not to splash manzanilla on the hospitable financiers, I squeezed with Barry onto a viewing balcony—gaping out over the sea of people as a current of nazarenos, those marching hermanos in their sinister, penitential hoods, came slowly advancing in the glow of the tall tapers they carried. And up behind, to the drums and shriek of trumpets of a marching band, a flower-engorged golden paso with a life-size Christ anguished on his cross inched along—past Zara, past Burger King.

But that was the opening act, for Christ overall plays a distinguished second fiddle in the week's spectacle devoted to him. Louder horns and drums swelled, and I gasped, as a Virgin's palio, her canopied float, came into view through clouds of incense—a vision in whites and creams out of some enchanted bridal salon. "*Virgen de la Salud*, a lesser virgin, but looking super guapa tonight," Rafa appraised behind us. The float paused right below to rest the costaleros, the bearers. Then at three loud knocks on its side, the palio was hefted once more. To the heart-catching shrill of triumphant music and the crowd's bursting applause, the Virgin swayed onward.

All around us bankers were displaying their goose bumps while munching jamon.

"This is the Baroque *alive and in motion*," enthused Manu, an artist friend of Rafa's. "With a soundtrack and an audience!"

Suddenly the Virgen de la Salud's band broke into a melodramatic tune, as if for a Hollywood kiss. A younger couple beside us started slow-dancing.

But Rafa looked restless. "The Virgins are best seen down in the streets," he cried. "Let's beat it!"

Which was how we found ourselves forcing our way through the densely packed sidewalks, trying to keep up with Rafa, until we were actually chasing his heels—the Baroque in motion—up streets through marching nazarenos—help!—and musicians. To my horror I knocked over a trumpeter's sheet music and—

And suddenly we were in a tight little plaza, so crowded I could barely breathe. In front of us the Rocío Virgin of the Hermandad de la Redención was making her slow, rocking, backward entrada (entry) into her home church. She stood inclined forward slightly, as if transfixed in her tender gesture of grief behind the blazing footlights of her candles—almost engulfed by her magnificent crown and vast embroidered cape, by her pale roses, by the gleaming silver columns and ornamented flaps of her canopy, which swayed in rhythm, ravishingly, almost lasciviously. The scent of orange trees mingled with the fumes of incense. A solo *saeta*, an "arrow"—a (supposedly) spontaneous flamenco-like song of devotion—pierced the night. A tremor of emotion went through our packed crowd—a mass of people hushed into a communal whole as the haunting wail soared above us. Tears streamed down my Jewish atheist cheeks. I'd have swooned, if I'd been able to move.

ON SEVILLE'S HOLY WEEK calendar, the processions that march from Holy Thursday night into Good Friday midday—La Madrugá—rank as the World Cup final.

Besides the grand, venerated Christ image of the Gran Poder, Seville's two great crosstown rival Virgins, La Macarena and Esperanza de Triana, are paraded in their full splendor. Our chance of getting close enough to glimpse either Virgin was zero. Cue Rafa to the rescue again. We'd watch La Macarena's entrada to her basilica late Friday morning at his sister's house on the processional route.

As for Holy Thursday afternoon, I shamelessly invited myself to Rafa's house in Triana—to see his mom prepare her prodigious potaje for the next day.

Potaje was a crucial final act of my tapas research. If jamon is

Spain's expensive national indulgence, a fiesta, then the variants of olla, or stewpot, are the national genus of family meal, casual but ripe with historical memory, be they expressed regionally as potaje, cocido, puchero, or pote. These multi-meat boiled dinners are pot-au-feu's Iberian cousins, of course, but more symbolic and vital somehow than their French relative. Especially here in Seville where every bar serves pringá, that iconic tapa of mashed-up olla meat leftovers inside little pressed rolls, a sort of Sevillian slider.

Rafa's mom, Señora Mercedes, must have been a voluptuous beauty in her time. Now in her huge dashing sunglasses and a long linen tunic, she looked smartly plump and maternal in Rafa's old-fashioned white-tiled kitchen. But I wasn't fooled. The nurturing histrionic Italian nonna, with her noisy kisses and sighs, is central to the Italian brand. But Spanish abuelas? Almost diametrically the opposite. Unsentimental, almost macho in their matter-of-factness, they relish their corridas, their late-morning tots at the barrio bar. In my decades of travels in Spain, I never stopped wondering why Spaniards don't make a cult about the cooking of their mothers or grandmothers. Perhaps it was the leaden Francoist past everyone prefers to reject and forget, with its improvised food, its patriarchal denigration of women simultaneous with a dictatorial nationalization of motherhood. Then again, even the Virgin long-worshipped here in Andalusia is the iconic Dolorosa typology: young, ravishing, solo, fetishistically overdressed. Not remotely maternal.

Señora Mercedes unfurled the brown paper parcels of her potaje supplies with an almost savage abuela efficiency. "Don't interrupt," she snapped at Rafa, who was proclaiming that potajes and ollas were simple, sure, but "muy complicado." No, Señora Mercedes wasn't about to stage any kind of *performance*.

The olla is both a dish and the iconic Spanish earthenware pot whose womb-like shape, the food writer Alicia Ríos suggests, unconsciously inspires in women "an urge to nurture and cook." Rafa's mom, however, swore by her pressure cooker—a convenience popularized by the Francoist Sección Femenina back in the 1950s. Into this potaje-express she tossed thin-skinned Andalusian garbanzos, chorizo Iberico—"not too overcured"—some ribs of the same pedigreed Iberico porkers, a few links of blood sausage, and a slab of papada, the dusky Spanish jowl bacon. Large pinches of cumin and smoked pimentón followed. Whereupon she quickly screwed on the cooker lid and settled down in the living room with a giant gin and tonic, to watch the bullfights on the tele.

While the potaje-express hissed in the kitchen and the corrida's pasodobles blared from the TV, Rafa showed Barry his autographed photos with soccer stars, and I sat on his orientalist patio, nibbling jamon and *seriously* pondering the quasi-mythical progenitor of all Spanish stews. Olla podrida. Rotten pot.

Carolyn Nadeau, author of a fascinating book of food in Cervantes, reports that the dish—fashionable in Hapsburg Spain of the sixteenth and seventeenth centuries, a.k.a. the Golden Age—represented "the culinary taste of nobles both for its ostentation and its opulence." But at the same time "everyone from kings to canons, to rectors and peasants enjoyed it," prepared according to their means. Here then was a rare bird, a "national culinary expression" that transcended class when European cuisines, not yet nationalized, were mostly meant for elites.

But why *podrida*, or "rotten"? Because the ingredients would disintegrate after hours of simmering? But just as likely from *poderida*, powerful, referring to the dish's amazing vitality.

I thought again of Cervantes, as one so often does in Spain—especially after Señora Mercedes declared that Barry, slender faced and goateed, was Don Quixote's spitting image (we heard this often in Spain). At the close of the sixteenth century, Cervantes shuffled in and out of Seville, working as an underpaid tax collector in Andalusia. Sevillians like to boast that *Don Quixote* was conceived in their rascal-crowded Royal Prison, where Cervantes spent time in 1597 on errant charges of tax fraud. Olla podrida features prominently in his great comic masterpiece, the world's most translated book after the Bible—and one of the world's most food-obsessed novels. There's its famous wedding scene where Sancho Panza ogles six simmering ollas "the size of wine vats," their gluttonously enumerated contents pretty much reproducing the 1599 recipe by royal cook Diego Granado, whose tome, *Libro del Arte de Cozina*, was lugged by conquistadores to the New World. There, the dish would develop its many colonial afterlives, as Cuban ajiaco, Colombian sancocho, Peruvian locro, and such.

And now, to Señora Mercedes's cries of *asesino!* in the living room at a matador's clumsy kill, the Inquisition reentered my thoughts. *Don Quixote* contains such a stew of coded references and sly food identity jokes that some *cervantistas* propose that the hero of Spain's most iconic work—ditto the author?—may in fact have been a converso. The fictitious "original" chronicler of Cervantes's knight-errant's adventures is an Arab historian writing in Arabic, one Cide Hamete Benengeli, whose name translates as Lord Eggplant—a vegetable that stigmatized not only Muslims but Jews, and occasionally featured in Inquisition proceedings. The novel's overall narrator (Cervantes?) finds Mr. Eggplant's manuscript, and in Toledo—a pre-Inquisition convivencia center of Jewish and Moorish cultures—enlists a young Morisco, a converted Moor, to translate it. Why does the Morisco guffaw reading how Quixote's ladylove Dulcinea has "the best hand at salting pork of any woman in La Mancha"? Maybe because Dulcinea's grubby village, Toboso, was well-known for being heavily Moorish. Her pork prowess would mock the Inquisition's dreaded "fake eating like Christians," as historian María Menocal argues. The overarching Cervantine joke? When he wrote *Don Quixote*, Arab manuscripts had long been outlawed and publicly burned. No Morisco translators wandered the streets of Toledo.

I stuck my head into the living room to ask Señora Mercedes about olla podrida. She took her eyes off a torero's capework a moment as *olés* chorused.

"Didn't it originate from *un guiso judío* [a Jewish stew]?" she suggested, before returning to the capework and *olés*. Meaning a dish called adafina, I reflected, back on the patio. That Sephardic olla of chickpeas, onions, mutton, and eggs also featured heavily in Inquisition reports. Another possible olla podrida source, though, was Muslim: a dish called Sinhājī, from a thirteenth-century Al-Andalus cookery book.

Olla was like a Baroque cathedral constructed on the foundations of a mosque and a synagogue. Or like the metafictional palimpsest that is *Don Quixote* itself, "written" by an Arab, "translated" into Castilian by a converted Moor, "annotated and edited" by a (truly?) Christian narrator.

Under Spain's Frenchified Bourbon rule after the Hapsburgs, olla podrida fell into disregard—only to regain its status in the late nineteenth century, when the battered country was trying to reassemble its identity. The dish found itself knighted into the service of nation-constructing—along with Cervantes. If a *"plato español por excelencia* ever existed," proclaimed Countess Pardo Bazán, "it's the one that gets such an honorable mention in *el Quixote*."

France's pot-au-feu and Spain's olla podrida/cocido/potaje got glorified in almost identical terms: unity in diversity, an empire of taste, a *national* potage. But such different historical contexts. Pot-au-feu represented the cuisine bourgeoise of a modern secular universalist France, "égalité-fraternité" in a soup pot for a cultural empire that was exporting culinary modernity the world over. Whereas Spain's intellectuals touted olla podrida as a nostalgic historical artifact evoking the country's past imperial might—the Golden Age of Cervantes and company, of the Baroque and the first apotheosis of Semana Santa's spectaculars.

And *Don Quixote* itself? At a time when Spain was suffering its identity crisis, the novel's massively observed 1905 tercentenary of publication was hailed by the period press with Quixotian hyperbole: the "most luminous and splendorous celebration that was ever held by any nation to honor the greatest glory of its own race, speech and national soul." Yet another invented tradition?

Finally Señora Mercedes's olla/potaje was ready.

It tasted nothing like the bland comfort of pot-au-feu with its clear Cartesian bouillon. Leaving most of it for La Macarena's big day tomorrow, Rafa ladled out small bowls of the buttery chickpeas in a ruddy-red pimentón-stained broth of such dense porky smokiness, you could almost slice the taste with a knife. Briskly, Señora Mercedes demonstrated just how to make a pringá. Vigorously mash up all the meats on a plate, squish spoonfuls between hunks of bread torn from long rolls—repeat. An explosion of flavor.

And suddenly it occurred to me that this was an exceedingly rare occasion. In three decades of roaming Spain, I could count on my fingers the times I'd been invited to a family meal. It seemed

ironic and lovely how my "meal" of moving from bar to bar ended
up with a sit-down *meal* proper. Except there was no white tablecloth here. No table as such. We ate the messy Quixotian sandwiches
on the couch in front of the tele. Rafa strummed a guitar, explaining the difference between flamenco's bulerías and alegrías. His
ten-year-old daughter, Sol, was trying on mantos (shawls), hoop earrings, and polka-dot dresses for the Feria, a weeklong carnival of
dancing and boozing that would follow Semana Santa almost immediately. On TV another bull was dying a panting death. "I'm a
huge animal lover," declared Señora Mercedes, "the kind of person
who'll save every kitten and bird. I adore my dogs. But I don't understand the animal rights fascists who want to ban the corrida! The
toro de lidia [fighting bull] has the most beautiful life, he dies like a
hero. They kill the *chickens* we eat—why this hypocrisy?"

The bull finally crumpled to its heroic knees and slumped in-
ertly on its side in a pool of blood in the sand. Señora Mercedes
applauded the deftly administered kill, along with the crowd on
TV. I turned my head away and stared at the floor.

AND NOW it's La Madrugá: Good Friday, late morning.

We've managed to squeeze and worm through ecstatic crowds
into the home of Rafa's sister, Rocío, to watch La Macarena's return to her basilica around the corner. Semana Santa reaches its
climax now, and Rocío's narrow street, Calle Parras, is one continuous indoor block party; every house a celebration, sidewalks
packed solid outside.

"La Macarena is best understood right in this barrio of hers,"
insists Rafa, bleary-eyed but revved up.

"This fiesta is like a second Christmas for all of us here," Rocío chimes in.

Tables around us hold honey-intensive, Arab-tasting fried pastries and the inevitable torrijas, the celebratory muscatel-soaked quasi–French toast. Besides her potaje, Rafa's mom has produced a vast cauldron of spinach and chickpeas and a huge pot of bacalao con tomate. We shuffle about eating pringá sandwiches between craning out the jammed front door for updates. Barry recognizes a signed wall photo of Manolete and is thunderstruck to learn that this tragically gored bullfighting legend was the godfather of Rocío's father-in-law.

"We consider again the 'living Baroque,'" muses Rafa's artist pal, Manu, cerveza in hand. "I say, come see La Macarena! Or perhaps our adulations hark back to something more ancient and pagan? To Roman times, when people had domestic altars here, and household gods and goddesses were the patres- and matres-familias."

"But she's also one of us, a barrio girl!" someone interrupts. "The identification is total."

Christ now comes inching past, accompanied by Roman centurions in extravagantly plumed helmets of bordador Rodríguez Ojeda's design. Then we hear *her* drums and trumpets. Her palio sways into view along the mobbed route as pink and scarlet rose petals shower down from balconies and roofs, turning the paving into a long frosted cake. Fifty yards away, she halts. A sudden hush turns the world silent—the obligatory saeta rings out.

"Now you must look in *her* face! Into *her* eyes!" implores Rafa, pulling at my sleeve as her palio starts up again to trumpets, erupting applause, cries of "Guapa! You beauty!"

I crouch by a window amid romping young kids. La Macarena

comes alongside, trailing her stupendous green cape. Through the half-melted candles and massed flowers and crimson, gold-embroidered undulating flaps of her canopy—our eyes meet. I swear she looks back at me. I gasp. It must be a hallucination. *Yes, isn't religion a collective delirium?* the Soviet girl in me faintly insists. But if La Macarena performed a miracle right here and now, I wouldn't join the doubters.

And just like that, it's all over. Exhausted costaleros plod into Rocío's house to eat jamon and tilt back Cruzcampos. Street cleaners are already out vacuuming up the rose petals with that slightly brute Spanish efficiency. This is modern Andalusia, where the magical and the matter-of-fact share the road. I stoop for a handful of rose petals on the paving before they're sucked away, and I inhale their fading perfume.

# OAXACA
## Maize, Mole, Mezcal

There is a moment in preparing Oaxaca's famed mole negro when things shoot up in flames—*la quemada de semillas*, "the burning of seeds."

Like a priestess at a ritual pyre, the petite dignified woman with raven-black hair stood by her comal, a pre-Hispanic earthenware griddle as big as the lid of a village well. Fire leapt toward the ceiling beams of the patio kitchen. I began coughing from the smoke.

In alarm I wondered if someone shouldn't call the *bomberos*.

"We're not talking charred," the woman intoned, "we want *ceniza absoluta*, total ash! Burnt!"

Whereupon chef Celia Florián of celebrated Las Quince Letras restaurant in Oaxaca de Juárez, the pastel-hued colonial capital of Mexico's most Indigenous state, flashed me a self-satisfied smile. She was well accustomed to wide-eyed journalists and their cell-phone cameras.

Flames having subsided, Celia now scooped the black pile of tortilla and chili seed ash into a beat-up zinc bucket with other, less

carbonized ingredients and handed the load to her obedient husband, Fidel, to take away to the molino, the mill, for grinding.

The quema is the sensational step in making black mole, the
syncretic Ibero-Amerindian showstopper that has fascinated me
since I first tasted it here decades ago. The arduously laborious step
is the tatemada, the slow toasting on the comal of some three dozen
ingredients. "Patience, *infinite patience*" was required, said Celia.
She wasn't kidding. For several hours, I'd hovered by her comal as
she coaxed out—from Mesoamerican cacao, tortillas, and chilies,
from Spanish colonial wheat bread, from Islamic Al-Andalus almonds, raisins, and sesame seeds—the multicultural universe of
flavor-layers demanded by black mole.

An ethnographic still life of chilies was already laid out for the
tatemada when I'd arrived early that morning, my first one back in
this city in its high-valley cradle in the mountains of southern Mexico. Here were bell-shaped chilhuacles negros—"sour-citrusy with
an elegant indirect heat"—grown by a handful of Indigenous farmers in Oaxaca's humid Cañada region, and so disease-prone and
finicky they were on the brink of extinction. Here, for their smoky
meatiness, were pasillas Mixes, cultivated in the rugged Sierra Norte
highlands by the Mixe people, the self-titled Ayüükjä'äy ("they who
speak the mountain language"). Besides these Celia had thrown in
more mundane chipotles and anchos, to roast their already dark
crinkly skins, then shake out the seeds for burning.

Toasting cacao pods and cinnamon sticks had filled the patio
kitchen with the chocolaty aromas of a Oaxacan breakfast. A whole
spice chest then met the comal: ginger, oregano, avocado and bay
leaves—plus the peppercorns, nutmeg, and cloves that historically
would have arrived in colonial Mexico on the Manila galleons, the
Spanish vessels that initiated the world's first globalized commerce.

A pantry's worth of dried fruit and nuts followed, all adding lush-
ness to Celia's mole, along with yellow bread rolls called molletes
(fried in oil) and plantains in their skins (roasted in embers). There
might have been charred tomatoes and onions, too, but I'd completely
lost track.

Her face haloed in spice haze, Celia slowly maneuvered ingredients around the comal with a palm leaf broomlet called an esco-
beta. I flapped at the smoke—and marveled, as I always did in
Oaxaca, at the absurdly backbreaking difficulty of a dish that remained an enigma to me still.

What was mole, really? That's what I wanted to learn, beyond the
prodigious literalness of a copious, aromatic sauce, ladled over bits
of protein (classically turkey), which always seemed like an after-
thought. Why was mole such a community ritual? How were Mexico's myriad moles, from grass green to tar black to mahogany red,
even related? "*Tan mexicana como el mole*," they say—equivalent to
our "as American as apple pie." But how did mole's special status as
a *símbolo de la Mexicanidad*—"often read as a proxy for the cultural origins of the national character," as one scholar noted—reflect
Mexico's complicated racial identity politics? In this age of globalization and decolonization, of the multiculturalism that Oaxaca has
grown famous for, what did mole represent today?

Celia's father is Zapotec, a member of Oaxaca's dominant Indigenous group. Her mother is mestiza, mixed race, which is Mexico's official identity. She grew up in a pueblo about fifteen miles
from Oaxaca City, the sort of place where girls got to play with
their dolls after a long day of kitchen chores. She made her first
atole (a pre-Hispanic maize drink) at eight, her first handmade

tortilla (that pre-Hispanic maize flatbread) at ten. The tortilla made
her feel grown-up and important, she told me, like a proper woman
of her community. When almost three decades ago she opened Las
Quince Letras a few blocks from the luridly syncretic Baroque
of the grand seventeenth-century temple of Santo Domingo de
Guzmán with its gold leaf and beheaded saints, it was the only *res-*
*taurante* in the vicinity. The early 1990s was also when I first came
to Oaxaca. It struck me then as enchantingly remote and dusty-
provincial, a folkloricized remnant visited mostly for its Indigenous
markets and the majestic ruins of Monte Albán, the grand capital
built by the Zapotecs 2,500 years before. Like Andalusia or Naples,
Oaxaca long embraced its own myth of exceptionalism—a Oax-
aqueñismo centered around the state's prodigious diversity. But unlike those iconic European locales, Oaxaca has remained until quite
recently on the periphery of Mexico's official national narrative,
one that belonged to Mexico City and its glorified Aztec history.

"And now we're *el nuevo centro gastronómico del mundo!*" Celia
laughed on her color-splashed kitchen patio, as she garnished a blue
corn tortilla for me with chapulines, or grasshoppers—"herbaceous
this time of year," salty, crunchy, not remotely repugnant. "Like you,
dear Anya, everyone wants to learn the secret of our moles," she said.
Indeed. Her street and the entire self-consciously prettified centro
were buzzing with restaurants, with hipster mezcalerías everywhere
you trod. As if on cue, a trio of very tall young Nordic chefs, burned
red by the winter sun, wandered in from the street. They announced
they wanted to learn about Celia's moles.

And here was a further delightful development. On my last
visit to Oaxaca a few years back, I wrote about its male chefs
and their liquid-nitrogenizing of arroz con leche or alchemizing
avocado-leaf-scented vapors—the influence of Spain's flashy nueva

cocina. Now cocineras tradicionales, traditional women cooks, some Indigenous, were claiming the spotlight. This made Celia extremely happy. After the Conquest, she told me and the Danes, Spanish women were scarce, so the colonizers took Indigenous wives, or at least employed them as cooks. For centuries Mexico's women had been the uncelebrated carriers of traditional cooking. Now their craft was being valued at long last.

"So that's my *meal* in Oaxaca!" I cried out to Celia. "Mole and maize masa [tortillas, tamales], prepared by women!"

Mole, I began to elaborate, representing the complicated hybridity of Mexican culture—

"—And masa," Celia completed my sentence, "*nuestras raíces indígenas!*" Our Indigenous roots.

To celebrate my *proyecto* Celia trotted out bottles of exquisite Real Minero mezcal made by our mutual friend, Graciela, a chingona (badass) and a fiery feminist.

"A nuestra querida Oaxaca," she said, lifting her glass.

"Stigibeu?" I attempted the traditional Zapotec toast.

"Skal," grinned the Danes, their eyes locking gleefully on the midday mezcal.

Was *that* what had really brought them to Oaxaca?

OAXACA STATE SITS at the convergence of two major mountain ranges, the Sierra Madre Oriental and the Sierra Madre del Sur. Its over 4 million inhabitants live amid such a wealth of cultural heritage and biodiversity that one important archeologist called Oaxaca "a virtual laboratory for human designs for living." Archeobotanists tout it as the probable birthplace of Mesoamerican plant domestication based on a local cave called Guilá Naquitz with its ten-millennia-old squash seeds and the earliest known examples of domesticated maize—teensy cobs from about 4,300 BCE. Of Mexico's sixty-four current landraces of maize (that is, unique cultivars), thirty-five are native to Oaxaca, as are some two dozen species of chilies and beans—all of them harvested together on small Indigenous farm plots called milpas, rain fed and ultrasustainable.

Linguists, meanwhile, bubble about how a state barely larger than Portugal has more tongues than the whole of Europe. Often promoted/branded as Mexico's "cradle of diversity," Oaxaca is home to sixteen ethnic groups—Zapotecs, Mixtecs, Zoques, Chatinos, Triques, and the like—all speaking unique languages. Zapotec alone boasts sixty known variants, so that stigibeu, or "cheers," the toast I tried not to mangle, might sound totally different in the high Central Valleys around Oaxaca City than in the tropical lowland of Tehuantepec Isthmus.

That's the sunny PR angle.

Beyond it, political scientists study Oaxaca's intense protest movements as sociologists research the effects of stark economic inequality, NAFTA, and climate change. Remittance from emigrants constitutes the second-biggest source of Oaxaca's income after tourism. Of the state's 570 municipalities, 356 (largely Indigenous) are nationally classified in the "extreme poverty" category.

In consequence, everything one eats here resonates with social issues: Indigenous rights, environmental justice, gender equality.

I WAS ROUSED from my mole and mezcal–induced slumber by the afternoon sun tatemadaing me through the tall bare windows. The

house we had rented was in Barrio de Jalatlaco—"sandbank" in
Nahuatl, once the lingua franca of the dominant Aztec empire.
Lying just east of the centro histórico, this was originally a Zapotec
settlement, then a Spanish colonial enclave, then a working-class
tanners' quarter. Now the Mexican press touted it as *el barrio más
chido del mundo*—the world's coolest hood. Sure enough, third-
wave coffee joints and organic mini-tiendas stood along the harsh
cobblestones beside rickety tables where families vended their memelas, thick maize cakes. In the mornings shy Zapotec women went door
to door bearing forty-pound baskets of handmade tortillas, trudging
past Instagrammers scoping out the indigo- and fuchsia-saturated
facades.

Our rental was in startling contrast to all such color-mad folk-
loricism. It was a newish compound, conceived in ruthlessly Nordic-
minimalist style by Danish textile artist Trine Ellitsgaard, the widow
of Francisco Toledo—Mexico's most prominent artist, who had passed
away a few months earlier and was still passionately mourned by
the city. On arrival in evening darkness, we looked around in shock.
It would be like camping in a vacated art gallery—for an entire
month?

But daylight revealed an inner-courtyard ziggurat-style staircase
flanked by a glowing, golden wall and another of lush cerise—a sudden, sumptuous homage to the colored planes of Mexico's great
modernist architect Luis Barragán. Under the sky of intense desert
blue waited a roof terrace flooded with pink bougainvillea, with
vistas of palm trees, church domes, and off beyond, the shadow
play of mountains.

Francisco Toledo designed the low terrace table where we'd finish our breakfast coffees. Around town he was simply known as El
Maestro, a charismatically modest celebrity in a campesino blouse,

hair and beard bushy and wild. From a Zapotec family rooted in the jungly Isthmus de Tehuantepec, he was an art-scene veteran of Paris, New York, and L.A., and not just a multitalent in the mold of Picasso but also an inexhaustible social activist and philanthropist. It was hard to move in Oaxaca without coming across something El Maestro helped create and fund: the Museum of Contemporary Arts, the Graphic Arts Institute. In 2002 he led a celebrated protest against a McDonald's planned for the arcades of the sixteenth-century zocalo—threatening to stand naked in front of it.

*Tamales, sí! McDonald's, no!* his supporters chanted, handing out Oaxacan tamales and atole. The Golden Arches backed down.

AFTER MY FIERY MOLE TUTORIAL, Celia left town on some extended promotional tour of Oaxaca. So I found my way to a cocinera named Olga Cabrera Oropeza. Olga was vivaciously lovely, with a heart-shaped cherubic face and a style that paired saucy movie-star eyeliner with the artisanal embroidered huipiles (traditional tunics) currently fashionable among local belles. We became instant friends.

Oaxaca being famed as the "Land of Seven Moles," I informed her that as part of my *gran proyecto* I intended to master all seven.

Olga couldn't stop laughing.

"Only seven? Oh, my dear Anyita. *Only seven?* Por qué?"

She began enumerating the canonical siete, including negro, rojo, amarillo, verde—black, red, yellow, and green. But these were just from the Central Valleys! All over the state? Two hundred moles at least. "You'll need a lifetime just to understand them, Anyita!"

Take only negro, for instance. In Cuicatlán in the north, the origin of chile chilhuacle, black mole has zero cacao, with no tatemada—and is thickened with galletas de animalitos, animal crackers. In Tlaxiaco nearby there, negro comes with sides of sweet-sour fruit picadillo and a hash of lamb innards and eggs.

Olga herself hailed from a dynasty of magnificent cooks in Mixteca, the rugged northwest region shared by Oaxaca and the states of Guerrero and Puebla. And so distinctive were some of her native moles that when twenty years ago she moved to Oaxaca City and opened a comedor (lunch canteen) to showcase Mixtecan cuisine, the urbanites here, accustomed to oversweet rich colonial flavors, snapped up her breaded chicken and meatballs but left her chileajos and pipianes untouched. Olga was heartbroken. Were her Mixteca flavors just too direct, too *picoso*? she wondered.

Olga tended to my mole education with a maternal zeal I found truly touching. Every few days I'd stroll a summer-hot winter mile across the centro's colonial grid, past ragtag taquerías and bright new mezcalerías, past gaudy juice stalls overflowing with cheri-moyas and carambolas; past peeling stucco facades with doorways hung with colored-bead curtains, behind which grandmothers sat in the blare of telenovelas. Olga would be waiting on the upper ter-race kitchen of her current restaurant, Tierra del Sol. It was a glorious place to learn about moles. The vista swept across the looming mauve ridges of the Sierra Madre del Sur, while right below us rose the imposing entrance to Oaxaca's famous Jardín Etnobo-tánico, in what was the old monastery garden of the temple of Santo Domingo. Like so much else hereabouts, the jardín began as a social-cultural project conceived by Francisco Toledo, who sparked fellow local artists to rescue the space from its fate as a convention center and parking lot. El Maestro and his compadres envisioned instead a botanical garden cum landscape-art installation, one that narrated Oaxaca's prodigious wealth of indigenous plants.

Olga's signature mole, called guaximole, was itself extremely etnobotánico. It featured peas from the pod of her native guaje tree (also spelled guaxe or huaje) blended with a puree of Mixteca's slender chiles costeños and simmered (non-indigenously) with pork ribs. Direct and picoso indeed.

Guaje made Olga hometown-nostalgic and patriotic—"*tan nuestro, tan lindo*," so ours, so lovely. She was born in the small city of Huajuapan de León, which means something like "guaje trees by a river" in Nahuatl (though oddly its Mixtec name is Nudeem, "land of the brave"). When the Spanish first reached this whole region in the sixteenth century, they found it called Huāxyacac—Nahuatl for "where the guaje tree grows"—which they dimly approximated as "Oaxaca." In California, Olga informed me, Mixtecan migrants plant guaje trees in their yards as an identity symbol. Mixteca, incidentally, is a prime exporter of human labor to the US.

Back in Huajuapan, Olga's mother is a celebrated panadera, a baker. While we extracted seeds from long, sticky, tightly closed guaje pods—Olga deftly using a hairpin, me tearing my nails—Olga spoke with great feeling about waking up as a kid to the comforting scent of her mom's pan de pulque and cinnamony pan de canela . . . eating these sweet bread rolls with ice cream and fruit and chocolate de agua.

I told her I was fascinated by Mexico's difference in attitude toward wheat and maize, bread and tortillas. It roughly reflected that of colonizer and colonized. Even in the mid-twentieth century, as maize was beginning to lose its "Indigenous" stigma, domestic reformers promoted wheat bread and cakes as paths to modernity, civilization, and better nutrition. In Oaxaca I kept noticing how bread halls at markets were airy and attractive, while tortilla vendors shyly skulked in dark passageways. But Olga didn't see it that way, as a racial or colonizer/colonized issue. Eating both bread and tortillas seemed to her like a great privilege of her mestizo identity.

That identity, of course, was complicated. And nowhere more than in Oaxaca. Olga had creamy bronze skin and softly Indigenous features; she often wore her hair in a long, traditional ribbon-laced braid.

Didn't she identify as Mixteca? I wondered.

"I couldn't," she began to explain. Until very recently, the Mexican census categorized race *culturally*. Identifying as *indígena* required you to be able to speak one of the country's Indigenous languages. "But where I'm from," Olga sighed, "we lost Mixteco generations ago . . . social pressure, discrimination. Anyway, we're a mixture," she said. "We look mestizo, we dress mestizo, we identify as mestizo. It's who we are. And our moles?"

She ladled out guaximole. It looked ruddy-red from the chilies, tasted sappy-green from the guajes, and had the rich fatty Catholic heft of Spanish costillas de puerco.

"*Puro mestizaje*," she smiled.

I'VE REFLECTED MUCH ALONG my journey how certain dishes get recruited to express their country's glorified inclusive identity—literal recipes for national unity. And mole, so I'd heard a thousand times, is the great symbol of Mexico because it represents mestizaje, the biocultural fusion of white colonizing Europeans and Amerindian natives.

Mexico is a nation where, in the most recent census, between half and two-thirds of its citizens claimed mestizo identity. Mestizaje has been variously described as an official narrative of national integration, as an idealized *esencia de la Mexicanidad*, and, crucially, as "a lived process," embraced and internalized.

From Late Latin mixticĭus ("mixed"), the term mestizo first began appearing in local church records in the late 1530s, around two decades after Spanish conquistador Hernán Cortés came ashore on Mexico's Gulf Coast and, aided by Indigenous allies, managed to topple the powerful Mexica (Aztec) empire of Moctezuma II. Mexican schoolchildren learn that their mestizo race descends from the union of Cortés and his Indigenous concubine/translator/enabler, Malintzin (La Malinche in Spanish), a character so controversial and fascinating as to inspire a whole subbranch of studies wherein she's variously portrayed as the symbolic mom of mestizos and a feminist icon; as a traitor-whore of her race; or, per Octavio Paz, as a passive rape victim (*la chingada*, the fucked one) who passed on her existential victimhood to the entire nation.

Historically, however, mestizos were illegitimate, marginal outcasts in an early colonial apartheid society, a society legally segregated into a república de españoles and a república de indios. Independence from Spain in 1821 failed to bring any cathartic decolonization. As food historian Jeffrey Pilcher reminds us, Mexico's Creole (local-born) urban elites might have proclaimed themselves heirs to Aztec aristocracy, but they continued to define national culture in European terms and dismiss "Indians" and "brown" rural mestizos as a national "problem." It was only in the decades after the ground-shifting 1910 Revolution, when a badly fragmented Mexico needed a unifying vision of patriotic common citizenship, that mestizaje was given its full-throttled promotion, elevated to an official state-building project.

Which is how the mestizo bastard of a caste-obsessed colonial society emerged, in the words of one scholar, as "the nation's archetypal hero." Manuel Gamio, father of modern Mexican anthropology, proclaimed mestizaje an "advanced and happy fusion of races, [that] constitutes the first and most solid basis of nationalism." José Vasconcelos, Oaxacan-born philosopher and a post-Revolution secretary of education—the champion and patron of Diego Rivera—raised mestizaje to all-transfiguring heights in his wacky but hugely influential 1925 pamphlet *La Raza Cósmica*, The Cosmic Race. In Vasconcelos's postracist utopia (his rebuke to the attitudes from the US and Europe), the birth in the Americas of a fifth human race, the superhuman bronze race, heralded "the moral and material basis for the union of all men . . . the fruit of all the previous ones and amelioration of everything past." (Even now Mexico celebrates Día de la Raza, or Race Day, every October 12.)

By the end of the twentieth century, however, this triumphalist narrative began to show cracks. In *México Profundo* (1987), his appraisal of deep, Mesoamerican Mexico, pensador (grand thinker) Guillermo Bonfil Batalla argued that the post-Revolution "mestizo" concept still followed a dominant European model, where a nation shared a common culture, language, and history. For Mexico, this required a highly *selective* history—one that, for example, elevated and glorified the Aztec past while ignoring the accomplishments and contributions of its numerous other pre-Columbian peoples.

For Bonfil Batalla, mestizaje ultimately meant the "de-Indianization" of Mexico. And more recent critics agree that the official narrative

of a supposedly inclusive and color-blind nation has consistently deni-
grated Indigenous people—and completely erased Afro-Mexicans.
Anthropologist Ronald Stutzman calls mestizaje "an all-inclusive
ideology of exclusion," fraught with the racial hierarchies of colonial times. To its harshest critics, mestizaje is complicit with white
supremacy.

The more I read, the more I wondered if mestizaje was about to
be canceled. And I wondered how some 80 million Mexicans who
proudly identify as mestizo, like Olga, would greet such a turn of
events.

But back to the food: Was there, in fact, one specific foundational
pre-Hispanic dish known as mole?

I wrangled with this issue on a Oaxacan restaurant trail that
veered from a coastal-style mole amarillo of incendiary chiles costeños thickened with masa and starring (gulp) black iguana (tasted
like chicken) to a luscious almendrado nutty with almonds and
sweet-tart with raisins, capers, and olives (straight out of medieval
Al-Andalus) back to a smoky ritualistic mole chichilo of the remote
Sierra Sur highlands, a version hauntingly bitter and burnt because
traditionally women made it for funerals while the coffin still sat in
the house.

I probed the matter further on Trine's ascetic couch at our aus-
terely beautiful rental, munching nísperos, loquats (tasted like tropical apricots), as I peered through a hefty scholarly roundup on
mole and discovered an extensive *family* of dishes etymologically
derived from *molli* or *mulli* in Nahuatl. Broadly the term means
sauce, mix, or stew, or even more broadly, food. (Guacamole?
*Ahuaca-mulli* in Nahuatl.) And these diverse preparations were

only loosely related—perhaps by the common use of chilies and likewise a particular kitchen technology. Contemporary historian José Monteagudo suggests mulli's story began more than five thousand years ago with the appearance of the first metates, the grinding stones "whose presence marked a change between nomadic and sedentary man."

We know about pre-Contact moles chiefly from one principal source. Bernardino de Sahagún was a Spanish Franciscan missionary, a friar cum proto–field anthropologist, who between 1529 and 1579 compiled a prodigious two-thousand-page encyclopedia of Aztec life, known as the Florentine Codex. "*Comían muchas maneras de cazuelas de chiles*," the friar informs us: they ate many manners of chili stews. One served to Moctezuma supposedly was called totolin patzcalmollo, a fowl cazuela with red chili, tomatoes, and ground squash seeds—today's pipián. As I read the friar's descriptions, I had a sudden urge to taste the pre-Hispanic unripe plum mulli with little white fish. Or the amaranth leaf mulli with yellow chilies—"very good to eat," we're promised.

And yet despite all this history, mole's canonization as a symbol of Mexicanness dates only from the country's post-Revolution "mestizo nation" push. What's more, its nationalist ur-origin myth still skews—yet again—pretty Euro-colonial-Catholic. It enshrines mole poblano, a super-baroque version with chocolate, supposedly concocted in Puebla, today Mexico's fourth-largest city—one founded in 1531 as a planned European-style settlement *for* Europeans.

First floated in the mid-1920s in Mexican newspapers, the legend of mole poblano stars a late-seventeenth-century nun named Sor Andrea de la Asunción, mother superior of Puebla's wealthy Convent of Santa Rosa de Lima. (Nowadays, the convent houses a striking museum of folklore replete with a grand vaulted and tiled kitchen.) Anxious to dazzle the visiting viceroy of New Spain with a wowza sauce for her chestnut-fed guajolote (Mesoamerican turkey), our good sister dipped into her various chili pots, then her spice and nuts chests—whereupon divine inspiration guided her to a jar in which the brides of Christ kept their chocolate tablets. With this mestizaje of ingredients, Sor Andrea knelt at a metate, grinding away as another sister exclaimed: "*Qué bien mole, su reverencia!*" How well you grind, your reverence! It's *muele*, not *mole*, Sor Andrea corrected her screwy grammar. But no use: this bad Spanish (misconjugated from *moler*, to grind) became the moniker that overrode the Nahuatl original, mulli. (How ironic, how purely Mexican this accidental linguistic syncretism.)

Naturally, there's no record of this Sor Andrea. Nor any mention of her divinely inspired chocolate in any mole recipe for yet another two centuries. (As it happens, one of Mexico's first written mole recipes, from the late 1600s, did come from a nun, the celebrated poet and feminist Sor Juana Inés de la Cruz. A spiced cazuela of pork, chorizo, and chicken laced with some chilies, it's actually closer to the Spanish olla podrida than any moles we know now.) But again, as the éminence grise of Mexican food history, Jeffrey Pilcher, insists, the glorifying of colonial moles as "mestizo" cuisine served the reconfigured nationalist sentiments of early-modern Mexico. Mole poblano offered a perfect culinary metaphor for the vision of indigenismo, an ideology which celebrated *selective* aspects of the pre-Columbian past, while aiming to whiten and acculturate living Indigenous people into mestizo society. "Mole poblano's glossy surface," writes Pilcher, "obscured the conflicted history of race mixture in Mexico."

Absent from the legend, I noted to myself: any mention of

African slaves owned by Mexican colonial nuns, who were usually the daughters of wealthy white families. Or of their Indigenous helpers, prohibited from becoming nuns until the mid-1700s despite making up the majority of Mexico's convent servants.

But as racial views of the nation changed and evolved, so, too, did the story of mole. Come the late twentieth century, competition erupted between Puebla and Oaxaca for the figurehead role in Mexico's gastronomy. The two states served more broadly, notes Pilcher, as "proxies for Mexico's European and indigenous heritage." Oaxacan cuisine, with its showcasing of folkloric native communities, proved better suited—more useful—to the country's turn to neoliberalism, as Mexico's ruling elites took Indigenous demands for self-determination as a pretense for abandoning Revolutionary welfare programs and adopting globalized market policies. Campesinos were recast as individual entrepreneurs/owners of their own cultural patrimony—while being left out in the cold economically. So mole poblano found itself eclipsed as a national symbol by the Indigenous diversity of the "seven moles" of Oaxaca. And Oaxaca, the country's most multicultural state, became a pilgrimage site for Mexican and international foodies seeking out a supposedly more authentic, pre-Hispanic cuisine with its heirloom agriculture and, in Pilcher's phrase, the "exoticized labor of indigenous women."

UNLIKE MOLES, so elaborate, so complex, the other edible symbol of *lo Mexicano* requires just three ingredients: maize, water, and, crucially, *cal*, lime slack in English. Mole is fiesta fare, a ceremonial community feast. The tortilla, on the other hand, is a daily essential, basic as running water, though even more accessible since plenty of remote Oaxacan comunidades don't have running water.

An average Mexican consumes over 150 pounds of tortillas a year, most of it edible cardboard these days, machine-pressed from Maseca, the national megabrand of dehydrated instant corn flour. Maseca's parent company, Gruma, achieved a near monopoly on Mexico's tortilla market through blatant political favoritism during the early-1990s neoliberal reign of president Carlos Salinas de Gortari. It's now a multibillion-dollar multinational behemoth pushing its products in over one hundred countries and fueling the international taste for burritos, quesadillas, and tacos.

But in Oaxaca, people spit on Maseca tortillas. Here, rural women make them by hand from fresh masa over live fire, while urban professionals buy them from such rural women who sell them for a living—at about twenty pesos, one buck, a kilo.

It was hard in Oaxaca to eat a tortilla or a tamale or a tlayuda (pizza-sized griddled tortilla) without someone patriotically blurting: *Somos gente de maíz*. We're people of corn. Or *Sin maíz no hay país*. Without corn there is no country. Or *Con maíz soy feliz*. With corn I am happy.

Corn = country = happiness.


Clearly, I needed to better understand Mexico's identity crop, to see how it was cultivated and processed. So on yet another bright morning, Barry and I headed out to visit maize farmers in Santa Ana Zegache, a Central Valleys comunidad an hour south of the city.

A new amigo, Julio César, accompanied us. Tall and bronze of face, with a gray man-bun under his flashy Stetson, JC displayed a lofty dignity to match his imperial name. Originally from Chiapas, the land of Zapatista insurgents, he had in fact a Marxist past of some kind, and a present as an anthropologist of Indigenous diets and occasional tour guide. He was also a restaurateur, dishing up very un-Marxist American Angus steaks to the Oaxacan bourgeoisie. My casual questions spurred him to extensive disquisitions.

Somewhere en route, we pulled over by an ordinary-looking modest field of maize. Still six months from harvest, its silky pink tassels stirred gently in the high-altitude sun against a backdrop of close foothills. JC pointed out the young vines of frijoles curling up the cornstalks, and closer to the ground, flowering squash vines. This field was in fact a roadside example of a milpa, the iconic local intercropped plot I'd been dying to see.

"The milpa," JC launched his exposition, "expresses the genius of our early Mesoamerican agriculture—the symbiotic complex where everything is beautifully, logically interconnected." So beans supply the soil with nitrogen, corn provides columns for climbing, low-growing squash vines trap moisture and inhibit weeds, while chilies additionally ward off pests. All their roots intertwine for mutual nourishment and reinforce the soil against erosion. Nutritionally, the beans-squash-maize triad makes a complete and brilliant package. What's more, a milpa holds a wealth of quelites, those wild edible greens long dismissed as indigenous weeds but now finally celebrated. JC plucked a grassy, antioxidant-rich quintonil (flowering amaranth). He pointed out tender round-leafed papalo, a natural laxative with the taste of super-sappy cilantro.

"La milpa is an *ecocultural construct*!" he proclaimed, now running his hands through the corn leaves. "A sacral space, to which campesinos will pray, reenacting millennial rites!"

It felt humid and tropical suddenly amid the maize. I walked out along its edge to the rasping of insects, wondering how a roadside cornfield could pack so much ecological and nutritional wisdom.

JC emerged holding a skinny green stalk.

"Teocintle," he announced, and I gasped.

So *that's* what it looked like. *Zea mays mexicana*, or teosinte in English. The wild grassy ur-ancestor of modern corn, the world's current number one grain crop.

I examined the plant. Long and pencil-thin, twisted like the braid of a baby Zapotec girl. Impossible, almost, to connect it to the fat, husk-swaddled, juicy corncobs we know—let alone with corn-based ethanol or laundry detergent.

JC took back the stalk and sucked it. "*Dulce*," he said. "Sweet."

Maize was domesticated around nine thousand years ago in the Balsas River valley of central Mexico, about four hundred miles from our milpa stop. For a good part of the twentieth century, its exact biological genesis was hotly debated, for reasons beyond just academic: identifying its genetic stock could boost the modern plant's productivity. Some scientists proposed that maize evolved from teosinte, transforming eventually via genetic mutation and human selection into primitive corn. Others argued that modern maize's ancestor must have been some archaic wild maize, either extinct or as yet unidentified. Then in the nineties, the teosinte hypothesis was confirmed through space-age genetic analysis and archeological findings.

But a question still nagged. Why *would* early Mesoamericans bother domesticating a puny stalk with so little nutritional promise? Was teosinte valued as a sweetener rather than a grain—appreciated raw, as by JC in the milpa, or fermented into an alcoholic tipple, perhaps? Or was teosinte simply different some nine thousand years ago?

Whatever the answer, the transformation of a grassy stalk into a corncob as we know it was, as JC put it, a *creación humana*, a human creation. Corn doesn't grow in the wild. Its husk prevents natural seed dispersion. Thousands of years ago, ancestors of the campesinos we were on our way to visit must have noticed teosinte's genetic mutation, stored the best-looking seeds, and bred them for desirable traits. As our milpa farmers *still* do, JC noted triumphantly.

Commercial corn (from hybrid or GMO seeds) is an international agro-industrial leviathan; its more than a billion tons of annual harvest account for over 20 percent of all human nutrition. Here in Mexico, maíz criollo or nativo—terms for the locally grown landrace varieties—was the source of the toasty handmade tortillas I'd been obsessing over in Oaxaca. In central and southern Mexico—JC was expounding again now; we were back in the car, bumping along a small road surrounded by ferric-red soil—such carefully evolved and nurtured criollo landraces were grown on rain-fed milpas by roughly 2.5 million smallhold farmers, mostly for *autoconsumo*. This kind of subsistence agriculture was something successive Mexican governments have long wanted gone, because it could never properly fit into any national market economy. Meanwhile, commercial domestic corn for "crappy supermercado tortillas"—JC practically sneered—was grown on high-yield, mechanized, chemically fertilized, and artificially irrigated farms, primarily in Mexico's flat northern states—from hybrid seeds "improved" through cross-pollination, sold by the likes of Monsanto.

ON THE SUN-BAKED ZOCALO of Santa Ana Zegache—Zapotec for "seven hills"—kids were chasing around an old plastic soccer ball. Goats roamed the drowsy unpaved streets past cactuses and electric-pink flowers. The local population, around three thousand, scraped by on small subsistence farming and remittances from Zegacheños gone north, to Mexico City, to California, to Oregon.

Elmer Gaspar Guerra, the fizzy young presidente municipal, greeted us at the bright, bare-bones ayuntamiento with a bag of huge empanadas stained yellow with mole amarillo. A political wunderkind who won his first term aged twenty-two and still resembled a pudgy college sophomore, Elmer brimmed with initiatives for improving life in his destitute municipio. Many of his schemes were gastronomic, to capitalize on Oaxaca's newfound status as Mexico's foodie cradle.

"Food has a power to transform our life here," he declared, taking us for a quick peek into the spanking new mercado nearby, where Zapotec women were aerating atole and chocolate.

Tiny Zegache had even made it into a *New York Times* article headlined "Oaxaca's Native Maize Embraced by Top Chefs in U.S. and Europe." Elmer was now organizing a women's collective to produce colored tortilla flour—rojo, morado, negro—that enjoyed great prestige at Oaxaca's *restaurantes gourmet*.

"The yuppies from Oaxaca City and CDMX [Mexico City]," he quipped, "come here pretending they're the ones who discovered maíz criollo tortillas. When it's our impoverished campesinos who've kept maize culture alive! Because if we don't, the community dies. *Maseca no entra aquí!*" he cried, raising a clenched fist to the corporate Godzilla. Then he led us out to the farmers we came for, and dashed off on some urgent municipal business.


Nati (Natividad) and Cayetano, the maize campesinos, were a middle-aged Zapotec couple. Their small compound on Zegache's outskirts held rudimentary living quarters, some service sheds, and a cluttered, ramshackle outdoor kitchen area, its sides loosely fenced with bamboo. Nati, in a mandil, the ubiquitous Zapotec apron, was making fiesta tamales with a chatty elderly neighbor, Elena. Chicken pecked about at corn kernels; giant squashes lay half-rotten by a gnarled tree.

Hospitable Cayetano showed us their earthen-floor living room, its pride of place occupied by the family altar with its colorized ancestral photos, bright oilcloths, and figurines of the Juquila Virgin with her long black lifelike hair. The Christmas manger was still up in February.

In the adjoining sparse bedroom, ears of corn lay heaped by the spartan bed. Corn was everywhere in the compound—mazorcas (ears) drying on straw mats, shucked kernels in blue plastic buckets, baled husks for tamales and chicken feed, dried-up scraped cobs to feed fires, zacate (dried maize plant leaves) to be mixed with animal dung for fertilizing the milpa.

And not even in Oaxaca City had I ever seen maize so gorgeous, so *baroque*: glowing orange, wine-burgundy, purplish black, some ears speckled. Their giant irregular kernels glimmered like multi-hued amber or polished pearl.

"*El maíz de Zegache tiene otro sabor*—has another flavor," Cayetano said dreamily, stroking his mazorcas as if they were kittens. He named the landraces: "Amarillo, negrito, pinto [speckled], bolita belatove"—the last a rare variety, recently on a brink of extinction, which produced a nutty purple-tinged masa.

Wiry and short, clad in a T-shirt, jeans, and a tall straw cowboy hat, his graying goatee trim and his grin gap-toothed, Cayetano had eyes that were both canny and gleeful. His Mexican sweet tooth for cozy diminutives was on full display when JC asked, anthropologically, about what he and Nati usually ate.

*Atolito* and *cafecito* (atole and coffee) for breakfast. *Un huevito criollo* (a free-range egg) with a *tostadita*, *frijolitos*, and *nopalitos* for lunch in the milpa; more of the same in the evening. For *fiestecitas* there were *tamalitos* and *molito*—tamales and mole for fiesta, the mole being amarillo or verde or a pipián from seeds of a calabaza called chompa. And then of course the quelites: *verdolaga* (lamb's lettuce), *quintoniles*, purple *alache*—all boiled *sin grasita*, without fat.

"A beautiful milpa diet," lauded JC. "Millenniums old, perfect nutrition."

(Was he, were we both, I suddenly wondered, perhaps romanticizing the idea of "Indigenous primitivity"?)

*Puro, natural, auténtico, todo orgánico*, Cayetano chimed in, fluent apparently in the globalized language of liberal foodism.

Cayetano learned the "orgánico" way ten years ago from Amado Leyva, a Oaxacan agricultural engineer, corn curator, and hyperpassionate apostle of biodiversity, much praised by foreign media. To Nati and Cayetano he was a beloved benefactor, the one who gave them their biodigester, which converts organic waste into fertilizer, and taught them how to sell extra seeds.

Amado also introduced them to chefs. "Once they came from thirty countries right here to learn about our maize!" Nati said proudly.

One important chef client was a certain chingón in Mexico City, the celebrity prophet of contemporary Mexican cooking, renowned for postmodern riffs on moles and maize. This same chingón chef, I learned now, paid Cayetano and Nati fifteen pesos (80¢) for a kilo of corn—which he then sold for eighty pesos (I noted mentally) at his chichi artisanal tortillería in Mexico City.

For the tortillería's much-publicized launch, Nati was invited to

CDMX to demonstrate her tortillas and her chepil tamales. She was paid five hundred pesos a day.

Twenty-two bucks.

How much did they think the chingón chef charged for a meal at his restaurants?

Cayetano laughed like a kid. "The kind of money I can't even *imagine*!"


Cayetano and Nati's seven-and-a-half-acre milpa a few miles away produced more than four tons of maize with good weather and a good harvest—an excellent yield, gracias, biodigester—which earned them about forty thousand pesos (under $2,000), in cash, per farming season. Again, weather permitting. Meanwhile, a regular family milpa could be just two and a half acres, producing less than a ton. With Oaxacan consumption of two hundred kilos yearly per capita, this kind of yield barely provided food for a subsistence household of six, and left nothing to sell. Which was why people were abandoning farms, Cayetano said sadly, especially now that the rainy season had become so unpredictable. This campesino outmigration, clarified JC, had already begun in the mid-twentieth century. It reached epidemic proportions with NAFTA and was now driven by climate change.

Elena, the elderly neighbor, meanwhile, who sometimes made tortillas for sale, enlightened me on rural tortillanomics. Two hundred tortillas took a grueling day to make and then sell in the city for two pesos apiece, less than a dime. Deducting the cost of the maize, the lime slack for nixtamal, the molino and firewood, the minibus to the market, that left her a profit of 140 pesos a day. About seven bucks—less than the price of a bowl of ramen in Tokyo or a pizza in Naples.

. . .

Would they want this life for their daughters? I asked the two women.

Both shook their heads vehemently.

As for Cayetano, he declared himself a *campesino feliz*. He loved arriving by six a.m. at the milpa, walking barefoot, bathing in the nearby river, having his early lunch there of tostadas and beans and nopales to the chirping of birds. (Was *he* romanticizing his life?)

"A happy farmer?" Nati snapped dourly. "It's *me* who gets up before five, hauls water from the well, makes his damn breakfast and delivers it to him on the moto!"

Come fall and the corn harvest, the couple could easily gather five hundred kilos a day just with baskets, sometimes hiring help. The dehusking and shucking took several days.

For firsthand experience, Cayetano had us try the *olotera*. This was a homespun shucking contraption of shortened dry corncobs pressed together inside a metal ring, like a coarse tambourine against which one scraped two corn ears, up and down. "*Todo a mano*, all by hand," proclaimed Cayetano, "if you want delicious tortillas!"

That was how they shucked four tons of maize.

By now Nati and Elena had produced a vast pile of mole verde tamales, wrists flicking, fingers a blur as they ensconced spoonfuls of mole and chicken in discs of masa and used a big leaf called hoja San Pablo to flip these into the corn husk totomoxtles.

"Tamales . . ." intoned JC. "From Nahuatl *tamalli* meaning 'wrapped.' Likely predating *even* tortillas." He tasted a spoonful of the verdant green mole filling—tomatillos, serrano chilies, epazote, and hojasanta leaf with a faintly liquorish scent, all ground on Nati's massive metate—and pronounced it *muy prehispánico.* "If you took away the onion, garlic, and cumin," he added, "and swapped the chicken for, say, iguana."

At lunch featuring these enormously labor-intensive Zapotec-style Central Valleys tamales, the verde filling had a direct, grassy intensity—so startlingly different from the opulent mestizaje colonial moles, an altogether different narrative of Mexican cuisine was evoked. Meanwhile, the steamed tamale masa, lacking mestizo lard or baking soda to render it fluffy, was jarringly gummy. Struggling in surprise, Barry and I desperately helped ourselves from the gallon of Coke enthroned on the table's dusty floral oilcloth.

Coca-Cola in a milpa kitchen?

"*Una maravilla!*" Cayetano exclaimed, his face almost rapturous. "*Mejor que el mezcal!*"

I remembered reading about the Coca-colonization of Indigenous Mexican life. How the soft drink had penetrated even communities without drinking water or milk—to be integrated into native rituals, fiestas, and church services.

Before leaving Zegache, we paid our respects to its Baroque jewel, the seventeenth-century church restored a few decades ago by the late, great local muralist-activist Rodolfo Morales. The eye-candy facade blazed like a vast 3-D tablecloth, riotous with marzipan-colored plaster flowers, seashells, polychrome plaster saints. Women in festive huipiles, their heads draped in rebozos, were streaming out of the church cradling life-size baby dolls. The dolls wore shimmery satin, brocaded velvets, tiaras, gold halos. They were *Niños Jesús,* baby Jesuses.

"Día de la Candelaria," explained Julio César. "The day when the Virgin presented her Holy Child at the temple."

Barry noticed one woman whose Niño featured denim overalls and a huge sparkling cross on its neck—and a backpack.

"*Niño migrante*," she told us shyly. Her husband and brother had left for Los Angeles twenty years ago, and had never returned.

IN *THE STORY OF CORN*, Betty Fussell makes an illuminating distinction between "corn" and "maize." The different "symbolic freight" of each term is profound. Capitalist North America built an industrial kingdom and a global empire on the economic power of corn. Whereas a thousand years before Christ, the Olmecs, oldest of Mesoamerican civilizations, founded a complete universe—language, calendar, mythos, and cosmos—on the symbolic power of maize. "If the one culture diminished a staple food to merchandise," wrote Fussell, "the other sanctified it as divine."

Commodity versus cosmogony.

The Aztecs (Mexica), the Maya, and the Zapotecs similarly venerated maize as the ur-stuff of existence, flesh and spirit both. Back in the car returning from Zegache, JC had quoted the most famous of Mesoamerica's maize origin stories, from the *Popol Vuh*, the creation epic of the K'iche' Maya: First *los dioses* created animals (useless, unable to praise their creators), then they tried shaping humans from mud (sad, sodden mush), then wood (dry, bloodless, soulless). Finally four men and four women were molded from maize.

"*From yellow corn and white corn was made their flesh . . .*" The words were known to every Mexican schoolkid. "*From masa were made their arms and legs.*"

. . .

Clearly, for campesinos like Cayetano and Nati, corn was a way of life, a quotidian cosmogony. Yet amazingly, given all the *sin maíz no hay país* current corn patriotism, from the arrival of Spaniards until well on into the twentieth-century maize "bore the stigma of defeat," as critical theorist Gabriela Méndez Cota puts it in her book *Disrupting Maize*—whose post-structuralisms I was now untangling mornings in Trine's courtyard, where the birds warbled cozily and pooped on our laundry line, and fallen bougainvillea petals made pink drifts on the ziggurat staircase. *The stigma of defeat* . . . the phrase stuck with me. In a society which until so recently equated whiteness and wheat with civilization and progress, maize represented indigenousness, backwardness, and underdevelopment.

The first Iberian colonists, notes Méndez Cota, took the prime agricultural terrain and left the natives the margins. Then, forced labor on Spanish wheat farms not only served as "the foundation for colonial usurpation of Indigenous lands in Mesoamerica" but, compounded by a series of imported epidemics, decimated the native population—by as much as 80 percent, according to the most drastic estimates.

Wheat was central to the Spanish colonial enterprise, and not least because wheat bread represented the body of Christ in the Catholic mass. But it wasn't simply religion, economics, or even nostalgia that drove the colonists to the massive trouble of supplying themselves with Iberian staples like wheat, wine, olive oil, red meat, dried fruit, and spices.

According to Rebecca Earle's *The Body of the Conquistador*, "food played a fundamental role in structuring the European categories of 'Spaniard' and 'Indian,'" in an era when the notion of race as biologically fixed hadn't yet emerged. Guided by Galenic-Hippocratic humoral theories, the colonizers viewed corporal identity as malleable by external forces—diet especially. Race, Earle argues provocatively, was in part a question of digestion. For transplanted Spaniards who'd used food to root out false converts back home, the phrase "You are what you eat" now carried an anxious *bodily* urgency. If new foods could generate new blood and humors, wouldn't a New World diet turn a vigorous, proud, bearded Spaniard into a timid, phlegmatic, dark-skinned, beardless Indian? And the reverse. Fray Sahagún, that great encyclopedist of pre-Conquest life, delivered a sermon in Nahuatl imploring the natives to eat "that which the Castilian people eat . . . You will become the same way if you eat their food."

Maize did unavoidably form the bulk of the settlers' diet, but often uneasily. Meanwhile, natives thought wheat bread tasted "like famine food . . like dried maize stalks."

And there was that other hotly debated issue. Was a maize tortilla suitable for Holy Communion? Some missionaries did say yes. Other churchmen dismissed all maize products as a demonic anti-bread, incapable of sacramental transubstantiation.

Colonial society would change, dietary theories shift. But maize still kept its stigma. Under the dictatorship of Oaxacan-born presidente Porfirio Díaz from 1876 until 1911, nutritional racialism took a social Darwinist turn. Don Porfirio—who was part Mixtec but reportedly fancied himself "Latin" and powdered his skin to appear more white—bent Mexican culture toward Europe, and dogmatically embraced industrial monopoly capitalism and foreign investment. His oligarchical banquets sometimes included moles, but mostly featured the *paupiettes de veau* and *glace dame blanche* of a Parisian chef. Meanwhile los científicos, as his brain trust of technocrats were dubbed, pushed French "scientific politics" and Herbert Spencer's racial ideology, in which Darwinian metrics were applied to society to declare white Europeans as evolution's obvious victors. The Porfiristas invoked the credo eternally dear to Mexico's elites: Indigenous campesinos hindered national progress. Some thought the solution was to whiten Mexico by bringing in Europeans. Others held "the social problem of the Indian race" to be solvable through acculturation, education—and the right nutrition.

"Let them eat more beef and less chile," admonished Justo Sierra, the most prominent Porfirian influencer.

And less maize, naturally.

"The most vicious anti-corn haranguer was Porfirian senator Francisco Bulnes," I informed Barry, as we strolled back one evening from the zocalo, where couples would slow-step old-style danzón to marimba bands weekly by the frilly bandstand, donated by Porfirio Díaz himself. The zocalo was also shared by the tent encampments of teachers protesting here since 2006—a long-standing, controversial reminder of Oaxaca's tumultuous political conflicts. Bulnes, I continued over street-table tlayudas, called maize the "eternal pacifier" of the Indigenous, that "lazy, evil, and intellectually inferior race." In an infamous treatise, the senator divided humanity into wheat, rice, and maize eaters, concluding that wheat eaters were the only "truly progressive" ones. After all, hadn't a small band of wheat-nourished Spanish bandoleros toppled the empires of the maize-fed Aztecs and Incas?

More and more, it seemed to me a miracle how corn tortillas had survived over five centuries of this negative onslaught. Even the Mexican Revolution with its slogan of Land and Liberty didn't produce any nationalist embrace of maize such as the one of today, though it brought land redistribution, farm subsidies, and regulated tortilla prices. Manuel Gamio, for instance, the great theorist of indigenismo who extolled the Aztec roots of Mexican food, insisted nevertheless that a diet of corn "victimized" Mexicans. He campaigned for soybeans instead (imagine a soybean tortilla).

And even as corn did begin losing its stigma, reformers continued to promote wheat, along with animal protein. By 1950 over half of Mexico consumed bread daily. "Eating bread, particularly manufactured bread," historian Sandra Aguilar writes, "became an act of cultural transformation through which a person stopped being part of the peasant or indigenous population and became a mestizo." And began suffering from obesity and the resulting ailments that exploded with NAFTA.

By the mid-twentieth century, a Mexican newspaper did feel able to trumpet "the end of antagonism between corn and wheat." Food scholar Jeffrey Pilcher quotes the "simple equation" for this rapprochement, supplied by one of Mexico's leading nutritionists: "people who ate only corn were Indians, those who only ate wheat were Spaniards, while Mexicans were fortunate enough to eat both grains."

Which was exactly, it occurred to me, what I'd been hearing from Olga.

ONE DAY OLGA announced it was time. Time for me to master tortillas.

"*Somos gente de maíz*," she declared, affirming the hoary mantra from the heart. Despite her affection for bread, Olga was such a lady of maize, she never took off her gold corncob-shaped earrings, and signed off her WhatsApps with a cute corn emoji.

The long mornings of tortilla making, I was already aware, required the labor of nixtamalization the day before. Water and *cal*—calcium hydroxide, 1 percent of the corn's weight—are mixed in a vast plastic tub, then maize is combined with this nejayote (alkaline water) to cook for an hour, and then sit overnight. Around five a.m., the slightly gelatinous glop must be carried to the molino for grinding—wet—into masa, that basic stuff of tortillas, tamales, tostadas, tlayudas, totopos, etc.

Olga, svelte in a brilliantly corn-yellow huipil, showed me the pre-molino part in the open breakfast kitchen on Tierra del Sol's ground floor.

"The process seems *basico*," she said, lifting a swollen soaked grano of Mixtecan white corn out of its chalky water. "But *cuidado*!" She squinted, assessing mysteriously. "Too much cal, the tortilla's too picante and yellow . . . too little, it's tough . . . Nixtamal takes years to truly master."

Why, how, and exactly when Mesoamericans discovered nixtamalization remains a great mystery. The only hint comes from traces of carbonized lime in 3,500-year-old Olmec cooking pots found in modern-day Guatemala. Did a corn cook accidently spill ashes or seashells into the pot? Were hot lime rocks used for heating liquids? Did people feel healthier after eating this alkaline maize, stop having certain diseases? How indeed does an ancient culture discover the nutritional value of something—which in nixtamalization's case was so transformative? Untreated mature corn is a dud, its goodness molecularly trapped inside each grain's hard casing. But the alkali process makes corn's niacin (a.k.a. $B_3$), six amino acids, and calcium readily accessible for human digestion, plus the softened hull is easier to grind into masa. More amazingly still: this corn + beans makes a complete protein.

"So superior is nixtamalized maize to the unprocessed kind," argues anthropologist Sophie Coe, "that it is tempting to see the rise of Mesoamerican civilization as a consequence of this invention."

And yet, I mused there in Olga's airy restaurant kitchen, for all of nixtamalization's miraculous power, it turned Mesoamerican women into ever-toiling Eves, cursed at birth to serve and preserve the hearth—to slave away producing the daily family quota of tortillas. I glanced over at Olga's enormous metate, which suggested a slightly sinister ritual bench. Historian Arnold Bauer notes that images from five thousand years ago showed both Ancient Egyptian and Teotihuacan women bent over such saddlestone manual grinders. Egypt eventually replaced this primitive device with mills, which had then spread to Europe. Mexico? Astoundingly, the stone-age metate remained. But why?

Well, for one thing, the wheel wasn't known in the pre-Hispanic Americas. More crucially, even when grain mills arrived with the colonists, they didn't work for the sticky soaked nixtamal. Yet Mexico didn't lack other engineering developments, such as sophisticated silver processing. Was it because tortillas were low-priority female Indigenous labor that not until 1859 did Mexico patent its first nixtamal mill—and it wasn't until much later that steam, gasoline-powered, and electric molinos become fully widespread, especially to rural communities?

"*Bendita invención!*" Blessed invention! cried the Mexican newspaper *El Faro* in 1902, about the nixtamal mill. "It comes to liberate the female sex of our land." Meanwhile, in the countryside, suspicious males were accusing it of being the "revolution of the women against the authority of the men."

The invention and diffusion of nixtamal mills was followed by tortilla-making machines, and eventually by that industrialized horror, instant Maseca.

But rural Oaxacan women never gave up the metate!" exclaimed Olga. "It's part of our identity."

And so during Tierra del Sol's mad breakfast rush, she was patiently trying to teach me how to give the molino-ground masa its crucial *segunda pasada*, the second hard press and roll on the metate, for ultimate smoothness.

Ever knelt at a metate? Any idea what handling its massively heavy mano (stone cylindrical roller) does to your shoulders and back? Ever attempted the wrist rotation, rolling the mano forward while at the same time pressing down *hard* with your palms? Twenty repetitive minutes of all this sent pain shooting through my wrists and fingers—can carpal tunnel syndrome set in immediately?— through my shoulders and knees.

Then it was time for Olga's comal, so treacherously pleasant-looking amid the azure tiles atop the artfully rústico cooking station.

I'm a wheat person. I've learned how to slap lavash on the sides of a tonir oven; I can stretch strudel dough paper-thin. The tortilla de maíz defeated me.

An hour passed, laboring and sweating, as sweet Olga murmured encouragements, as morning customers stared from their memelas, tetelas, eggs in gusano worm salsa, and frothy chocolate de agua. I glowed red and redder with embarrassment.

I kept getting overmatched by the basic sequence: roll out my masa ball; flatten it, leaning really hard on the lever of the blue tortilladora press; smooth my resulting mutant tortilla by hand three times between sheets of plastic, flipping it once; unpeel the sheets of plastic; swiftly drape them over the tortilladora with one hand while with the other holding my "tortilla" (torn-edged, ugly) without crinkling it, then lay it gently—slap too hard, air bubbles will form—on the comal so it lands perfectly straight. (Sure!) Wait about forty-five seconds, then flip it while avoiding (how?) burning myself on the 700°F clay surface. For professional tortilleras, this vuelta, the flip, is the trickiest. Too soon and the inside will be raw; too late and it's too dry. And of course, the masa needs constant hydration or your tortillas won't inflate.

When it does, what a beautiful moment, a tiny miracle really, the steam trapped inside swelling from the heat, so the tortilla breathes and undulates and balloons like a delicate primeval life form. When one of mine actually managed to do this, I watched in awe. With a sigh of relief Olga snatched it up, deftly slit it, slipped a whole raw egg inside, and tossed it back on the comal—a breakfast of champions. Then she showed me the most elemental and most beloved local snack, taquito de sal, a tortilla sprinkled with salt and rolled into a tight tube with an earthy primordial taste of . . .

And I paused, sweating and sore.

How easy it was to idealize a handmade tortilla of native heirloom corn. So artisanal, so deeply rooted in pre-Hispanic identity, a rebuke to colonialism and industrial agriculture that has—improbably, how?—survived for millennia in its pretty original form.

Yes, wasn't this tortilla the bedrock of family life and pride, the very essence of Indigenous Mexicanness?

But then, my God . . . for many, many women, what endless daily grueling toil . . .

I FOUND MYSELF OBSESSED with this issue of tortilla and female Indigenous labor—so essential, yet so often ignored in the current consumerist adulation of heirloom maize on both sides of the border.

Is the tortilla *empoderamiento o esclavitud*? Empowerment or slavery?

Olga, startled by the question at first, thought for a while, then declared, Yes, slavery—despite all the special power, domestic and cultural, that the tortilla conferred on a woman. She herself was a liberated modern cook, after all, who ultimately valued her licuadora (blender) more than any metate ("La licuadora helped moles survive!"). She welcomed any innovation or shortcut that helped local women be "feliz con maíz"—happy with corn.

Slavery, agreed sociologist Dr. Gloria Zafra, author of the influential study *Mujer, Trabajo y Salud en Oaxaca* (Women, Labor, and Health in Oaxaca). And what's more, a chronic health hazard, causing metate-related shoulder and knee injuries and lung damage from inhaling comal wood smoke. But then, without opportunities, Zafra countered, without education, what were our Indigenous women to do? Consider Oaxaca's professional tortilla vendors, those "living tortilla machines" enduring brutal work, terrible pay, three to four hours a day just in colectivo taxis. Yet theirs were usually family businesses with cousins, aunts, sisters all chipping in. Ultimately, such a model offered more freedom, and yes, empowerment even, than slaving as *empleadas* (employees), abused and discriminated against, for more or less the same pay.

. . .

To my surprise, even Eufrosina Cruz Mendoza seemed of two minds in answering my "Empowerment or slavery?" question. And hers was the opinion I especially sought.

Eufrosina, as she's simply known, is one of Mexico's most dynamic Indigenous politicians and women's rights activists. What they call a super-chingona. I felt extremely lucky she found an hour to meet at the jazzy mezcal-bar patio of a just-opened design hotel in Oaxaca. Where I had to strain to imagine how this intimidatingly glamorous, powerful woman, urgent and polished, a wine-colored rebozo draped stylishly over her little black dress, had grown up in a village seven long hours from here by steep winding roads—speaking only Zapotec, sleeping on a dirt floor, being lectured by her father that women were only good for making tortillas and babies.

"That life was my supposed destiny," she began after a cursory sip of mezcal. "The destiny of every Indigenous woman in such a comunidad. Being indígena, female, and poor in Mexico—*cabrón*, you're triply screwed."

*That life.* Fetching water predawn . . . waiting for the nixtamal mill to open . . . kneeling for hours at the metate . . . slapping tortillas on the comal . . . boiling nixtamal for next day. "I'm forty," she said. "My son Diego is six. Back home every woman my age is a grandma, married at twelve."

At eleven, Eufrosina heard of her dad's plans to marry her off and ran away from this destiny. She moved in with relatives in a bigger pueblo and learned Spanish, supporting herself selling fruit and chewing gum on the street. Aged twenty-seven, with a college degree from Oaxaca City, she returned to her comunidad to enter political life—still haunted by "the sadness, the injustice on the faces of our women, their hands hardened by nixtamal and scarred by comal."

In the 1990s, Oaxaca became the first Mexican state to be granted the right for its Indigenous communities to elect their leaders through usos y costumbres (literally, "uses and customs"), whereby both voters and candidates "earn" their right to take part through public service activities. Of Oaxaca's 570 municipios, 418 elect leaders this way. And in most municipalities, women were excluded from participating.

"Usos y costumbres," scoffed Eufrosina. "Usos y abusos de women!"

In 2007 she ran for presidente municipal of her comunidad, and apparently won. Whereupon the incumbent declared that "women are created to assist men," to prepare meals and raise kids, not govern. Ballots marked for her were destroyed. Her supporters were harassed, slandered as idiots, drunkards, and gays. "I'm not a crier," said Eufrosina, "but those words made me weep. Zapotec insults sting." Appealing to Oaxaca's state congress, she received death threats. But her plight made national news and her story was heard by Mexico's then president Felipe Calderón. Suddenly a celebrity, she found herself becoming the first-ever Indigenous woman elected to the Oaxacan state congress, and then to Mexico's national Chamber of Deputies. Her major achievement so far? A federal constitutional amendment recognizing the right of Indigenous women to vote—later replicated globally by the UN.

At the time of our meeting Eufrosina headed SEPIA, the Secretariat for Indigenous and Afro-Mexican Peoples, in Oaxaca's state government. One of her debut actions was to change the name of her office, formerly the Oficina de Asuntos Indígenas. "Asuntos?" she snorted. "Indigenous Affairs—a term so bureaucratic, so passive."

She waved a hand. "Even our well-meaning mestizo liberals still treat los indígenas as sweet helpless dolls . . . *los vulnerables*, a 'national problem.' Oaxaca's Central Valleys with their markets and crafts, they're seen as some sort of open-air living museum. But we are people, not an 'affair' or folkloric artifacts waiting for handouts. We've just been denied opportunities!"

She leaned forward. "Write this down, Anya! *'La mujer indígena* can be *empoderada, chingona, y valiente'*—empowered, badass, and brave!"

All of which brought on my next question: How to reconcile hard-won Indigenous rights of cultural and political autonomy with a feminist vision?

Contesting traditional laws wasn't the answer, Eufrosina responded impatiently. Changes had to come through community conversation, education, transparency. "Our pueblos have many virtues," she said. "Beautiful fiestas, tamales for Christmas, sharing, planting, and eating together. These are my values, too, I fight to defend them."

And the tortilla issue? I pressed.

"Look," she replied, "I don't cook. I refuse to touch nixtamal."

Given who I'd been spending time with in Oaxaca—women all drawing their power from food making—these were distinctive words.

"But in my village," Eufrosina continued, "I do it! To show my respect for community life. But I draw the line at human rights violations. Indigenous rights and human rights need not be incompatible. And we keep making progress." There were many more women municipal presidents now, and a female quota in cabildos, the state's local assemblies.

"But you ask me, Anya," she pondered further, "if tortilla is slavery . . ."

Her answer was that it was not. Maize was and is the alimentary base of Indigenous comunidades, their subsistence and culture. Machine-made tortillas are scorned, Maseca regarded as contaminated.

"What needs changing," Eufrosina insisted emphatically, "is the prejudice that the tortilla is solely women's work. We try to educate villagers to involve the whole family. The señor can fetch firewood for the comal—why can't he?" She tapped through her cell phone to show photos of her delivering family-size nixtamal mills to small groups of village women, a program she launched called Mujeres de Maíz, so women don't have to wait at dawn for men to open the communal molino whenever they want, another form of abuse. "Through these small molinos, sisterhoods are created."

Rising to leave, she said she was still mulling my tortilla question. She herself had made a life choice involving zero tortillas. But if a woman chose that life, she needed to be respected for it. "And ultimately," she added, smiling coolly, adjusting her rebozo, "the tortilla *is* power. A woman can tell her dude, If you don't respect me I will deprive you, I will go on strike. Nixtamal is our strength. Sin maíz no hay país, as they say!"

And with that she hurried off.

POSSIBLY THE WORST HISTORIC assault on Mesoamerican maize culture was dealt by NAFTA, the 1994 free trade agreement between the US, Canada—and Mexico, where a majority lived and still live in poverty. For its Mexican champion, president Carlos Salinas, an economist, NAFTA marked the triumph of the neoliberalism embraced after the country's crippling 1982 debt crisis.

Salinas and his free-market evangelists abandoned the Revolutionary promise of a welfare state and turned instead toward manufacturing, privatization, and large agribusinesses.

The countryside suffered particularly. By most estimates, Mexico cut agricultural support by 90 percent over NAFTA's first seven years. Worse, the government reduced protective tariffs on maize almost immediately, sending farmers into shock. American agribusinesses meanwhile began dumping industrial corn here (mostly for animal feed) at *below* production cost, even as the US government continued to heavily subsidize its own corn producers. In the first decade of NAFTA, the price of Mexico's domestic corn crashed by nearly 70 percent. Farm laborers' income plummeted. (It's one-third of its pre-NAFTA level even today.) Consumer tortilla prices shot up nearly 300 percent. Despairing campesinos sold or abandoned their land, setting in motion a mass exodus now estimated at anywhere between 2 million and 5 million people.

The last straw from NAFTA's injuries and indignities—and paradoxically, the catalyst of today's nationalist celebration of maize—was the so-called corn scandal of 2001. That year a pair of University of California, Berkeley scientists doing fieldwork in Oaxaca discovered a high level of gene flow from industrial GMO corn into local criollo crops.

Meaning NAFTA, having flooded Mexico with cut-rate US corn, was now tainting the national gene pool?

Published in *Nature*, the Berkeley scientists' findings set off an international uproar and a furious counterattack funded by the likes of Monsanto. A subsequent exhaustive study from the Commission for Environmental Cooperation (CEC) confirmed the gene flow—adding that its "impact on landraces has become entwined with historical issues and grievances affecting rural Mexicans."

To say the least.

"We thought we were facing an apocalypse—a possible extinction event!" the prominent Oaxacan maize scientist Flavio Aragón Cuevas emphasized as he showed me the germoplasm bank at the National Institute for Research in Forestry, Farming and Animal Husbandry north of Oaxaca City. Here seeds of some two hundred local species of maize were being preserved. "*El nuestro Arca de Noé*," he joked.

The corn scandal spread its panic through farming communities already savaged by NAFTA. "Maize is *el centro de la Mexicanidad*," Aragón repeated the mantra, and the unique landraces selectively bred for millennia were being threatened by transgenes that could cross-pollinate so easily as to overrun them completely.

"And what's at stake?" Aragón asked somberly. "Our genetic treasure, our biodiversity—our cuisine, culture, and patrimony!"

Mercifully, no long-term damage to Oaxacan maize has been observed following the 2001 alarm. But the maize issue went to Mexico's soul, to the fabric of its rural communities, the livelihood of its Indigenous farmers—those campesinos marginalized for so long but now touted as stewards of the nation's foundational heritage.

*Sin Maíz No Hay País* was the title of the 2003 exhibition at the National Museum of Popular Cultures in Mexico City, accompanied by odes and paeans to the grain from top intellectuals. That same year some 100,000 protestors flooded the capital demanding a renegotiation of NAFTA, as farmers marched naked through the streets or formed "tractorcades." *Sin Maíz* was also the slogan of La Red en Defensa del Maíz, an influential anti-GMO network founded in 2002 with some three hundred mostly Mexican activists and still important today.

And so it's been going. Over the past two decades, over five hundred organizations have taken part in the various campaigns. Against the backdrop of the anti-neoliberal Zapatista insurgency, such grassroots movements have brought together campesinos, urban chefs and consumers, Indigenous activists, NGOs, and fancy international scientists. The response from Mexican governments? The usual evasions and half measures, primarily, though currently transgenics are being phased out, and López Obrador, Mexico's populist president, has loudly promised campesino support. But public awareness and consumer patriotism have been created; small-scale farmers and producers have been educating themselves; the media have been roused to the cause.

Mexico even got its Día Nacional del Maíz. The twenty-ninth of September.

Leaving the maize scientist and his germoplasmic Ark, I strolled through the mercado in the small nearby town of Etla, where campesinos stood stoically by their crates of multicolored maize in the fierce sun and narrow shadows. How, I wondered, did this new corn patriotism affect national attitudes toward such farmers? Were they still seen as "nostalgically folkloric remnants of underdevelopment," in the words of one scholar? Or were the likes of Cayetano and Nati amid their rough-jewel maize in Zegache now considered independent proprietors of culture and patrimony? Or were they tiny cogs in the neoliberal marketing machine, promotional props of heritage tourism? And what did the future hold for them? The global explosion of eco-conscious consumerism has created a demand for heirloom corn that could easily overpower production capacities—as has happened with mezcal. And if social and educational programs championed by the likes of Eufrosina succeeded— what would restrain campesinos from quitting their milpas and integrating into mestizo society?

High in the hills above Etla, Francisco Toledo refashioned a textile mill into an ecological art center. There I bought a few striking anti-GMO posters of El Maestro's design. The one that now hangs in my office in New York depicts Benito Juárez—the nineteenth-century Zapotec from Oaxaca who became a revered, liberalizing president of Mexico—asleep on a pile of criollo corncobs. *"Despierta Benito!"* ("Wake up, Benito!") urges a caption. *"Y di no al maíz transgénico!"* ("And say no to GMO maize!")

INEVITABLY, any food story set in Oaxaca will turn for its crowning scene to a mole-lavished fiesta of one kind or another. Many delightful dichos (sayings) invoke mole's deep-woven role in Mexican social life. For instance: *"Para cuándo el mole?"* When's the mole for? As in: When's the boda (wedding)?

Never in a million years did I dream that such a boda fiesta would feature Barry and me, exchanging vows at a shamanic Zapotec ceremony on Olga's terraza.

And yet here was Olga excitedly drawing up guest lists and menu plans. "Imagine, Anyita!" she cooed. "You'll make your own wedding moles!"

This was to be my meal in Oaxaca, after all. My own wedding moles.

Olga had seven in mind, but nothing canonic or national. Together we'd make her family recipes, such as a clove-scented mole de clavo from her abuelita, Chonita, who runs a famous comedor in Huajuapan. The pièce de résistance would be a fruity bridal-white mole blanco of nearly thirty ingredients that Olga herself had invented after months of trial and error. It required, in part, alchemically blanching calabaza seeds with water and ash.

And who knows, maybe I'd even somehow manage to slap up some tortillas.

My unexpected marital plans were all the result of mezcal. More precisely, of a visit to the mezcal palenque (distillery) owned by Olga's business partner and our new friend, Jorge Vera, a London-trained former economist turned palenquero—very mestizo. His palenque, Convite, lay a long hour's drive southeast of Oaxaca City, some six thousand feet aloft in the Sierra Madre del Sur just outside the modest pueblo of San Baltazar Guelavila. This is the Zapotec heart of mezcal country, where Mexico's largest diversity of agave abounds.

Despite the high price of its product, the Convite facility consisted mainly of a large mostly open-air platform set into a slopeside, at whose rear a soil-and-stone roasting pit was loaded up, covered high with earth and log weights. Freshly cut agave hearts, piñas, sat heaped close by like pale monster pineapples awaiting their turn roasting. Or more like monster asparagus stubs, since agave (maguey) is actually a member of the Asparagaceae family. Beside these stood the tahona, the traditional grinding wheel for crushing the cooked piñas, powered by a plodding circling burro. Big oaken vats of tepache (agave mash) bubbled and foamed nearby . . . slowly, spookily.

After a show-around, we tasted a 120-proof new distillate straight from the alambique (still) with Tucho Hernández, one of Convite's master distillers along with his older brother, Daniel. The Hernándezes are a well-known family dynasty in San Baltazar, where recent decades have made celebrities of Zapotec mezcaleros, as the best small-batch distilleries were being snapped up by multi-nationals like Pernod Ricard and Campari. Beyond us the wintry slopes rolled away in faded grays and browns, with their scattered wild agaves making spiky eruptions of green.

Tucho was especially proud of his jabalí (boar) mezcal—*muy difícil* because the jabalí maguey grows on steep cliffsides, takes twenty-five years to mature, and requires some one hundred kilos for a single distilled liter.

"But drinking it can fuck with your mind," he cautioned. "Give you moods."

"Tucho" means "wild" in Zapotec, and the nickname suited. Around forty, with fierce Emiliano Zapata good looks featuring a dashing wide mustache, Tucho seemed to have a shamanic relation-ship to agave and mezcal and the sierra. He could just eye a loca-tion, he told us, and know what maguey would grow there, how its mezcal would taste. Every now and then he'd disappear into the mountains for several days with only a bottle of distillate and some mushrooms, "and talk to the birds." He had his special way of doing things—a Tucho life-approach. For instance, how he got himself married. He was kicking a ball around with some pals one day and it landed by a girl. "And I said to myself, she's the one," he recounted. It was love. "Will you be mine?" he asked—just like that. "Can I think about it?" replied the girl. "No, not really, but okay. I need your answer tomorrow," he said. Then he asked for her name.

For some reason Tucho seemed fascinated by Barry. "He's *old*," he declared, turning our scrutiny of him back the other direction. "But surprisingly *spry* . . . How long have you two been married?"

He was shocked to hear we weren't, after twenty-five years of "courtship."

"Our accountant said it was a terrible idea financially," I told him, with the frivolous chuckle I always produce when explaining our relationship status.

Tucho frowned.

"It is time you got married," he pronounced with solemn intensity. "Marriage will teach you new responsibilities."

"Tucho can marry you!" piped up Jorge, our host. He was grinning, but clearly a little dazed by what he might be setting in motion.

It turned out Tucho was a bona fide Zapotec shaman, entitled to preside over spiritual ceremonies. He'd married people before.

Barry and I looked at each other.

"Why not?" we gulped. Dazed, for real, by what the palenque and its 120-proof jabalí had wrought.


Before the marriage itself, though, there was a preliminary ceremony to be undergone: la pedida, the entreaty. A father figure for Barry had to formally petition my mother figure for my hand.

And before la pedida, there was the gauntlet of earthy folkloric jesting to be run, which we brought on by announcing brightly to all and sundry that we planned to get married Zapotec-style.

Windburned, work-haggard faces immediately lit up with bawdy mirth. Ladies asked shrewdly how I was with the metate. Men asked lewdly how I was on the petate (straw mat).

"*Him?*" a couple of Mixteca abuelas cackled at the Friday market at Ocotlán, referring to Barry. "Better the other, *he* looks like a rich gringo!" Meaning our tall regal amigo Julio César. The Ocotlán market, famous for its live turkey trade, was where I bought my white wedding huipil.

Barry's entreaty for my hand took place early one evening at the same jazzy hotel mezcal bar where I'd met Eufrosina. Olga's friend Mari Paz, the hotel's genial general manager, accompanied me as stand-in mother. I sat beside her, silently as required, a crimson rebozo modestly covering my head while Barry's father stand-in, Jorge Vera, the instigator, launched with surprising eloquence into the spousal virtues—and deficiencies, granted—of the long-in-the-tooth "son" beside him (some twenty years older than his "father"). Mari Paz eyed the pair with protective suspicion. Barry was accoutered in a debonair, but odd, outfit: a pseudo-campesino blouse, a bright purple bandana, and a large floppy black hat. Once Jorge was done, Barry stood and squawked out a mariachi classic he'd revised especially for me, to applause from the ten friends gathered as witnesses. Then he went down on one knee and asked for my hand after presenting his requisite pedida offerings of chocolate, cigarettes, mezcal, pan de yema, and a mini-metate—plus the fattest virility-suggestive vela (candle) he could find in Oaxaca. By local tradition, the groom's worth and quality is measured by the price and weight of this vela. My hand was granted. We kissed.

We toasted our mezcal-wrought betrothal and impending

marriage. It was a process we had embraced, to be honest, as sort of playful folkloric cosplay, a lark. But now, raising our vasos velado-ras, the traditional squat church-candle glasses for mezcal, we found ourselves filled with emotion. Our betrothal was, in truth, a salute to the Oaxacan community web that had so richly and gener-ously gathered us in these past weeks. That's what we toasted most deeply and sincerely. Even if one of us resembled an escapee from an operetta.

TEOTITLÁN DEL VALLE, a prosperous Zapotec weaving village, lies under El Picacho, a starkly peaked sacred hill in the Sierra Juárez near Oaxaca. A few days before our boda zapoteca was to take place, I came here to call on Abigail Mendoza, and, among other things, invite her to our wedding.

In Oaxaca, Doña Abigail is less a cook than a Zapotec cultural treasure. Diana Kennedy borrowed her recipes, Anthony Bourdain came to pay his respects. Mexican *Vogue* put her on its cover. When she was still a young cocidera (a traditional cook for fiestas and weddings), unmarried Teotitlán women such as her weren't allowed to shop at the market or drink mezcal (she still doesn't). With much anguish and shame, she defied village traditions, and then defied the contractors who built Tlamanalli—the restaurant, named for the Zapotec kitchen god, she founded with her five sisters thirty years ago—who refused to take orders from a woman. Now she sat on the village council and presided over Teotitlán's new Commu-nity Cultural Center.

In her sturdy fifties, with a round laughing face and red-ribboned braids coiled on her head like a rumpled tiara, Doña

Abigail waited for me at the rambling magical-realist house she shares with her two likewise unwed sisters, Adelina and Rufina. The huge central courtyard presented a realm of exotic blossoms, comals galore, bubbling pots over live fire—a happy Camelot of women, which made me momentarily reconsider my marriage plans. On the arcaded porch, though, among the looms, straw baskets, and pottery, I counted seven daunting presences: metates. Separate ones, Abigail noted, for chilies and chocolate, spices and beans, so flavors didn't mix.

When Abigail was five, her dad made her a practice mini-metate from river stone. At six she made her first real tortillas, tiny mis-shapen ones, and when her mom tossed them to the chickens, she wept. At nine, she had to drop out of school because it was all getting too much, the weaving, helping with younger siblings, scrambling to deliver nixtamal to the molino at recess, dashing back to her mother with the masa, then back to class.

"Aha!" I jumped in with my irrepressible "So tortilla equals slavery?"

"Part of me thinks, yes," Abigail allowed, after the inevitable bemused pause. "But if we all went instead to school and got jobs, who'd make the tortillas? *Sin tortillas*, family as we know it will end!"

We sat around a long table now in the lush shady calm of the patio, dabbing the ur-local mole cegueza that I'd been so wanting to try onto giant tlayudas, stiff charred discs of maize cratered like moons.

"*El primer mole de nosotros*, our number one mole," Abigail said of cegueza.

"*De nuestros ancestros prehispánicos!*" chimed in Rufina.

Indeed, there was something truly archaic about this cegueza.

No Iberian onions, no garlic, no imported spices. No sweetness. Large frijolones (beans) were its main content for everyday eating, while pork innards and neck featured for fiestas, the Catholic porker replacing native deer or wild hare. But ultimately, it occurred to me, cegueza was a *mole of maíz*. Thickened with maíz quebrado (comal-toasted dried corn kernels coarsely ground on metate), it was the closest I'd come in my quest for a pre-Conquest mulli: less a sauce than a haunting pre-Hispanic polenta alive with tomatoes, ruddy chilcostle chilies, and the licorice hit of fresh hoja santa.

I told the sisters that my mole journey had taken me in a reverse historic chronology—from the Baroque-colonial mestizaje of my first negro with Celia, to this austere Zapotec mulli of their ancient ancestors here.

I further explained about my wedding, noting some of the moles Olga and I were making, and extended my invitation.

Abigail chuckled, nodding along as I spoke. Then she spoke herself. She spoke of how in the life of a Zapotec woman, moles represented something deep, something profoundly personal. Moles were the book of a woman's days, of the cycle of life with its community fiestas, its joys, its intimate sorrows. There were the gentle chili-less moles verdes local mothers fed to their babies. The mole zapoteco of chiles chilcostles and toasted breadcrumbs, unique to Teotitlán, that she'd prepared for her siblings' fandangos (grand wedding feasts). The ritual mole amarillo of beef served nine days after the death of her father.

And none of this, I thought to myself as I listened, featured in any mestizaje national narratives.

Then Abigail announced that she had a surprise for me.

*Chocolate-atole.*

Apparently, news of my boda zapoteca had already reached

Teotitlán. And though Abigail and her sisters, alas, couldn't attend, this was their gift: a foamy fiesta potion Abigail had branded with entrepreneurial savvy as "Zapotec cappuccino."

"Not having married," she declared, her smile wide and contented, "I am very happy no man is bothering us. But if it is your sincere decision to wed, you shall have our bebida de dioses. Drink of the gods!"

Atole—from Nahuatl *atl*, "water," and *ollin*, "movement"—is the daily breakfast of campesinos, part maize gruel, part drink. *Chocolate*, on the other hand, was the potion pre-Hispanic elites served in beautiful vessels, flavored with chilies or agave honey or cinnamon, and frothy. "Chocolate-atole marries luxury (chocolate) and daily sustenance (maize)," Abigail said. "And for us here, frothy drinks are as important as tamales and moles."

Certain recipes are epic narratives of conquest and battle; certain others are fleeting haikus. Chocolate-atole, I thought, as Abigail commenced a recitation, is an incantation, a spell.

"Chocolate-atole has many pasos, or steps," she began, "of which the first and most difficult is the fermentation of cacao pataxte, white cacao we call it. Nothing to do with brown chocolate.

"You buy pataxte from mujeres de Sierra de Chiapas," she chanted now, "from a trusted seller, paying whatever she asks—never stint—and soak the pods for two weeks. Meanwhile on rocky land make a square pit, fill it with water. Then wait. When the water stagnates, add the cacao. Close the pit with wood, straw, and earth, leaving a hole; every day check how much water is absorbed, and refill; every week take out all the cacao, wash it—bury it again. Six months will pass, maybe eight, the water will rot and develop maggots and worms, the cacao skins darken. When the stench and worms disappear, dry the pods—not in the sun, but *not* in shade or the cacao will rot. You will know when the pataxte is ready *only* if you are one of the chosen women who knows . . . In my comunidad there are just five such women."

Here she paused to show me the already fermented pataxte pods, chalky and lightweight inside fragile black shells. I took a taste. There was the faint savor of earth, not entirely pleasant.

I couldn't hide my astonishment. Nine months for *this*? Just like pregnancy. *Why?*

"Because chocolate-atole is sacral magic," answered Abigail, suddenly grave. "Through chocolate-atole for special fiestas and weddings, we preserve sacred rites. Now listen and don't interrupt."

The recipe unfurled onward for almost an hour, involving toasting and soaking the pods, and having a small army of helpers peel them with very clean hands—no grease or cream. All this could take up to a week. At long last, the pataxte was ground and blended with comal-toasted wheat, corn, rice, cinnamon sticks, and brown cacao, and this *pasta* was set out to dry in the sun until hard as a rock.

"And now comes the last paso, *día de fiesta*," Abigail announced, her voice swelling with the drama. "Your wedding day, dear Anya! The house is full, you've killed chickens and turkeys and pigs, made your bizcochos and regular chocolate de agua for arriving guests. Now in this crowded chaotic house you find a special corner for you and your eight metates and your twelve helpers: six to grind, and six to do the *batida*, the foam beating, in special ollas that have never touched meat or sugar or grasa—or the espuma is ruined!"

Abigail now hurried over to kneel before the metate and start smashing the rock-hard cacao pasta with the metate's mano, splashing on water, grinding away with the expertise perfected across the decades since childhood. Her forearms, I noticed, were those of a weightlifter.

Rufina and Adelina meanwhile simmered the liquid base: milky atole blanco of white maize tiziahual, a special un-nixtamalized masa.

"So they're grinding and grinding, and other girls are beating and beating espuma," Abigail narrated away, working faster and faster, approaching a ritual climax. "They scoop the espumas finally into jícaras [gourds], always terrified of the evil eye, *mal de ojo*."

Now she was up again, beating the pasta herself in an earthenware olla, rubbing and turning her wooden ridged molinillo with a dervish dance of the hands.

And there I finally saw it, a pale foam slowly emerging. Big frail bubbles at first, then a dense lather that gleamed and glinted like oxygenated jewelry.

Ancient Zapotecs had a concept of vital living force, *pi*, meaning "breath" or "spirit" or "wind." According to archeologists Joyce Marcus and Kent Flannery, anything with pi—a flooding river, a rain cloud, the foam on top of a cup of chocolate—"was considered alive and therefore sacred, addressed with special respect during ritual."

One consumes chocolate-atole by spooning the sweetened espuma over a cup of still-warm atole. The world prizes Mexican food for its bold, spicy energy. But chocolate-atole, the vital elixir from so much grueling fairy-tale labor, was exactly the opposite. Ephemeral . . . faint. It was something, I had to sigh to myself, I guess I'd never understand as an outsider.

"You're a lucky bride," said Rufina, "to have such a gift."

"And your *novio*, your boyfriend," Abigail added graciously, "is most lucky to wed you."

# ISTANBUL
## The Ottoman Potluck

In 1459, six years after realizing his dream of seizing Constantinople, the Ottoman sultan Mehmed II, "the Conqueror," commissioned a palace on the site of an ancient Byzantine citadel overlooking three waters and two continents. For the next four centuries, until a new palace supplanted it, Topkapi ("cannon gate") Palace would serve as the command center of an enormous empire that stretched at its zenith from Algeria east to the Persian Gulf, from Crimea westward to Hungary.

In the mid-1960s, four decades after the empire's moth-eaten collapse, a sloppy six-story apartment building went up on a steep street in a fairly raffish district on Istanbul's European shore. Since 2007 Barry and I have owned a pied-à-terre walk-up at the top of that building, a slapdash place but with a drop-dead view of the Bosporus, the strait that both separates and joins Europe and Asia. My neighborhood, Cihangir, takes its name from Sultan Süleyman the Magnificent's sad hunchback son, whose circumcision feast in 1539 lasted fifty-two days and depleted the imperial treasury. Over two hundred dishes were served, some of which—soups and pilafs and such simple stuff—I'd been taste-testing now for a while in my kitchen. I was trying to pin down a perfect historical (but still vital) menu for an Ottoman-inspired dinner I'd been plotting with my friend Gamze, a compulsively hospitable modern dancer turned chef.

In Topkapi's Second Courtyard, entered through the castle-like Gate of Salutation, visitors behold the Matbah-ı Amire, the Imperial Kitchen complex that occupies the courtyard's entire south flank. In a palace whose intimate scale subverts Western expectations of grandeur, the kitchen is a strikingly monumental sight. The expansive many-domed silhouette is even visible from the Marmara Sea. It was meant to project to arrivals an image: the image of the empire's largesse and its Koranic commitment to feeding the hungry.

The Matbah-ı Amire fed up to five thousand people a day. Foreign envoys, humble petitioners, even pet monkeys, *anyone* who entered Topkapi got a free lunch on the sultan. There were feasts for the Sultan's Sadness (taziye) or Sultan's Joy (isar-i urs); feasts for reaching legal decisions; "helvah socials" to relieve the boredom of winter, illuminated by candles attached to live turtles. For royal weddings and circumcisions, the Matbah borrowed pots from nearby mosques and staged citywide extravaganzas over at the Hippodrome, where the Byzantines once raced their chariots. At these feasts, pashas and commoners, Greek wine tavern owners and Jewish poll tax collectors, Armenian silk merchants and Sufi dervishes, all shared the same yogurt soups, pilafs, peacock and partridge kebabs, dolmas, and mastic-scented puddings. It was as if the sultan's soup was the social glue that held together the complicated layers of his multicultural, multiconfessional capital.

Now, on a pretty June day following our early spring in Oaxaca,

I was browsing Ottoman cookbooks, still frustrated over the perfect menu for my symbolic Istanbul meal. Putting my reading aside, I reached into a cupboard and tugged out a large tray. It was plastic, from the global empire of today called IKEA, but manufactured here in Turkey. I fell to pondering its Ottomanesque blue-white-and-red pattern. And then it dawned on me.

I rushed to text Gamze.

"Let's do a çilingir sofrası *potluck*!"

Çilingir sofrası is Turkish for a tray laden with meze (small plates) to accompany the anisey liquor called raki. It would be like a Spanish tapeo, with each tiny taste telling a story, but without the manic shuffling from bar to bar.

"*Harika canim!* Fantastic, my dear!" Gamze texted back. "It shall be OUR celebration of OUR Istanbul."

OUR ISTANBUL. Ex-Constantinople, ex-capital of Roman, Byzantine, and Ottoman empires.

Whenever people ask why I bought an apartment here—busted elevator, leaky roof—I mention the Bosporus view, of course, and the food. On my first visit here back in the mid-1980s, I prowled the city in a kind of lyrical, ravenous daze, taking in the oily perfume of mackerel sandwiches grilled by the ferry docks, inhaling the dime-sized dumplings called manti at homey, tattered esnaf lokantas, the tradesmen's eateries of the bazaar quarters. I still remember the exact taste of the ambrosial peach, one I devoured on the Galata Bridge over the Golden Horn while gaping at the grand domes and minarets of Aya Sofia and the imperial mosques. The city seemed like one never-ending orientalist cliché, but a cliché made poignant by what I now recognize as *hüzün*, that free-floating tristesse of depletion and loss of a cosmopolitan texture, which Orhan Pamuk has turned into a kind of official city emotion.

Visiting the year before me, the Russian poet Joseph Brodsky misanthropically kvetched about Istanbul's "crooked, filthy streets," which reminded him of Astrakhan and Samarkand, then still Soviet. I was reminded of Soviet places as well—but in a bittersweet way. Even the food, for all its exoticism, seemed completely familiar from my travels through the USSR's own creaking empirium, in eastern Europe, and other places where the Ottomans passed. In Turkish köfte (grilled meatballs), I recognized the ćevapčići I'd tasted in Skopje. Versions of dolma (stuffed vegetables) I'd eaten in Ukraine and Armenia, pahlava (baklava) in Azerbaijan, guvetch (claypot vegetable stew) in Moldova. For me, someone raised and fed on the hoary Soviet myth of the "friendship of nations" of its numerous subject realms, Istanbul's edible fusion made perfect sense—a Pan-Eurasian melting pot formed by conquests, migrations, and trade. Given the Ottoman empire's sheer geographic scope, was its cuisine arguably among the world's most influential, though in a totally different manner than French?

Nowadays, over three decades later, neo-Ottomanism is decidedly in fashion in Turkey, relentlessly stoked by the ruling Islamicist party and its main man, President Recep Tayyip Erdoğan, a humbly born devout Muslim with sultanic ambitions. But back then, in the 1980s, hardly anyone mentioned the Ottomans. Memories of the dynasty, founded in 1281 by an Anatolian Turcoman warlord called Osman, hovered wanly about Istanbul like a dishonored ghost, exiled by Mustafa Kemal Atatürk—"Father Turk," an officially awarded honorific—the creator of a secular modern nation from the ruins of the Islamic empire after its humiliating defeat in World War I, followed by the Turkish War of Independence, which he brilliantly led. Upon establishing the Republic of Turkey, with new borders officially recognized by the 1923 Treaty of Lausanne, Mustafa Kemal wasted no time forcing through his vision for the nation-state and its citizenry, based on the French republican ideals of ethnic nationalism, positivism, and laicism. The caliphate was dissolved, fez and harem abolished. From water-lapped Constantinople—now officially Istanbul—with its ideologically suspect imperial hodgepodge of cultures, the capital was transferred to Ankara, off in the Anatolian plains. The Ottoman language, rich in Persian and Arabic borrowings and written in Arabic script, was discarded for a modernized Turkish written in the Latin alphabet. Even clocks were reset to the Western Gregorian calendar. For decades, former Ottoman subjects could barely read a book or tell time. Meanwhile, writes historian Charles King, new generations of Turkish students would be taught "to see their distant ancestors as Turkic tribesmen, even if their grandfathers had actually been Salonican greengrocers or Sarajevan tailors."

It goes without saying that the elaborate palace cuisine of the shunned empire was barely mentioned.


Istanbul looked different to me when I began returning in the nineties and aughts.

Cleaner now, more prosperous, economically opened up to the world by successive neoliberal governments. Tourism was surging. There were malls now and McDonald's and pizza—even restaurants promising the "treasures and mysteries of the Ottoman kitchen."

My favorite evenings, though, involved raki and meze at meyhane, the dark smoky taverns clustered around newly pedestrianized Istiklal Avenue in the European Beyoğlu district, the former Pera of earlier times. An inebriated historian once explained that meyhane dated back to the city's Byzantine past. They were portside dens where sailors could get a drink, a dame, and a haircut to boot. Wine houses at first (mey is Persian for wine, hane for house), they were run in Ottoman times by non-Muslim minorities allowed to sell alcohol, and were only precariously legal. Under hard-drinking Atatürk, however, meyhane flourished as symbols of secularism. Raki, the "lion's milk" dear to "Father Turk," flowed as the *milli içki*, the "national drink." Atatürk's portraits gazed down from meyhane walls, often with glass in hand.

The original meyhane served only rudimentary snacks—pickled cabbage, bowls of leblebi (roasted chickpeas), and the like. But with neoliberal prosperity, the meze trays of çilingir sofrası (çilingir means lock; sofra is the round, low Ottoman tray table) morphed into fantastical edible memoryscapes that now gathered together the strands of Istanbul's multicultural heritage. At a Beyoğlu meyhane, one ate Arnavut ciğeri, fried cubes of "Albanian liver," tossed with wisps of raw onion, and the mayonnaise-laden "Russian salad" I knew as Salat Olivier from my Moscow childhood. Greek—Byzantine?—taramasalata and dried fish called çiroz shared the tray with yogurt dips harking back to the Anatolian nomadic past, alongside distinctly Armenian topik, a compound of mashed chickpeas and richly caramelized onions.

How enchantingly nostalgic, I thought it all was . . . Small fleeting tastes of an imperial polyglot past mosaicked in front of me, as chain-smoking bohemians brooded over their raki and a bespectacled Armenian busker called Madame Anahit rendered "La Vie en Rose" on her battered accordion. She was so painfully out of tune regulars paid her not to play.

And so, I bought an apartment in Istanbul.

*"POTLUCK—*I LOVE IT, canim!"

Gamze was practically jumping off her rickety red plastic stool in excitement. We were in a murky alley near the Balik Pazari, Beyoğlu's produce and fish market, indulging in a hard-core Istanbul ritual: kelle söğüş sandviç. A sheep's-head sandwich.

I was feeling delighted myself. Here in Istanbul, the idea of an imperial mingling of cultures at table persisted even through republican "Turkification." Cultural polyphony remains one of this city's particular and most enduring foundational myths.

Gamze, for her part, kept on repeating, *Potluck!* The term that to me evoked tuna casseroles was to her the perfect metaphor for a cuisine whose benevolent subtext was that everyone was welcome at table. And so here was the plan—a gastronomic homage to Istanbul's melting-pot legacy by means of each guest contributing a dish.

On a paper napkin Gamze scribbled an invite list. Takuhi Tovmasyan, an Armenian memoirist, would bring her famous topik. Deniz Alphan, our Jewish friend, would contribute a Sephardic eggplant börek. Zeynep "the Albanian" would bring the Albanian liver. I volunteered Russian salad, and since I've actually *been* to the Caucasus, a Circassian chicken in walnut sauce, by legend prepared by the fair-haired favorites of the harem. Gamze, with her Ottoman DNA—her great-grandfather was an honest-to-god Ottoman pasha, assassinated while serving at the court of that degenerate defeatist Abdülhamīd II, the penultimate sultan—promised one of her family recipes.

. . .

I'd met Gamze a few years before, after I'd been half living in Istanbul for almost a decade, and Erdoğan's mounting Islamicist authoritarianism was battering the once-surging optimism about Turkey's democracy. A refined curly-haired beauty, Gamze was a part of my ever-expanding circle of friends from the food scene: women mostly, all worldly and elegant, all proud Istanbullus heartbroken at *our* city's ongoing ruination by toxic political forces, and ever nostalgic for that past—that hazy, mythical past—where Armenians, Greeks, Muslims, and Jews exchanged food during holidays. This city, *our* city, with its memory of a thousand and one palace-born dishes and its rich minority foodways, was utterly special, I was repeatedly told.

"Istanbul cuisine has a particular *savor*," Gamze repeated again, as we ambled past Balik Pazari's early June bounty of mulberries, favas, and artichoke hearts bobbing in blue plastic tubs of vinegared water. "Mild, seasonal, delicate . . ."

And that savor, I said with a loud, poignant sigh, just kept eluding me in my own kitchen.

"But then, canim, I have an idea!" Gamze exclaimed. She insisted that we go right now to her house nearby, and together make kelek dolma, stuffing unripe green striped melons the size of a tennis ball with an Ottoman filling of meat, rice, and nuts. Gamze even offered a quick tutorial on zeytinyağlı ("with olive oil" literally)—seasonal veggies such as artichokes, leeks, or green beans slowly braised in rivers of oil. A preparation, she insisted, "fundamental to Istanbul."

At her house we sat scooping out pale-green cucumber-like flesh from the kelek, while Gamze reminisced about her childhood, a magical one, in a yali, a wooden waterside villa on the city's Asian shore. There she fished in the Bosporus and swam with packs of neighborhood kids in the cold treacherous currents. During full moons local families threw parties on *sandals* (traditional fishing boats) illuminated by kerosene lanterns; singalongs echoed across the dark oily waters. Gamze's paternal grandmother, daughter of that assassinated Ottoman pasha, was a marvelous cook, precise and refined. She braised eggplants with sour cherries until the lot was luscious as pudding, and she prepared Istanbul's best iç pilav, rice studded with nuggets of chicken livers and currants, delicately aromatic with allspice and cinnamon and threaded with succulent shreds of roast poultry. On Saturdays there were puf börek parties featuring ethereal puffs of meat-filled fried dough. During the fleeting unripe fig season in April, the fruit was blanched and dry-toasted with sugar, then wrapped in crescents of yufka pastry so thin one could almost see through it.

Later, as a young woman, Gamze shuttled between Paris and New York, dancing in Robert Wilson's experimental productions. All the while she spent fortunes on phone calls to Grandma to record and recapture her flavors as the genteel Istanbul of her youth was becoming unrecognizable. In 1994 she moved back to the city, started entertaining like crazy and then consulting for restaurants. These days, she was famous for the exquisitely choreographed meals she organized at international food festivals.

It was from her grandmother that Gamze learned the "sautéing ceremony" she was showing to me now: slowly, meticulously melting down masses of onions in fat—the cornerstone of most Ottoman dishes. For our zeytinyağlı (zey-thin-yah-lih), a wondrous silken veggie confit eaten at room temperature, Gamze transformed the onions into a translucent jam before adding favas and artichokes. The whole were to braise with secret pinches of sugar in olive oil to a texture Istanbullus call "helmelenmek," meaning something like "perfectly melting." For the kelek dolma filling, we sautéed onions to a particular shade of pale golden. To these Gamze added blanched almonds and pine nuts and kıyma (minced meat), and we spooned the allspice-scented filling into the melon globes after meticulously rubbing the cavities with plenty of butter—as Gamze's grandmother had done.

The finished dishes had a restrained but voluptuous elegance, worlds apart from the bold spicy tastes brought to the city by Eastern Anatolian migrants.

Which reminded me suddenly . . . "Wait, shouldn't our potluck feature meze like hummus?" I wondered. Or maybe muhammara—the chili-laced dip of red peppers, walnuts, and pomegranate molasses?

Gamze frowned. An elegantly complicated frown.

Despite foreigners' stereotypes of Turkish cuisine, such dishes, along with kebabs and bulgur and pizzalike lahmacun, were considered "arabesk" specialties—in no way natural to Istanbul.

"Canim, when I was growing up," Gamze declared, "we'd *never* had these."

Indeed. Until the migrations from Eastern Anatolia and the Black Sea that started in the 1950s, exploding the city from a million-plus souls to the current almost 15 million, most secular westernized Istanbullus had never set foot in a *kebapçı* (kebab house). Hummus? It was something utterly alien. Ara Guler, the grand old Armenian photographer of world-famous Istanbul images from the mid-twentieth century, expressed a lament about migrants quite savagely in a 1997 interview: "We have been overrun by villagers from Anatolia who don't understand the poetry or the romance of Istanbul. They don't even know the great pleasures of civilization, like how to eat well."

My friends were more liberally spoken. They loved hummus, actually, and tirelessly researched Eastern Anatolian foodways. The problem was Erdoğan and the identity politics tearing the city, and the country, apart. Conservative Anatolian Muslims with their bulgur balls and kebabs and their headscarves had gone from being Kara Türkler ("Black Turks"), marginalized by the haughty Kemalism of Atatürk's legacy, to being the domineering powers-that-be. They were Erdoğan people; now it was the "secular elites" who were feeling—rightly?—oppressed.

I told Gamze I understood.

Back at home, I sat with the windows open wide on the Bosporus view. Tankers inched north and south in the last light, dwarfing the ferries that would glow like paper lanterns come nightfall. Barry and I grazed from my inspirational IKEA tray; I'd loaded it with the Balik Pazari's fresh milky-fleshed almonds, Aegean olives the size of a baby's fist, and stinky tulum cheese aged in goatskins in Turkey's northeastern province of Erzincan.

The cries of the muezzins seemed particularly urgent in the evening air, rising and falling, stopping, then resuming at an almost anguished pitch. Across on the Asian shore loomed, like an enormous plaster souvenir, the imitation-Ottoman megamosque erected by Erdoğan on Istanbul's highest hill—a not-so-gentle reminder of this city's and country's jarring transformation over my time here. So, for that matter, was the cloudy raki in our glasses; taxes on it had gone up 665 percent since 2003, the year after Erdoğan came to power. All mention of alcohol was now banned from the media. These days meyhane, those palimpsests of Byzantine, Ottoman, and republican drinking cultures, felt like an endangered species, hunching under the shadows.

It had been so hopeful for a while. Early on in his ascension, after decades of army interventions and Kemalism's heavy hand, Erdoğan seemed to offer the path to Turkey's democratization and tolerance—a breakthrough model of moderate Islam. And "Istancool," as this city of West and East was dubbed by the international press, was reveling in a hedonistic heyday. I felt smug: *living* in a place everyone was dying to visit. But then the politics darkened. "*Get out! Now!*" my mother pleaded after the 2016 coup attempt rocked the country and the sonic booms of low-flying fighter jets shattered my stairwell's big window. Then came the crackdown on all opposition, purges on a scale that seemed almost Stalinist, the relentless assault on the rights of the Kurds in the country's southeast. But I couldn't abandon this city, its watery poetry and the friendships that were like family here, even if the politics felt so wounding and personal.

I stared again at my IKEA tray, would-be symbol of bygone diversity, now strewn with olive pits and clumps of uneaten cheese. What then of Istanbul's long and often anguished ethnic-religious complexity, under the Byzantines, the Ottomans, Kemalism, and Erdoğan? You could, it occurred to me, find entirely different resonances in the very çilingir meze mosaic I was planning. Tasting the Armenian topik, for example, could summon the cries of women and children as they were being hauled off to the death marches of 1915. Greek taramasalata could evoke the infamous September weekend in 1955 when a whirlwind pogrom drove the last age-old worldly breath out of the city. No, I resolved to myself: we wouldn't

just cook lovely meze and celebrate Istanbul's erstwhile cosmopolitan soul. I would seek out members from the dwindling Rum
(Greek), Jewish, Albanian, and Armenian communities, to draw
out the stories and histories that came with the recipes.

And there was a question that lurked behind it all:

*What happens to the cuisine of a multicultural empire, when it
becomes an aggressively nationalist state?*

ON CONQUERING Constantinople in 1453, twenty-year-old sultan
Mehmed II faced the stark challenge of reviving an emaciated "city
of the world's desire." Europe's largest and grandest metropolis
over many centuries had shrunk to a mere 50,000 inhabitants.
Mehmed's solution was radical and far-reaching. Diverse populations and their skills were brought in, by command if necessary,
from across the Ottoman lands. "Like the spices which arrived in
the city's markets from every corner of the empire," writes historian
Heath Lowry, "the new arrivals brought with them their own flavors and aromas."

To handle its enormous patchwork of subject ethnicities, the
officially Muslim empire developed a distinctive administrative
system of millets (from Arabic, meaning "nation"), which divided
the various followers of religions—Muslims, Jews, Greek Orthodox
Christians, Armenian Apostolic Christians—into self-governing
units. The millets were left to their own rules and infrastructures in
spiritual and social matters, and were allowed their own languages.
A sense of local identity, then, was fitted into an overarching identification as an Ottoman subject. In the fantastically polyglot imperial capital, to be a "Turk" was to be just one of its over seventy

nationalities, and by no means the highest in status. Ara Guler's harsh words weren't new. Until the mid-nineteenth century, "Turk" described country bumpkins from the Anatolian outback "more comfortable astride a donkey," wrote one historian, "than in the sophisticated environs of Istanbul."

By Mehmed's death in 1481, 40 percent of his prized city was non-Muslim, a ratio that prevailed into the early twentieth century—then shrank to 36 percent by the late 1920s, now withered to a fraction of 1 percent.

And there was nothing called "Turkish" cuisine. Until Atatürk willed into being a country called Türkiye, borrowing Turchia, the name, from Medieval Latin.

THESE DAYS OTTOMAN TOLERANCE toward its minorities is often exaggerated, in reaction no doubt to the early republican nationalist fervor for homogenizing the hell out of its diverse population. In reality, until the Ottoman citizenship reforms of 1869, members of non-Islamic millets paid higher taxes and couldn't serve in the army. Their houses couldn't be as large as Muslim houses. They weren't allowed to ride saddled horses. Their meyhane could be closed down in a flash if a Muslim neighbor complained of, say, an imam being dragged in and forced to drink gavur (infidel) wine. Such complaints were common, apparently.

On my way now to talk with our potluck's Sephardic Jewish representative, Deniz Alphan, I recalled a story about Yeni Cami, or New Mosque, whose somber gray bulk dominates the Spice Bazaar neighborhood. Before New Mosque's construction in the early seventeenth century—supposedly to Islamize a commercially valuable Golden Horn port area—this was a dense Jewish merchant quarter replete with a synagogue.

"And not only did Jews not get compensated for their expropriated property," I exclaimed to Deniz when I arrived, "they were *charged rent* on their demolished temple while the mosque was being constructed!"

"A very contemporary situation, my dear," she replied tartly.

In her sixties, vivid of feature and easy to laugh, Deniz, an old dear friend, was hosting me in her airy flat in the very Parisian-looking Nisantasi district. We'd be preparing "some Jewish dishes," she promised. A legendary former newspaper editor, Deniz had written an influential book about Sephardic Turkish cuisine and more recently produced a documentary about Ladino, the Judeo-Spanish language that Turkish Jews had miraculously preserved for five centuries—until today.

Deniz's ancestors came to the Ottoman territories under Sultan Bayezid II, the scholarly son of Mehmed the Conqueror. When Ferdinand and Isabella kicked out Spanish Jews the year Columbus sailed off, Bayezid sent a fleet to their rescue. "You venture to call Ferdinand a wise ruler," the sultan famously quipped, "he who has impoverished his own country and enriched mine!" Indeed. Jews, for example, established Constantinople's first printing press.

"And upon arriving," said Deniz, sounding tickled, "the Jews got a tasty surprise!" Much of Ottoman food must have tasted very familiar. Both fifteenth-century Judeo-Arabic-Spanish cuisine and Ottoman cuisine were heavily influenced by Persian and Arab court cooking. Both had countless eggplant preparations—"Ladino has a poem about 'thirty-six ways to cook eggplant'!"—along with tart flavors from pomegranates and sour plums, loads of savory pastries, and the medieval habit of adding sugar to savory dishes.

"What were Ottoman böreks," exclaimed Deniz, "but Spanish empanadas?"

"Or what are Turkish köfte," I added, "but Spanish albóndigas [meatballs], from Arabic al-bunduq, hazelnut, as I'd learned back in Spain?"

So was it language, then, I wondered, as Deniz led me into her kitchen, that saved Sephardic cuisine from totally blending in with Ottoman (and later Turkish) cooking? Was language a key, a home, an identity? Did a coiled pie Turks know as *gül* (rose) börek taste different when you called it bulemas de carne?

Deniz was showing me now how to make a kind of börek called almodrote de berencena, the dish she'd be bringing to our potluck. It was a fluffy bake of mashed eggplant, eggs, and plenty of kashkaval—a.k.a. "Jewish cheese"—a dish that already shows up in a slightly different version in *Llibre de Sent Soví*, the medieval Catalan cookbook. As Deniz sautéed the creamy pale baked eggplant flesh with pounded garlic and onion, I had a sudden feeling of falling down some culinary historical rabbit hole and emerging in the land of Isabella and Ferdinand. In Catholic Spain, as I'd learned in Seville, eggplant was stereotypically identified as Jewish or Muslim; it even featured in the Inquisition's ethnic profiling of infidels. Most likely almodrote was a Shabbas dish, Deniz confirmed, cooked on Friday to be eaten on Saturday, clandestinely. "The Inquisition," she chortled, "supposedly they could find secret Jews by the sound of the eggplant frying in oil."

Almodrote now in the oven, Deniz offered me lakerda, the fatty salt-cured bonito common to all Istanbul meze trays. "Turkish Jews think it's from Ladino for *la kerida*, or dear one," she noted. "Maybe because they love it so much!"

Then we sat on Deniz's white couch in the living room to watch some of her documentary about Ladino. It was poignantly subtitled "A Fading Language, a Fading Cuisine."

Deniz's mother spoke Ladino at home but French with her sister, Deniz's aunt. Both women had been educated at Alliance Israélite Universelle, one of the schools established in the empire in the 1860s by Jews living in France, with the idea that their backward Ottoman coreligionists were in need of Gallic enlightenment. Deniz was proud of her mom's beautiful French—and embarrassed by her god-awful Turkish. Most Jewish women spoke Turkish badly. For centuries their female progenitors had just stayed at home in their Jewish quarters of Ottoman cities while the men ventured out.

"But those French schools, they weakened Ladino!" Deniz exclaimed. "The Alliance-educated Jews began to snub Ladino speakers."

A worse blow than Francophone snobbery came from Atatürk's insistence on a revamped Turkish—its new Latin script developed, incidentally, by an Armenian—as this long-polyglot land's sole official language. (Nationalistic self-exaltation would reach new heights in the 1930s with the republican pseudoscientific Sun Language Theory, which asserted that all tongues derived from Turkish.) With the "Citizens, Speak Turkish" campaign of 1928, speakers of minority languages now faced harassment or fines or even arrest. "They even Turkified Jewish names," said Deniz. "Cohen became Oz-kohen or Guzel-kohen or Er-kohen."

And the Turkification continued.

In 1934 Deniz's grandparents were forced out of their city, Kirklareli in eastern Turkey, by an organized pogrom known as the Thrace Incidents. Some fifteen thousand Jews fled to Istanbul.

And then came the *varlık vergisi*—the notorious 1942 wealth tax dividing taxpayers into groups by religion, hitting Jews and Armenian and Greek Christians so heavily and disproportionately that fortunes and businesses collapsed overnight. Deniz's grandfather lost almost everything.

"Still," said Deniz, with a smile nevertheless, "there were lots of bright days." Despite all, her parents, like those of so many people I knew here, remained ardent Kemalists, followers and admirers of Atatürk's new vision. "They loved loved loved Atatürk. Myself, I was raised feeling Turkish. My mom, like all Turkish moms, made dolma and pilaf."

We watched more of the Ladino documentary. There were sepia-toned family photo stills, footage of old women preparing labor-intensive holiday dishes—and children lamenting not learning about the food and the language until it was too late.

Deniz sighed. "For the younger generation, who barely speak Ladino at all, the names of the food are their only tangible link to the culture."

A fading culture. Turkish Jews numbered some 81,500 at the birth of the Turkish Republic; today, they're a scant 15,000. After 1948, many people moved to Israel. Even more moved with the fresh political troubles of the seventies.

And now . . . now *everyone* wanted to move.

"Ladino? I guess it's a useless language," said Deniz, with a resigned little grin. "Not even like Yiddish, which has real literature." As for the food, the few remaining kosher butchers in Istanbul were actually Muslim, and for bar mitzvahs Jewish boys insisted on kosher sujuk sausage on their pizza, and kosher kebabs and kosher lahmacun.

"Almodrote de berencena . . ." She nodded at the eggplant bake

puffy-hot from the oven. Another rueful grin. "Who even remembers?"

"WHAT'S IN THE NAME of a dish?" I mused, as the taxi home swung
past the leafy slopes and late-Ottoman pavilions of Yildiz Park,
where that penultimate sultan, the paranoid Abdülhamīd II, re-
treated behind high walls as his empire went bust. Down on the
Bosporus road, traffic crawled past the outsize photographs of
Atatürk fixed to the park's street-side wall, like billboards for a
grand silent-movie star, part Valentino, part Bela Lugosi.

The driver meanwhile had turned up the volume on an Erdoğan
speech on his crackly radio.

"*Memleket neresi, kaptan?*" I shouted over Erdoğan's usual
bombastic harangue. "Where're you from, captain?"

It's a question you ask all Istanbul taxi drivers (as opposed to
asking if there are seat belts, the answer always being no). This kaptan's father, I learned, was from Hatay, a partly Arabic-speaking
region on Turkey's Syrian border known for its brilliant, spicy
cuisine; his mother hailed from Gaziantep, a rival southeastern
food mecca where Turkish is spoken.

"Which food's better?" I shouted.

"Food kinda the same," the driver yelled back. "In Hatay, dishes
have Arabic names, in Gaziantep, Turkish."

"BUT," I yelled louder, "does that change the taste *AT ALL*,
depending on which language is used?"

The driver threw up his hands from the wheel so the taxi almost
swerved into oncoming traffic. "BİLMİYORUM, ABLA? [How
would I know, sister?]" he bellowed, and turned up his radio.

My question wasn't preposterous, though. Taste is not only deeply subjective but also associative, as psycholinguists inform us; hence, advertisers spend millions devising the catchiest labels for sodas or sweets. Names of foods influence flavor perception, so to me a *kebap* (Turkish) will never taste the same as *shashlik* (Russian): the words conjure up different associations and cultural memories.

And so we get gastronationalist food fights.

Recently I'd been to Armenia. In Yerevan I met a middle-aged chef named Sedrak Mamulyan, who, with his starched toque, gregarious mustache, and insistence that even medieval Armenian dishes taste better with Slavic sour cream, was a classic old-school Soviet type. Except he now ran an NGO called Development and Preservation of Armenian Culinary Traditions.

Upon hearing of my Turkish connection, Mamulyan launched into a speech about dolma, stuffed vegetables, a name which most people believe derives from the Turkish *dolmak*, to "fill up." (On my very first visit to Istanbul, I'd found it delightful that dolma shared an etymology with dolmuş, or shared taxi, the battered vintage Chevys and Studebakers stuffed full with sweaty lovers of dolmas.) Mamulyan wagged an angry finger at me. The correct pronunciation, he insisted, was *tolma*. From *toli* ("grape leaf") and *ma*, meaning something like "wrapped" in Urartu, the ancient language of Lake Van proto-Armenians.

I protested meekly that in Turkish stuffed grape leaves, as opposed to, say, tomatoes or peppers, are called sarma—from Turkic for "wrap."

"Nonsense!" snapped Mamulyan, then he diverted to a tirade

against UNESCO's decision to add keshkek—a chicken and pounded wheat stew—to its list of *Turkey's* intangible cultural heritage. "It's *completely* Armenian!!" he thundered, eyes hot with rage. "*Kashi* means to 'pull' and *ka* to 'take out'—and when the whole porridge is cooked and then stirred we call it harissa. From *harel* or 'stir.'"

"Yes, but—but—" I protested again, lost in this etymological mush and remembering faintly that the word harissa was actually Persian. "Wheat porridges like keshkek—and harissa—are extremely ancient, Mesopotamian possibly. Cooked long before Armenia as a country even existed."

"*Armenia*," corrected Mamulyan, with great dignity, "has *always* existed."

Of course for UNESCO's designation of lavash bread as *Armenia's* intangible heritage, he had nothing but praise. Never mind that Turkey, Azerbaijan, Iran, Kazakhstan, and Kyrgyzstan instantly launched a joint nomination request to register lavash as *their* common heritage. "We Lost Lavash to Armenia," and "They Appropriated Our National Bread," ran the Turkish press headlines.

But who owns a recipe, really?

I thought once again about the "problematic obviousness" of national food cultures. Perhaps it was easy enough to define one in Mexico with its unique singular moles, or France, which pretty much invented this very idea. And who'd ever dispute pizza's Neapolitan origins? But modern Turkey belonged to a vast geographical region where people cooked similar foods centuries before nation-states came into being. The collapse of the Austro-Hungarian and

Ottoman empires, and more recently the USSR, created over four dozen new nations; some had nothing remotely resembling a previous national consciousness, let alone a distinct cuisine. So whose hummus was it? Whose baklava or dolma? Whose demitasse of dark sugary coffee: Türk, Bosanska (Bosnian), Kypriakos (Cypriot), or Elliniko (Greek)? The current storms in a coffee cup over ownership of keshkek or lavash—weren't they serving as fledgling proxies for deeper, much stormier geopolitical conflicts?

So really, UNESCO, what were you thinking when recently awarding dolma to *Azerbaijan*, Armenia's formerly friendly fellow Soviet republic turned mortal enemy after the Nagorno-Karabakh conflict erupted in the nineties (and reerupted just recently). Upon learning the dolma news I could just imagine the glee on the face of my Azeri acquaintance Tahir Amiraslanov, author of a book charmingly titled *Culinary Kleptomania: How Armenians Plagiarized Azeri Cuisine* with a preface by Azerbaijan's kleptocratic president, Ilham Aliyev.

"National food cultures," anthropologist Mary Douglas once wrote, "become a blinding fetish which, if disregarded, may be as dangerous as an explosion."

BUT THEN WHAT *DOES* happen to the cuisine of a multiethnic, wide-spanning entity with no use for nationalism, when it becomes a *national* food culture?

Given the intensive social engineering of the Turkish Republic's early decades, I expected a feast of ideological policy details—the ingredients for a grand theory, maybe. *Food as a mirror of post-Ottoman Turkish identity.*

"So what happened to cuisine in the republican era?"

I shot my eager question at Zafer Yenal, an important sociologist who writes about such matters.

"Umm . . . umm . . ." mumbled Zafer. My question had caught him with his mouth full of Gamze's tart yogurt dip flourished with burnt sheep's butter and walnuts. We were on her terrace with its sweeping Bosporus–meets–Golden Horn vista; she was throwing a kind of pre-potluck rehearsal dinner.

Zafer swallowed. "Nothing really," he said.

"*Nothing?*"

"National cuisines . . ." He shrugged, glancing longingly at Gamze's majestic whole sea bass. "Ever read Sidney Mintz on the subject?"

I had. Mintz, an American anthropologist and author of the seminal book *Sweetness and Power*, argued that a national cuisine is a "holistic artifice"—a construct, essentially, as I knew so well from my own journey, based on food found within the scope of a particular political system and defined by a specific community characterized by common cultural features.

"But that's my point," I said. "What happened to Turkey's cuisine after the huge change in *its* political system?"

"I read your book about Soviet food," Zafer replied. "Crazy how those Soviets turned even food into a top-down political project. But here in Turkey?"

Nothing like that happened in Turkey.

"I'm afraid, dear Anya," concluded Zafer, whose grandly Ottomanesque mustache gave him the look of a kindly intellectual janissary. "I'm afraid you're chasing a phantom." He said it very gently, as if breaking some terrible news.

Meanwhile a different conversation was taking place between

Zafer's wife, Biray, herself a sociologist, and our dear friends Armine and Ihsan, a young Armenian-Kurdish couple. Armine and Ihsan were leaving Turkey for an extended while—such were the chilling effects of Turkey's *current* political system. Armine's boss, an internationally known "Red Millionaire" who ran a number of progressive NGOs, had been arrested on preposterous charges. The human rights journalist from whom I'd bought my apartment had spent months in jail. With tears in her eyes, Biray talked of the existential dilemma she and people in our liberal circle were facing. Stay and risk prison, or forsake all *this*. She gestured at the panorama beyond us. The last of the sun cast a gold-orange gloss on the Bosporus and the mouth of the Golden Horn; Aya Sofia loomed in profile next to Topkapi's Ottoman turret. Northward up the Bosporus, fairy lights lit up the bridge linking continents. "All this, and for what? An exile in some German or American university town?"

Our terrace table fell silent.

The next day Zafer emailed me some of his articles. Does baklava have a national identity? wondered one. Answer: "Such a question is utter nonsense."

But another article, titled "'Cooking' the Nation," offered a partial response to my particular question. In it Zafer examined the Girls' Institutes established at the beginning of the republic and popular still well into the 1970s. These vocational schools were a part of the radical Kemalist reforms replacing Sharia law with the Swiss civil code, outlawing polygamy, banning headscarves at public institutions, granting women equal rights in divorce, in voting, in property—all meant to turn young Turkish women into members of the contemporary "Western world." Or into "educated housewives" at least. By midcentury the institutes' home economics and cooking curriculum was extremely westernized: chocolate pudding, fish with mayonnaise, schnitzel, roast beef with spinach pasta, along with nifty tricks to Europeanize and lighten up Turkish dishes.

To Zafer this showed that for Turkey's republican ideologues the modernizing of women meant westernization of the *domestic* as well as public sphere. In contrast, new postcolonial nationalisms, such as India's, were faulted by feminist scholars for treating home and hearth as principal venues of a national culture's traditional qualities—with women as keepers of the "inner spirituality of indigenous life."

But none of the schnitzels and tarts taught at the institutes to upper- and middle-class ladies made it into any "national" food canon. How come?

*So what happened to food in the republican era?"*

Professor Özge Samancı, considered the world's foremost expert in nineteenth-century Ottoman cuisine, looked up from her manti. We were eating these teensy dumplings cloaked with rich, creamy buffalo yogurt at a hip New Anatolian spot at the very Dubaiesque Kanyon shopping mall.

"*Nothing* much happened . . ." came the answer again.

By the end of the empire, Özge explained, the cuisine of the Ottoman elites was already pretty westernized—or was a fusion at least of *alafranga* (foreign and modern) and *alaturka* (Eastern old-fashioned). "The menus of Atatürk's state banquets and the late-Ottoman court banquets were surprisingly similar!"

This sort of made sense . . . Atatürk's sweeping westernization appeared less revolutionary when you considered the Ottoman modernizing reforms known as the Tanzimat (Reorganization), enacted between the 1830s and 1870s to counter the empire's alarming military and economic decline—and formulated, as with Atatürk, on European models.

Culturally, Özge went on, the Tanzimat ushered in an appetite for all things *alafranga*—"in clothing, food, art, interior decorating." Exhibit A: in 1856 the Ottoman dynasty abandoned its low-slung palace of Topkapi for Dolmabahçe, an insanely expensive alafranga-heavy lollapalooza on the Bosporus shore right by my house. For centuries the Ottomans sat cross-legged, eating with their hands around moveable sofra trays. Now they showed off dining tables, cutlery, and white Dresden-ware porcelain—and *frenk aşçıbaşı* (foreign chefs) alongside traditional Ottoman cooks. The new palace's first official banquet—to celebrate the Crimean war victory—was an alafranga-alaturka mashup: börek and dainty French pastries, baklava and *croustade d'ananas*, pilafs and *foie gras à la Lucullus*. Among the dishes, I noted excitedly, was *suprême de faisan à la circassian*—a fancy pheasant version of the Circassian chicken on my çilingir potluck menu.

Dolmabahçe's foodways trickled down to wealthy homes and to the patisseries, cafés, and restaurants of Istanbul's longtime European district of Pera (now Beyoğlu). Late-Ottoman cookbooks brimmed with pâtés, crèmes (krema), biscuits (biskuvi), and grilled cutlets—like so many nineteenth-century cookbooks, from Mexico to Poland to Egypt, all products of the worldwide Frenchification at table.

Suddenly I noticed that Özge seemed distracted by something. "Weird, come to think of it," she puzzled over her sour cherry–soaked bread pudding. "How *no one* here works on republican-period cuisine . . . I know this because I supervise all the dissertations . . ."

. . .

$B$ut how could it be, I kept on puzzling for my part, that a radical young republic that dictated to New Turks as to religion, language, music, hygiene, hats, calendar, clocks, how could it have left food out of its social-engineering agenda? Stalin had a food commissar, Mikoyan, an Armenian who sponsored a socialist-realist kitchen bible and established a centralized recipe system called GOST. Mussolini, no foodie, staged his famous *Battaglia del Grano* campaign, the Battle for Grain, to liberate Italians from foreign wheat slavery. Il Duce even penned a terrible poem, "Amate il Pane" ("Love Bread"), and urged Italian women to cook cheaply and locally.

And yet any Google digging into "Atatürk + food" mostly yielded descriptions of dining facilities at the erstwhile Atatürk Airport. (Which filled me with sadness: that old ramshackle hub had just been replaced with Erdoğan's new faraway megacolossus, which had required the destruction of a forest.) Indeed, the venerated and beloved Father Turk, who personally modeled Western ways to set an example, himself "took no interest in food, eating what came," according to one biographer, "with a preference for such plain peasant dishes as dried beans and pilaf."

True, Atatürk's preferred plain kuru fasulye bean stew came as close as Turkey has to a national dish, served at schools and cooked at many homes on his death day, November 10. But did Atatürk ever *promote* it in his writings and speeches? Where were republican food policies on school lunches or army rations, the kind of details that seem insignificant but actually help forge a national food consciousness? Unlike most other countries, Turkey didn't even have anything resembling a foundational cookbook that created "imagined communities"—perhaps because the contenders, those popular late-Ottoman kitchen bibles full of alafranga-alaturca recipe tips, weren't translated into modern Turkish until the 1980s. Amazingly, there wasn't a cookbook with "Turkish" in its title until the 1970s.

Was there *no* history, then? Or no historiography? Why *weren't* Turkish scholars, as Özge attested, writing about the cuisine of the hugely transformative republican era?

The main obstacle, it turned out?

There were no archives.

"*No archives?*"

I sat in astonishment under the slow-stirring fans of a battered, historic meyhane festooned with Atatürk paraphernalia and old-timey raki bottles, in the company of a young professor named Işıl Çokuğraş. Işıl had spent a fruitless year chasing documents for a book about republican-era beer halls, which she finally abandoned to write a study of eighteenth-century meyhane instead. "Because where taxes on alcohol were concerned," she explained, "the Ottomans at least kept their accounting ledgers in order. Very taxation-centric, those Ottomans."

"*But no republican archives?*" I muttered on, gripping my head. "*None?*"

"Look, Anya!" said Işıl. "Turks have a different, non-Occidental, relationship to written knowledge."

I thought of France and its relentless abundance of gastroencyclopedic treatises and literary gastrophilosophizing . . .

Using a VPN that evening—the current Turkish relationship to knowledge includes banning Wikipedia; and more darkly, leading the world in jailed journalists—I reeled at the combination I found of censorship, erasure of history, and sheer neglect. It wasn't just the destruction of archives relating to the Armenian genocide. It was the fifty tons of Ottoman documents sold as scrap paper in 1931—to Bulgaria. The "confidential documents" of the Ministry of Foreign Affairs discovered in the late nineties at a scrap-paper dealer in Ankara. The "accidental destruction" of state senate archives from 1960 to 1980. The Directorate of Republican Archives? Established only in 1976—over half a century after the republic's founding. No wonder, the liberal *Radikal* newspaper once wrote, professors couldn't find graduate students willing to research the twentieth century overall. *Radikal* itself? Shut down in 2016, along with numerous other liberal media outlets—and now almost forgotten.

A CHEERILY AEGEAN RESTAURANT named Mezedaki sat between SushiCo and BurgerLab in a flashy mall complex called Uniq, which sat in turn in a leafy zone by the construction-boom skyscrapers clogging Maslak, one of Istanbul's prime new business areas on the European side. It wasn't exactly a site to inspire postempire hüzün.

But it was in the spirit of recovering memory—and collecting some Greek meze recipes to feature in my potluck project—that I came here to meet Mezedaki's proprietor, Meri Çevik Simyonidis.

In her fifties, self-assured and auburn haired, a journalist as well as a restaurateur, Meri is a member of Istanbul's tiny Rum (Greek) community, the so-called Polites, short for Konstantinoupolites. Less than 2,000 remained from the more than 300,000 who made up a quarter of Istanbul's population before World War I—and accounted for the vast majority of the city's commerce.

Meri became immersed in the food and history of the Polites while working at the Greek consulate here back in the aughts. People approached her spontaneously with their recipes and reminiscences—to "transfer the food and the memories to the next generation," as she put it, "and talk about the tragedy of forced migrations." She had published two books of interviews and profiles of Rum taverna, meyhane, and patisserie owners. That is to say, the *entire* restaurant culture of Istanbul before 1955, which was 90 percent Greek.

At Mezedaki now, she'd brought along her nephew, Ari, an earnest NYU student home for the holidays. Between them they'd start a sentence in demotic Greek—the language of Polites—and finish in Turkish, or vice versa. Then Ari would laboriously translate to English for me.

Meri followed her first book with a volume of interviews with the Rums who left after 1955 and settled in Greece. Baylan, Inci, Savoy, Bahar . . . she tossed off names of pastry shops I patronized almost daily for their dainty alafranga cookies, sponge cakes, and chocolate bonbons.

"All Greek?" I exclaimed.

"They *were*, before the *katastrofi*."

Meri and Ari repeated that word a lot: katastrofi. Also known in Greek as Septemvriana or Exodus, it meant Turkey's Kristallnacht, the pogrom against Istanbul's Rums that exploded on the night of September 6–7, 1955. Nationalist Turkish mobs ran amok pillaging and terrorizing Greek-owned businesses, churches, schools, houses. More than thirty people were killed, hundreds raped. By daylight, Beyoğlu's bustling thoroughfare, Istiklal Avenue, a ten-minute climb from my apartment, was a smashed, acrid sea of devastation.

The rioting was an apparently spontaneous frenzy at the news (false) of a bombing at Atatürk's birthplace in Thessaloníki (part of Greece since 1913). Tensions were already raw between Turkey and Greece over competing claims regarding the island of Cyprus. But it became clear the mobs were at least partly organized and that Prime Minister Adnan Menderes was complicit, though to what extent is still debated. At any rate, Menderes and two ministers were hanged in 1960. Thirty years later, Turkey's parliament absolved the three of all guilt and gave them a ceremonial state reinterment.

The katastrofi's most lasting damage, according to Aykan Erdemir, a Turkish commentator, was to the ideal of equal citizenship in Turkey—"not only for the *Polites* but also for the country's other non-Muslim minorities."

Istanbul's Rums began to leave. In 1923 they'd been exempted from the population exchange between Greece and the brand-new nation-state of Turkey mandated by the Treaty of Lausanne. Based solely on religion, 1.5 million Greeks were expelled from Turkey; half a million Turks likewise from Greece. All were sent to "home" countries entirely foreign to them.

In Athens, I'd heard this forced resettling described as a foundational twentieth-century trauma: a first katastrofi. Besides the great suffering, the transfer swelled Greece's population by over 20 percent, as cosmopolitan people from cities like Smyrna (Izmir), with their bourgeois culture and cooking, flooded into a then-backward land. Turks hardly mentioned the population exchange, however. To them it was another migration in an era of mass migrations. Atatürk's legacy has constructed a triumphalist narrative of the nation's foundation. Meanwhile, the Greek view of history: a litany of grievances and historic injustices.

"*Sent away from Turkey like Greeks and received in Greece*

*like Turks . . ."* At Mezedaki, Meri repeated this well-worn summary of forced shifts. Only she was referring to a multiplicity of migrations, post-1955, and then post-1964, when more Greeks had left after another dispute over Cyprus. What broke Meri's heart, Ari translated awkwardly, was interviewing Rums in exile in Athens. "Always strangers. Doubly alienated." This "second trauma" startled Meri the most. "Often there were such tears of joy," she recalled, "when people talked about their beautiful childhoods in Konstantinoupoli." (That's how Greeks still call Istanbul, the former Byzantium that got taken away in 1453—but remains the seat of the nominal head of the Eastern Orthodox Church and retains an everlasting hold on the whole Hellenic psyche.)

More than anything there were the *whys*.

*Giati?* in Greek. *Neden?* in Turkish. *Why??*

*Why* did heartbroken Istanbul Polites have to abandon their seat of great empires, to leave behind the Aya Sofia for a former cowtown dominated by a strange alien ruin?

Our meze arrived. "A cultural mosaic of Istanbul!" declared Meri, of the familiar constellation of tastes encoded in Istanbul's DNA—the very same meze from our own potluck çilingir tray. Here were sarmdakia, a Rum rendition of sarma, stuffed grape leaves, bright with lemon and herbs. Here were several types of zeytinyağlı, the "olive oil vegetables"—classically Lenten specialties of Christian millets. Armenian topik showed up beside Albanian liver and Circassian chicken. Meri pointed to the "possibly Byzantine" tarama, the "probably Jewish" lakerda, the "definitely Hellenic-Aegean" fava bean mash.

Could one even begin, I asked, shaking my head, to truly untangle the origins?

*"Hepsi karışık."* Meri smiled in agreement. "All mixed up." The

identity markers, if any, were religious. The abundant meatless dishes such as yalanci (liar's) dolma stuffed with grain were Lenten fare; Muslims used meat. The insistence on olive oil was non-Muslim, as opposed to clarified butter. The traditional profusion of un-halal shellfish was from the tables of Rums and Armenians.

"But wait—was there even such a *thing* then as distinctive 'Rum cooking'?"

I had the sudden anxious feeling I might be chasing another phantom.

Meri shrugged introspectively. "A subtle savor, perhaps. A somewhat distinct table culture . . ." Rums covered their tables at home with meze, whereas Armenians ate meze at meyhane. Armenians, maybe they favored spices where Greeks might prefer a little more herbs. But then again: "Cinnamon, sugar, lemon, those were the three pillars of Istanbul Rum cooking—plus rivers of olive oil."

"And the Rums who left, were they angry?" I asked, going back to that topic. "Did they hate Turks?"

"No, no, they were *nostalgic*!" Meri insisted. "Filled with a terrible longing that overwhelmed them!"

Her books were not meant to assign blame or to point fingers. Rather, she wanted to heal: "To show how much Istanbullus, too, suffered from this rupture."

When the katastrofi occurred, Meri's mother and her uncle were young; a Turkish neighbor hid them and Meri's grandmother in her attic "à la Anne Frank." I'd heard many such stories, stories of the "good Turks" standing up to the angry mobs with "There are no Rums. We are all Turks here." Many Istanbullus still believed the rioters were mostly bused in. When the Greek exodus began, Meri's grandmother was too poor to leave. She waited things out and gradually life went back to normal. Except that it hadn't. Come

1964, thousands of remaining Greeks were outright deported with "twenty dollars and twenty kilos of luggage." More left in 1974 after the Turkish army entered northern Cyprus.

Istanbul's Greeks were the public face of the city: its florists and tailors, its hoteliers and waiters and restaurateurs. They were Istanbul's cultural bridge between East and West, importers of alafranga fashions and food mores—the creators of *atmósfaira*, the cosmopolitan atmosphere. They fished in the Bosporus, filled the street with the twang of bouzouki, presided over glamorous displays of profiteroles and éclairs at patisseries. Since early Ottoman days, they were also Istanbul's chief meyhaneci, or tavern keepers.

Without Rums, it suddenly occurred to me, there *would* be no çilingir meze trays.

"Come, let's go visit my elderly Turkish friend Fistik Ahmet," Meri proposed. "A day doesn't pass still that he doesn't talk of the trauma. How his neighborhood was suddenly emptied of laughter. How overnight all his childhood friends were gone. He's never stopped mourning."

Giritli in Sultanahmet; Zorba Taverna in Gayrettepe . . . just a handful of the old Rum places remained. They, and the memories of beautiful waitresses named Eleni or Zoe, and gregarious chefs named Kostas or Giorgos roasting aromatic spring lamb for Easter.

*Giati? Neden?* repeated Meri. Why? echoed young Ari.

AS DAYS WENT BY and summer thunderstorms threw wild curtains of rain over the Bosporus and my roof began to leak yet again, my own whys kept piling up—a cascading series of them. My potluck had started out as a clever tactic, really, to throw a nice get-together and probe the deeper narratives of various Istanbul dishes. But it had plunged me into a landscape of longing and cultural cleansing, a terrain shadowed with dark and darker memories.

On a muggy late afternoon, I decided to ride the tram across the Galata Bridge to Topkapi Palace—for respite, and perhaps to glean some fresh insights from the gilded vestiges of the Ottoman past.

The abode of sultans looked nothing like the melancholy sprawl I'd encountered on my first visit to Istanbul. Its pavilions and jasmine-scented gardens now sparkled with restored beauty. Thanks to a wildly popular Turkish telenovela, *The Magnificent Century*, about Sultan Süleyman the Magnificent and his scheming wife, Roxelana, the grounds were mobbed with Roxelanaphiles from Moldova, Azerbaijan, and Ukraine. I entered the ten-domed Matbah-ı Amire, the Imperial Kitchen. After a long renovation it had reopened with much neo-Ottoman pomp and now resembled a very expensive dinnerware showroom: lustrous celadonware, goblets scooped from whole pieces of turquoise, the jeweled hoşaf (compote) bowls adored by the ladies of the imperial harem. How graceful they looked compared with the neo-rococo alafranga stuff transferred here from the Dolmabahçe Palace.

I found a bit of space for myself amid the Second Courtyard's flowerbeds and gazed at the restored Matbah's tall rhythmic chimneys, designed by the Michelangelo of Ottoman architects, Mimar Sinan. What does a palace kitchen tell us about power? Why was this particular kitchen such a strikingly monumental facility, in a palace whose squat pavilions and kiosks resembled, fancifully, a series of stony encampments—a nod to the Ottomans' nomadic past? Why did the sultans, who completely secluded themselves after conquering Constantinople to express the new absolutism of their power—who ate alone but for deafened and muted servants with whom they communicated in sign language—why did these secluded sultans put on some of the world's most lavish and efficient spectacles of hospitality?

And it wasn't just the feasts the Matbah threw in the capital. From Belgrade to Baghdad the Ottomans set up vast purpose-built soup kitchens called imarets, which were savvily bureaucratized charity food institutions often feeding five hundred comers a day. In newly conquered lands the imarets showed, and showed off, the benevolent face of Ottoman colonization. The menus were pretty much identical: rice soup for breakfast, bulgur wheat soup for supper, always chickpeas and bread, honeycombs as a welcome, mutton on Friday, zerde rice pudding for dessert. All was distributed free to "fire-worshippers and heathens, Christians, Jews, Copts, Europeans . . . even Gypsies and the destitute," as the famous seventeenth-century Ottoman traveler Evliya Çelebi observed.

There is, of course, no such thing as a truly free lunch; hospitality ensnares recipients in a spider's web of obligation and gratitude. The Ottomans knew this. They conquered by the sword, but legitimized and manipulated their power through soup.

I drifted out through the Imperial Gate in the purple-pink twilight. It was the last days of Ramadan. Banners proclaiming "Ramadan Is Sharing" twinkled between the minarets of the Blue Mosque. On the main square of the historic Sultanahmet district, the AKP, Erdoğan's party, had set up long iftar (fast-breaking) tables. A few years ago, a government-sponsored public iftar would have utterly scandalized Atatürk's secularist republic; even in Ottoman days iftars were hosted by private individuals or by mosques. Now the AKP was showing Istanbullus who exactly buttered their bread— neo-Ottoman style—except that the wrong half of the city was no longer invited. Maybe the early republican leaders failed to exploit the power of food. But Erdoğan—he who sold simit bread rings as a boy, and had now revived the sultanic practice of having his meals tested for poison—doesn't miss any such opportunity. He lectures on the merits of köy ekmek (country bread) and declares that Turkey's national drink is no longer raki but rather the salty thin yogurt-based ayran (a declaration causing a huge spike in Turkish dairy stocks). During election rallies, he promises to build cafés serving free tea and cake.

As I approached it now, I realized that the AKP iftar was in fact an *invitation-only* affair, completely violating the "sharing" Ramadan principle. Curious, I mumbled *gazeteci* ("journalist") and slipped inside a VIP tent. Fleshy AKP matrons in shiny polyester hijabs fixed unbenevolent gazes on my uncovered head. Feeling doubly a gate-crasher, I picked at the Ramadan dates and bread, skipped the lentil soup, chickpeas, and pilaf, then found my way to another, more populist iftar, where large trucks unloaded mountains of boxed Ramadan meals with conspicuous efficiency.

Soup, bread, pilaf, beans, rice pudding, cheese, olives . . . Was *this* it, then? The *milli yemek*, the national meal, all shrink-wrapped in plastic?

National for half the nation, that is.

*You ate Erdoğan's dates and bread?"*

At a cocktail gathering of fooderati the following evening, my friends were howling at me as I recounted my iftar adventures. So much for the idea of food as a binding benevolence between people.

I wanted to understand something about *türk mutfagi*, Turkish cuisine, I bleated.

*Türk mutfagi?* Civan Er, a young chef known for his smart

modern meze, winced at my words. The adjective "Turk," he informed me, was politically incorrect and reactionarily Kemalist, leaving out Laz, Armenians, Abkhazians, Bosnians, Jews—*especially* Kurds.

I blinked hard at the handsome, thoughtful Civan, incredulous but somehow not surprised. Yes, this was Turkey, where even an obvious term could harbor a witches' brew of identity politics.

"So how would you call the cuisine of this country where you live?"

"*Türkiyeli*," replied Civan. "*Of* Turkey."

This adjective, I later discovered, was already proposed to describe citizenship during the republic's foundation, but then lost out to the more aggressively nationalist "Türk." Türkiyeli resurfaced again—as a political statement among young progressives—in the liberalizing nineties, when conversation around identity was opening up and multiculturalism became à la mode.

"Me, I prefer *Anadolu*, 'of Anatolia,'" put in another young chef. "Actually," he added, "*New Anatolian*."

An older, imperious cookbook author drew me aside. She's the kind of hard-core nationalist who calls Kurds "Mountain Turks" and bristles at any mention of the "Armenian issue." "Don't listen to them," she instructed. "*All* our dishes are *Turkish*. And I get so *angry*," she moaned fiercely, "that Chobani—owned by a Turk!—markets *our* yogurt as *Greek* all over America!"

I thought it best not to point out that Hamdi Ulukaya, Chobani's founder, is Kurdish.

FOR EVERY GASTRONATIONALIST claim of *my* yogurt, *my* baklava, there's a universalist counterclaim that all foods belong to all people. Both arguments are in their way fictions, as I'd learned, mythologies created by the different imagined communities. In Istanbul my liberal friends, the tribe of the Türkiyeli persuasion, often repeated an identical phrase: *There are no nations in food, only geographies.* Where did this oft-repeated homily come from? I kept wondering. Then one day Gamze told me.

"It's from my Armenian friend Takuhi Tovmasyan," she said, "the one who'll be bringing topik to our potluck."

The one who in 2004 had written a slim, much-loved book called *Sofranız Şen Olsun*—May Your Table Be Jolly.

*I do not know*, begins Takuhi's fairy tale–like food memoir, *to what extent these dishes are Armenian, to what extent Greek, to what extent Turkish, to what extent Albanian, to what extent Circassian, to what extent Patriyot, to what extent Gypsy. But there is one thing I know and it is that I have learned these recipes from my Akabi and Takuhi yayas . . . my grandmothers.*

Takuhi's yayas both hailed from Çorlu, a small city west of Istanbul, where Armenians cooked food strikingly different, nevertheless, from their great-city brethren, and more different still from the foods of what eventually became the post-Soviet Republic of Armenia on the other side of Turkey. Takuhi herself grew up in Istanbul, in Yedikule (Seven Towers), an ancient neighborhood on the city's southern Marmara seashore, dominated by the crumbling fifth-century Theodosian walls that once protected Byzantine Constantinople. Today Yedikule is poor and deeply Muslim, but back in Takuhi's mid-twentieth-century childhood, it was a thriving place resounding with Greek and Armenian voices. Before the new year its sloping streets would reek of onions from Armenian matriarchs caramelizing mountains of them, a key ingredient for topik, the sine qua non of their holiday tables. Summers, Yedikule turned smoky from barbecued mackerel—çiroz (air-cured fish) drying on lines by fishermen's houses. The midye (mussels) were so abundant in the Marmara Sea, you gathered them just by sticking your hands in the water—then made midye dolma filled with sweetly spiced rice, currants, and pine nuts.

Slowly cooked onions, mackerel, the aroma of allspice . . . the old Armenian households of Istanbul.

In her book, which I devoured in an evening, Takuhi writes of the priests who shared recipe tips with the ladies during Armenian potlucks called "Can/Sevgi Yemekleri" (Soul/Love Dinners). Of her father, Bedros—a real Yedikuleli, a Yedikule gentleman—grating big bars of soap into water on laundry days while the women prepared fasulye paçası, a "bean trotter" stew. For the Virgin's Assumption, Akabi Yaya decorated the "petaluda" cookies with grapes that children were forbidden to touch until the last Sunday in August. Come Christmas the Tovmasyans sent anuşabur, their cinnamon-scented ritual wheat pudding, to their Greek neighbors, the Apostolakis. The Rums returned the plate, as tradition dictated, with their own Christmas sweet, while the families exchanged *bereket* (blessings) for wealth and abundance.

Then suddenly the Apostolakis went away. And nothing ever tasted the same. "Not the dried apricots or figs or jujubes . . . Not the Olimpos brand lemonade they'd spike with vermouth . . ."

Behind Takuhi's charming fairy-tale evocations of a world that will never return, there hover—purposefully elliptical but vivid to the right readers—the crimes of actual history.

Just beyond the Byzantine gates of Yedikule, Takuhi's grandfather Gazaros Efendi ran a meyhane where the whole neighborhood gathered for raki and meze prepared by Takuhi Yaya, his wife. The wealth tax of 1942 led to such crushing debt that he was forced to sell his beloved meyhane after the Second World War. From heartbreak and stress, he suffered a stroke, eventually dying paralyzed and bedridden.

And then deeper and darker: when Takuhi Yaya had accepted the marriage proposal of Gazaros Efendi, a widower, he told her of his two children. Only on their wedding night did she learn of a third, a toddler boy named Mardik. Takuhi Yaya was livid. "You said you had two children and I accepted them," she told her new husband. "If you'd said three, I'd have accepted that, too. But I wish you didn't trick me!" And so little toddler Mardik, the trick one, the undisclosed third child, was sent off to live with his grandparents in Çorlu.

It was 1915. The Ottoman tehcir (deportations) were about to begin.

That year, amid the upheaval of World War I, leaders of the collapsing Ottoman state unleashed an ethnic cleansing campaign against Armenians, everywhere except for Constantinople. Accusation: traitorous Armenians planned to join enemy Russia in destroying the empire. Armenians were tortured, drowned, executed in mass graves. During death marches into the Syrian desert, they perished in unspeakable numbers. By war's end, close to a million Armenians had died in one of the first mass atrocities of the twentieth century, widely recognized as the "Armenian genocide." Recognized everywhere, that is, but in Turkey, where it's been deleted from official history: made mute.

How do you talk about such a traumatic past in a society that denies that past's existence? A society where schoolkids are taught that Armenians betrayed their generous Ottoman hosts? Where

Armenian schools and churches have been systematically destroyed, parents too scared to reveal to their children their Armenian heritage?

I met Takuhi, finally, at the farewell party for our departing Kurdish-Armenian friends, Ihsan and Armine. Green-eyed, her gray hair styled short, she radiated a kind of regally modest grace. I admired the Armenian anuşabur ritual wheat pudding she'd brought. "It's Armenian only in name," she corrected me gently. "Turks call it aşure, Greeks kolliva, Georgians gorgot." I asked about the memoir, and she told me she'd never set out to write a heartbreaking book, or even to publish one at all. "I intended a scrapbook of stories and family recipes," she said very softly, "to pass down to my children." But as she wrote, the tears came, the words turned into something else.

"They turned into a mevlet, a prayer, for the souls of those who departed."

Around Takuhi's family table, even without explicit design, those who had passed on were commemorated through their favorite foods. And so her memoir's little recipe chapters are eulogies: to Gazaros Efendi and his favorite bean pilaki, to Uncle Yeğya, who loved çullama (chicken pastry), to Uncle Krikor, fancier of eggplant kebab with garlicky yogurt.

And having endured the tribulations of 1915, Takuhi wrote, "some forgot what had happened on the roads of exile. Some never talked about it, came to terms with it, or pretended to come to terms with it." And some, like her uncle Yeğya, "had never forgotten it, never came to terms with it, and left this world just like that."

Little Mardik, the toddler who was sent away, vanished in

the deportations of 1915. Haunted by grief and remorse, Takuhi Yaya searched for him for the rest of her life. When she died at eighty, still brokenhearted, her quest and trauma were passed on to Takuhi's parents, Bedros and Maria. All *their* lives they looked in vain for Mardik, for news of him. The voices and recipes in the book, Takuhi told me now, were not hers: "I just channeled my relatives."

But the very last recipe in the book belongs to Takuhi herself. It's the recipe for irmik helva, the semolina sweet that one roasts for the souls of the dead. "Refusing to accept he was truly gone, my older family members never made irmik helva for little Mardik," she said to me, her sad, serene words almost drowned out by the party chatter.

"I finally made the helva myself and said a prayer for him. I put little Mardik to rest. So I don't have to pass on the trauma of loss and guilt to my children."

TAKUHI'S MEMOIR ENDS with helva, but it begins with topik.

In Turkish, topik means "little ball": a mashed chickpea dumpling filled with sweetly spiced onions and pine nuts then boiled in a muslin cloth that, by legend, every Armenian girl had in her dowry. But, as Takuhi noted to me, topik's original Armenian name is more noble: vardapet ("priest"). Before migrating to Istanbul as a meze, it was a Lenten main course at Armenian monasteries in Eastern Anatolia.

I still remember my own first topik encounter in the mid-1990s. It was at Boncuk, a raucous Beyoğlu meyhane that proudly advertised itself as Armenian. Back then I hadn't a clue that a fashion for those nostalgically inclusive meze trays, along with a new interest in minorities' cultures, along with a revival of Ottoman cooking and heritage—all were products of the political and social liberalization kick-started the previous decade by a man named Turgut Özal.

A devout, at least partly Kurdish Muslim and an ardent evangelist of free markets, the portly, exuberant Özal led Turkey as prime minister and then president from 1983 until his unexpected death in 1993—a death variously ascribed to poisoning (by the Kemalist "deep state"?) or a heart attack from consuming an entire roast lamb during a tour of Central Asia. Gluttony is an apt metaphor for the neoliberal Özalist era. But he is remembered for more profound doings: bringing Islam back into public life, privatizing Turkey's lumbering state-owned industries to unleash the floodgate of global commodity capitalism (and massive corruption). Another turning point was a full-blown reassessment of Ottoman history, though unlike Erdoğan's narrow and aggressive Islamicist vision, Özal's Ottomania was more pragmatic and inclusive by far. More Ottoman. Which is how a whole bouquet of previously repressed identities was readmitted as part of Turkey's vibrant new openness in the age of globalization—readmitted and packaged, as sociologist Yael Navaro puts it, "to assume a commodity form." (That familiar refrain of commodification . . .)

After decades of forced amnesia and taboos (on religion, ethnicity, imperial history), young urban types began feverishly pulling family photos from attics, or rummaging through antique shops of newly gentrified Christian enclaves for mementoes left behind by those purged and exiled. Albanian and Circassian cultural associations sprang up, along with Greek and Armenian publishing houses. Now the very minorities formerly branded as betrayers of the Turkish nation-state were being celebrated—up to a point—as a nostalgic cultural asset, part of Brand Istanbul, vital to its new global image as a tolerant, pluralistic neo-Ottoman paradise.

Which brings us back to topik.

The dish was featured on those "mosaic of Istanbul" meze trays of Beyoğlu meyhane that so enchanted me in the newly *nostaljik* nineties, as all around me mansions, covered arcades, and cafés were being restored to show off the Beyoğlu belle epoque glamour of yore.

"Topik . . ."

Takuhi the memoirist smiled warily. Apparently topik became such a hit among the young cosmopolitans that a local Armenian artist published an irreverent little book of cartoons called *Ben Topik Değilim*—I Am Not Topik. It summed up the Armenian sentiment, said Takuhi. About all those nice newly liberal yuppies showing their open-mindedness by praising Armenian food, and by insisting that their aunts always drank cherry liqueur with Armenian neighbors—here in a country where the mention of genocide still remained a transgression, and the history of discrimination was never officially acknowledged.

"Topik and cherry liqueur . . ." Takuhi repeated quietly. "An entire culture, a past, reduced to this pair of stereotypes . . ."

AS THE EVENING of our potluck drew near, I found myself thinking more and more about the cosmopolitan nostalgia cult, that particular form of Istanbul mythmaking reanimated in the neoliberal nineties. It was all part of a worldwide boom in what scholars call "nostalgic consumption"—from Mexico's vogue for Indigenous campesino cuisine to Italian Slow Food evocations of a rural utopian past to Japan's consumerist obsession with furusato ("old village," literally), the idealized "native home." All these movements were a reaction, of course, to the onrush of globalization and homogenization. But they were also products of a late-capitalist cultural logic that treats identities, belonging, heritage, and origin myths as commodities subject to the rule of the marketplace.

And wasn't such consumerism a privilege of white urban classes? Had Istanbullus *really* always treasured the days when Greeks and Armenians and Jews exchanged foods on holidays? How inclusive, really, were these Beyoğlu meze trays? Where were the dishes of the Kurds and the Roma, displaced by the nineties gentrification? Of the Alevis, with their disrespected non-Sunni faith? Of the rural Eastern Anatolian migrants whose very presence in Istanbul inspired, in large part, the sighing for the "civilized" past before their arrival?

I began to wonder if we shouldn't just bag the whole nostalgia exercise, and book a restaurant table in Aksaray. Aksaray, just beyond the Grand Bazaar in the historic peninsula, was the neighborhood where Mehmed II settled some of his forced immigrants for repopulating Constantinople. Now it was Istanbul's *current* multicultural heart. Arabic signs touted falafel franchises from Beirut and bakery chains from Damascus; Moroccans and Uyghurs, Syrians and escapees from ex-Soviet republics flocked here looking for quick work and cheap housing. Aksaray harbored its own version of postimperial nostalgia, too—but of a different flavor. This was where I came to buy faux-USSR chocolates and chacha, the homemade Georgian grappa snuck in by bus from the ex-Soviet Caucasus. At Aksaray's dodgy makeshift cafés, my former compatriots noshed fatty kolbasa, our socialist madeleine, and complained about exile in Russian, that "great language of Stalin and Brezhnev," as one refugee from Turkmenistan once put to me.

But I didn't raise any of this with Gamze. Gamze was having literal potluck struggles.

Last-minute cancellations, for one thing, which is how we lost Meri and her Rum taramasalata, and Zeynep, an Albanian friend, and her Arnavut ciğeri, the fried cubes of "Albanian liver" tossed with red onion. Then a gas cut at Gamze's on the morning of the party sent us scrambling off for emergency takeout. Off Istiklal Avenue, at Balik Pazari, we stopped at Gamze's favorite fishmonger for blobs of glistening mullet roe for taramasalata and for the Jewish (Byzantine?) lakerda, that buttery cured bonito. Next door sat our main destination, the worn narrow shopfront of a pristine old ciğerci (Ottoman for offal shop), where two ancient gents with identical gray curly hair presided over garlands of small intestines, lacy folds of honeycomb tripe, and sheep trotters resembling squeaky-clean babies. The men, Orhan bey and Kamil bey, were Albanian—cousins.

I asked about Arnavut ciğeri, the liver. "A famous Albanian recipe, yes?"

Kamil bey, the older one, laughed. "Everyone thinks so," he said. Most Albanians, he explained, arrived here after the Balkan wars—yet more wars that rearranged people's destinies early last century—and established themselves as the dying empire's best cattle breeders, offal butchers, and slaughterhouse owners. "You wanted *best* liver? You bought it from Albanians. And so this name, 'Albanian liver'—for a recipe unknown in Albania!"

We arranged to have this unknown-in-Albania liver cooked and delivered, and suddenly Orhan bey, the younger one, turned

nostalgic. "Our customers used to be *civilized* . . . Men in suits, ladies in beautiful dresses. All the vendors hereabouts, even the
Turks, spoke Greek and some French. But then came 1955 . . ." He
trailed off with a sigh, his old hands spread. Sensitive Gamze sighed,
too, almost in tears. We all knew how *that* story ended. "And now?"
Kamil bey gestured at a group of sullen guys sitting outside, hunched
over plastic plates of kokoreç, roasted intestines. Their bloodied,
shaved scalps were wrapped in sinister black bandages.

"Gang members?" I whispered, alarmed.

"Worse! *Hair transplant tourists* from the Gulf States!"

Gamze headed home, and I left the market through Çiçek Pasajı,
or "Flower Passage," next door. This ostentatious Parisian-style
covered arcade, packed these days with unloved touristic meyhane,
was commissioned in 1876 by a Greek banker and originally called
Cité de Pera. Its renaming derived from its White Russian flower
sellers, the destitute aristocrats who fled to Constantinople from
the Bolshevik Revolution. And the Russian salad that came with
those refugees, that I'd be bringing to our potluck? With America's
Marshall Plan and virulent anticommunism post-WWII, the salad
was renamed Amerikan salatası, "American salad."

Istanbul: a capital of renamings.

Slowly I drifted home along Istiklal (which means Republic),
taking in this former Grande Rue de Pera, the bygone Champs-
Élysées of alafranga late-Ottoman aspirations, of embassies, music
halls, *bon marché* shops, and *cafés chantants*—an astounding
thoroughfare, wrote an English traveler in 1893, "of no land and
all lands . . . a place of dancing dervishes, water sellers and sedan
bearers . . . Albanian wood-cutters from Asia Minor, Persian
donkey drivers, Croats and native Turks from a polyglot population
unparalleled in the world."

I paused by the site of the former Inci Pastanesi (now moved), founded by an Albanian Greek, and recalled the guilty pleasures of its lethally caloric profiteroles from my own early Istanbul days. And here was Markiz, another sweet mecca, once owned by a portly Armenian; Istanbul literati used to gather for Parisian chocolates under its famous Art Nouveau ceramic panels of half the seasons, L'Automne and Le Printemps. These days, still paneled but emptied of all cultural memory, it existed as a fast-food joint called Yemek Kulübü (Meal Club), its graceful windows plastered with posters for daily burger-and-fries specials. And here were the sahaflar, used-books passages, living relics of Walter Benjamin's Parisian arcades. Living, but how fading and ghostly they seemed, mustily awaiting the arrival of developers' sledgehammers.

In Orhan Pamuk's 1990 novel, *Black Book*, Istanbul appears as a kind of Borgesian double city: a surface one of ersatz imitation and an underground one of ruins that gathers the "old, discarded objects that . . . make us who we are." *Black Book* is Pamuk's familiar, hüzün-filled meditation on the erasure of the Ottoman texture of the former capital by Kemalist westernization. Except that today, just ahead in Taksim Square, a new mosque was rising in triumph across the wide expanse from a former sixties modernist landmark, a cultural center demolished and just replaced by a flashy updated replica of . . . itself. While in the narrow alleys around Istiklal, boozy dens of "Istancool" times were being edged out by faux-oriental narghilleh cafés for abstemious Saudi tourists.

*Nostalji* . . . This city, *our* city—it was a kind of water-lapped nostalgia factory, forever generating and regenerating endless cycles of loss. That sense of an overcrowded but depleted metropolis was especially acute now, when layers of past civilizations—Byzantine, Ottoman, Kemalist, even neoliberal globalist—were being submerged under the wave of a slick and censorious Islamist autocracy, one with its own neoliberal economics. I had the image of vast archives being cast away again, drowned into oblivion. So who was I, then, I thought, as just a doting part-timer here, to doubt my friends' melancholy about their past, their stubborn attachment to the rose-colored myth of a cosmopolitan, *civilized* city.

Turning downslope finally toward my apartment, I saw that our courtly neighborhood tailor had put yet another portrait of Atatürk in his window. How oddly reassuring it was, that steely, elegant figure: a rallying symbol of our endangered secular lifestyle, of women's emancipation. Until one remembered, of course, the hypernationalism, the anti-Kurdish repressions, Atatürk's own erasures of history and heterogeneity. These days they seemed like a lesser evil, I guess. I trudged up my six flights of ramshackle stairs, heartbroken at having to choose between two such heavy-handed modes, religious and secular. Then I peeled the potatoes and started dicing them for my Russian—American?—salad. Out my window, the Bosporus rippled like coarse silk in the afternoon breeze.

IT WAS WELL PAST MIDNIGHT when Barry and I left Gamze's apartment. Outside on the cobblestones, the massive stony column of the fourteenth-century Galata Tower, built by Genovese traders, thrust its pointed cap at the almost-full moon. Old as Constantinople itself, Galata had always been a foreigners' enclave—and a red-light district, one of infidel "vice and depravity." Latifi a fifteenth-century Ottoman poet, called it the biggest meyhane in the world.

Upholding Galata's reputation, we were finely drunk on Gamze's hundred-proof raki, on the strange inky Süryani wines produced in Turkey's southeast by Christian-Orthodox Assyrians who still speak a form of Aramaic—the language of Christ.

Our çilingir sofrasi turned out to be one of the loveliest parties in memory, not a stage-managed show of diversity out of an ESL class of my Philadelphia childhood but a celebration of friendship and a shared devotion to Istanbul. Everyone circled Gamze's artfully laden table in awe. On my IKEA tray, she had arranged a formal raki service attended by rosy-skinned plump pistachios and dark curls of basturma, the Ottoman precursor of pastrami, which even back in the seventeenth century was cured by Armenians. A salty cloud of Greek taramasalata glistened with a topping of fish eggs: "Sultan Mahmud II, the Tanzimat reformer, loved caviar!" Gamze noted. She'd sprinkled intricate cinnamon patterns on Takuhi's topik, and scattered fried pine nuts and dill fronds on Deniz's puffy Sephardic eggplant almodrote.

Unexpectedly, our Kurdish friend Ihsan showed up, bearing a huge aromatic pile of midye dolma, stuffed mussels. Armine, his wife, had already begun her graduate studies in Boston. Ihsan should have left, too, but here he was, procrastinating, inventing every excuse to stay on and guzzle raki with friends.

"*So whose dish is it?*" Ihsan philosophized tipsily, scooping cinnamon-scented rice out of the mussel shells. Stuffed mussels, he answered himself, were a great specialty of Christian meyhane before Greeks and Armenians disappeared from Istanbul's restaurants. The dish might have vanished with them, but it was adopted as a street food by Istanbul's Kurdish migrants from the southeastern region of Mardin, who'd been fleeing poverty and the unspoken civil war against Kurds since the eighties. And so for economic reasons inevitably entwined with politics, Mardin Kurds became the city's *midye dolmacılar*, streetside stuffed-mussel sellers. Their mussels were modest totems of a new cultural fusion.

Hepsi karışık, all mixed up, I thought to myself, echoing the phrase of Meri the Rum chronicler. Yes: *Whose food?* At some stops along my journey, the answer appeared refreshingly obvious. But now, way past midnight, here in this crossroads-palimpsest of civilizations over millennia, the quest to assign ur-identities to particular dishes and disentangle their complicated entwinings seemed like sheer absurdity.

We'd smoked too much on Gamze's balcony, watching fireworks for some rich people's wedding shimmering over the Bosporus, along with the raki and Assyrian wine. Arda, Gamze's husband, an amateur DJ with a PhD from the Sorbonne, blasted Roza Eskenazi— a Jewish singer born in Constantinople who became the Queen of Greek Rebetiko, the blues music of Turks exiled to Greece in the population exchange. Roza wailed so loudly some new neighbors called the police.

"Well, canim," Gamze concluded, kissing us good night, "I guess this means the party is a success!"

# EPILOGUE
## National Dish

On February 25, 2022, I woke up after a turbulent night checking news updates about Putin's invasion of Ukraine, and amid the shock and bouts of crying and adrenalized doom scrolling, a seemingly trivial yet intimately unsettling thought entered my mind. I realized that after these years of investigating national cuisines and identities, I no longer knew how to think or talk about borsch, a beet soup that both Ukraine and Russia claimed as their own. I grew up in Soviet Moscow eating borsch—борщ in Cyrillic, no "t" at the end, that's a Yiddish addition—at least twice a week; for better or worse it always signified for me the despotic difficult home we had left. Here in Queens a big pot my mother just made sat in my fridge. But who *did* have the right to claim it as heritage? That tangled question of cultural ownership I'd been reflecting on for so long had landed on my own table with an intensity that suddenly felt viscerally, searingly personal.

Back in Moscow at the height of Brezhnev's "stagnation," I never regarded borsch as any people's "national dish." It was just *there*, a piece of our shared Soviet reality like the brown winter snow or the buses filled with hangover breath or my scratchy wool school uniform. Our socialist borsch came in different guises. Institutional borsch with its reek of stale cabbage was to be endured indistinguishably at kindergartens, hospitals, and workers' canteens across the eleven time zones of our vast Union of Soviet Socialist Republics. Personal borsch, on the other hand, brought out every Soviet mother's and grandmother's sweet ingenuity— although to me it all tasted kind of the same in the end. My mom was inordinately proud of her hot, super-quick vegetarian version. I still have an image of her in our trim Moscow kitchen, phone tucked under her chin, shredding the carrots, cabbage, and beets on a clunky box grater right into our chipped enamel family pot. It was *her* recipe, she always insisted, a miracle of a shortage economy conjured from a can of tomato paste and some withered root veggies. In the fall she'd add a tart Antonovka apple; in winter maybe a glob of alien American ketchup for a piquant, faintly dissident non-Soviet touch. I never had the heart to tell her that I preferred her make-believe pot-au-feu, or her cold borsch that came with the dacha season, a salad inside a magenta chilled liquid, alive with the cucumber-scallion-radish crunch of the fleeting short northern summer.

Ukraine became an independent state in 1991, having been an original republic of the USSR, and part of the Russian empire since the late 1700s. The earliest known mention of borsch dates from 1584, in the diary of a German merchant who traveled to Kyiv when most of present-day Ukraine belonged to the Polish-Lithuanian Commonwealth—well before Ukraine *or* Russia developed any modern-style national consciousness. For that matter, the Slavic word borsch most likely referred to hogweed back then, a common plant thereabouts that was often fermented and used for a sour green potage. The deep-red soup we all know must have developed toward the eighteenth century as the cultivation of beetroot in Eastern Europe took off. From then on, mentions of borsch in Russian cookbooks became fairly common, although often referencing "Malorossiya" (Little Russia)—the imperial term for Ukraine.

The Soviets themselves never denied borsch its Ukrainian origins. In fact, parallel to our frugal, quotidian beet soup was a dish the propaganda-puffed recipe books about the diverse cuisines of our Soviet republics presented as the *real* Ukrainian borsch. A baroque meal in a bowl, thick enough to stand a spoon in, it brimmed with all kinds of meats—meats!—nobody ever saw at a store. Although that borsch supposedly celebrated Ukrainianness, it was a socialist-realist fiction, of course, a Sovietized folkloric-kitsch rebranding of Ukraine as our scarlet empire's happy wholesome breadbasket and sugar bowl—a Ukraine scrubbed of the horrors of Stalin's collectivization and Holodomor (state-induced famines), of the repressions of its language, culture, and any authentic expressions of nationalism. In a political system that dictated and socially engineered ethno-identities and assigned cultural heritage, that borsch was an imperial possession of almighty Moscow. As was Ukraine itself, implicitly always a lesser nation than Russia, or perhaps not even a nation at all, as Putin now would have us believe.

I'd never thought much about that "real" Ukrainian borsch until 1989, fifteen years after my mom and I immigrated to the US, when I wrote my first cookbook, *Please to the Table*. My book, too, meant to celebrate the culinary diversity of the Soviet republics—an imperialist-tainted project, perhaps? as I now uneasily ponder in retrospect. A deeply ironic one, for sure, because Gorbachev's creaking imperium was coming apart at the seams as my book went into print and the Soviet republics kept asserting their independence. Researching borsch in Western Ukraine those twilight days of the USSR, I was shocked to discover versions I never suspected existed: borsch with white sugar beets and porcini mushrooms; with fermented beet kvass; with smoky dried pears and wild game shot by a hunter we'd met on the road. Returning to New York I interviewed the Ukrainian diaspora here, generous people who fed me fragrant honey cakes and Christmas borsch with tiny dumplings called vushki. And then wrote angry letters when my publisher decided to subtitle *Please to the Table*: the *Russian* cookbook.

MY MOM'S "super-quick vegetarian" borsch featured in *Please to the Table*, along with a handful of other borsch recipes. And by some strange twist of fate almost three decades later, it became for her a kind of salvation. After her darkest, hopeless days under Trump and the pandemic, in early 2021 she miraculously sprang back to life when she started teaching cooking on Zoom for a wonderful multicultural school called the League of Kitchens. For her class, Mom plumped for her Moscow veggie borsch accompanied by herb- and garlic-smothered dinner rolls called pampushky. And as soon as her menu promising "iconic Russian dishes" went up on LOK's website, an angry email arrived from a Ukrainian-American journalist.

"To say borsch is a Russian dish is not accurate and could be seen as offensive to a lot of people," said the email. "There has been an ongoing fight over borsch in recent years as part of the backdrop to the continuing very real war between Russia and Ukraine."

Indeed. The first real political flare-up over borsch broke out in 2019, five years after Putin annexed Crimea and started a war in Eastern Ukraine. That year the Russian Federation's ministry of foreign affairs provocatively tweeted: "A timeless classic! #Borsch is one of Russia's most famous & beloved #dishes & a symbol of traditional cuisine." Ukrainian social media responded with outrage and scorn at this weaponizing of soup as part of Russia's wartime propaganda. "As if stealing Crimea wasn't enough," seethed one commentator, "you had to go and steal borsch from Ukraine as well." "Cultural appropriation!" cried Ukrainians interviewed on the subject. "[The Russians] will not take our borsch," vowed a young activist chef in Kyiv, Ievgen Klopotenko, as he launched a crusade to have it inscribed into UNESCO's Intangible Cultural Heritage list.

"Like the food fight between the Arabs and Israelis over who owns hummus," *The New York Times* opined, "the dispute sadly divides two neighboring cultures over traditions that might have united them."

For her part, my passionately anti-Putin anti-imperialist mom was much pained by the Ukrainian journalist's email. Cooking for her was always politically conscious. She garnished her LOK classes with memories of Soviet repressions and the endless, humiliating food queues. She told of fleeing the hated Soviet regime at age forty with only me and two suitcases and no right of return, of how she made her borsch in our new still-bare apartment in alien far-away Philadelphia. But she refused to assign a single identity to a dish that she, along with vast myriads of people across multiple borders, have been cooking for generations, have internalized as their own. "There are *many* types of borsch," she would insist, grating her carrots and beetroots: "Russian, Polish, Lithuanian, Moldovan, Karelian, diaspora Jewish—and, yes, yes, Ukrainian." Across the giant span of the USSR, she'd further insist, borsch was a comfort food that connected people who shared not just the dishes but also the tragedies of Soviet fate—Stalin's gulags, for instance, which didn't spare a single group or ethnicity. Anyway, it was *her*, *Larisa's*, recipe, full of her personal touches. Resonant with so many memories.

I wasn't about to argue with Mom about whose dish it "really" was. My years of work on this issue had left me wary of essentialist gastronationalist claims, where knee-jerk nationalism was inevitably entangled with nation-branding and profit. Similarly the overused concept of cultural appropriation. I agreed with philosopher Kwame Anthony Appiah on his insistence that it casts cultural practices as something like corporate intellectual property. Whereas in reality, as he put it, "All cultural practices and objects are mobile; they like to spread, and almost all are themselves creations of intermixture."

THEN FEBRUARY 24, 2022 HAPPENED.

That night, my mom, Barry, and I sat in silence gripped by grief, rage, despair—and utter disbelief—watching live CNN footage of Putin launching his full-scale invasion. There were air-raid sirens blaring in Kyiv that night, missile strikes, explosions rocking several other major Ukrainian cities. My mom was ashen-faced. She barely spoke, but I'm pretty sure she was flashing back to the sunny day of June 22, 1941, when she was seven and the Nazi invasion of the Soviet Union was unleashed.

Over the following weeks the news brought a surreal split screen of two countries collapsing in different ways: Ukraine all smoke, haze, and wreckage from Putin's missiles and artillery; Russia ominously freezing itself back to the cold war USSR of my childhood—extreme censorship, toxic state-sponsored patriotism. As if one needed any further reminder that allegiances and identities can shift overnight, Soviet émigrés from our circles who considered themselves culturally Jewish-Russian-American started acutely remembering all the family members they had in Ukraine. So did we. My mom's dad was from Dnepropetrovsk (now Dnipro); her entire maternal clan was from Odesa, the city of our sunburned summer vacations. Now in that Black Sea port where she herself was born and lived very briefly, acquaintances who used to grimace at Ukrainian nationalism switched their social media feeds to Ukrainian and railed against Moscow's brutality. Meanwhile close friends of ours here, worldly people born in Soviet Ukraine, were posting diatribes on Facebook savaging "Great Russian Culture." Some gloated over images of dead Russian soldiers, just boys, splayed in the snow. It was shocking to see; but deep down I shared in their naked rage. Every Russian—including myself—seemed somehow complicit to me. I felt guilty for thinking in the imperialist language of Putin's aggression, for the volumes by Pushkin and Tolstoy on my bookshelves. And yes, for my previous thoughts about borsch.

And if I started my national dish project comfortable with my own globalized cosmopolitanism, I felt existentially bereft now, a gaping emptiness where my mental safe happy places should be. Turkey, the country I loved, was being strangled by authoritarianism. In the US, years of Trump and Trumpism were poisoning the country that opened its doors to my mom and myself back in 1974. My ancestral homeland? A genocidal terrorist state. I couldn't imagine now ever returning to Moscow, even to visit the graves of my younger brother and my father who had died the previous year.

It's an evergreen cliché that in times of crisis the foods we grew up with provide a comforting sense of home and security, reconnect us to who we are, where we come from. But just thinking of borsch brought more heartache. *Who owns borsch?* The question hung in the air like an accusatory pall. The soup of my childhood had become a symbol of Putin's assault on Ukrainian land, culture, and heritage, of his drive to plunder Ukraine—to obliterate even the very concept of it.


By April Russia's atrocities in Bucha were being uncovered, millions of Ukrainians had turned into refugees, and entire towns and cities lay in ruin. Meanwhile Russia's foreign ministry spokesperson, Maria Zakharova, a ferociously Putinist blonde, delivered a bizarre drunken tirade about borsch. "It had to belong to just one people, just one nationality," she ranted about Ukrainian insistence that borsch was their national dish. "But for it to be shared? . . . No! They didn't want to compromise. This is exactly what we are talking about, xenophobia, Nazism, extremism in all forms!" In the service of an unprovoked horrific invasion she was grotesquely co-opting the universalist notion that food should be shared.

By then my mom, who'd been so traumatized by the early days of the war, had found in her borsch an emotional anchor and a new political meaning. Together with LOK she was using her Zoom classes to raise money for Ukraine, to speak out in our local media, even on Japanese television, against Putin's horror show. The struggle transformed her. At eighty-eight years of age she became a modest, heartfelt part of the global "stand with Ukraine" movement, where borsch was no longer just soup but a fundraising force and a solidarity symbol. "Anyone who cooks borsch today gets closer to us," declared Ievgen Klopotenko, the young Kyiv chef who petitioned for the dish's inscription in the UNESCO ICH list. In London, my friend Olia Hercules, a brilliant Ukrainian food-writer-turned-crusader, started the "cookforukraine" drive with her Russian émigré colleague Alissa Timoshkina, raising nearly two million pounds and the profiles of Ukrainian culture and food. In New York, iconic East Village restaurant Veselka became an activism hub, with all its borsch profits going to Ukrainian charities. Soon the social media of my food friends all over the world was a tide of blue-yellow flags, of photos of varenyky dumplings and stuffed cabbage—and the same borsch and pampushky my mom made for her class.

My mother now spoke about borsch with a newfound authority and moral clarity. It didn't matter who exactly "invented" the soup, she insisted; it mattered even less which exact territory it first appeared in. What was crucial was how borsch figured in a *national narrative*. And for Ukrainians under an unspeakably brutal assault from their neighbors, it was a powerful symbol of unity. "Borsch," she told one radio interviewer, "stands for home, generosity, the richness of land, and family ties . . . And all these things are being now taken away from Ukrainians."

This was pretty much UNESCO's justification for an unprecedented emergency move to fast-track the ICH application for Ukraine submitted back in 2019. On July 1, day 128 of the invasion—as Russian missiles killed more than twenty people near Odesa—UNESCO declared the Culture of Ukrainian Borsch an "intangible cultural heritage in need of safeguarding."

"The victory in the war for borsch is ours!" Ukraine's culture minister Oleksandr Dyachenko posted on Telegram: "Remember and be sure: We will win this war like we did the war for borsch."

LATE THAT SUMMER, six months into Russia's assault, I called Aurora Ogorodnyk, a food researcher in Lviv, who is writing a book about borsch with an anthropologist named Marianna Dushar.

I wanted to ask her thoughts on the dish as a Ukrainian national symbol, a role supercharged by Putin's invasion.

"But borsch has long been symbolically important for us," Aurora responded. "We cook it for baptisms, weddings, and funerals, we serve it in public communal pots during political protests—we even prepare it in dried form as rations for our soldiers since 2014." She paused, then added simply: "It's who we are, our DNA. Red like our blood. And now Ukrainians eat it when they return to their ruined cities and villages."

I'd met Aurora in the sunny Before era, at an international food conference. These days she was mostly homebound in Lviv in western Ukraine, well away from the major fighting in the country's south and east, yet always under threat of a missile strike. "Daily life goes on here," she told me, sounding eerily calm, "but with the ever-present backdrop of a sudden air raid . . . the realization that any moment you, too, can be killed."

I wondered to her if perhaps now wasn't the right moment to talk so much about soup, while civilians were being slaughtered and cities destroyed?

"No, now *is* the moment!" Aurora insisted forcefully. "To finally banish those Russian/Soviet colonialist optics. Because it was fine having us as funny folksy Ukrainians with our borsch and our salo

[lard] when we were part of the USSR, which Russia controlled. But once we began to assert our independence, they decided to remind us, no, borsch *doesn't* belong to you, actually.

"So borsch," she said, "is also an emblem of separation for us. A red line—red as borsch—where we cut them off and say *enough to colonialism.*"

There were a thousand things more I planned to ask Aurora. But instead I suddenly found myself profusely apologizing. Then apologizing for narcissistically going on about the guilt I was feeling, my own rage at the Russians, my loss of identity, my sheepishness for not yet learning Ukrainian and having to speak Russian to her.

With the quiet authority of a trauma counselor, Aurora offered me a way forward in my dilemma. "I understand your rage, I share it, Anya. And when you're far away it's easy to get engulfed by despair. But all you need is a moment of reflection—just one. Then stop dwelling on hatred and guilt. Spread love and compassion through your cooking and writing. Do what you can to support us.

"And really," she added. "How is any of this your personal fault?"

At the end I asked Aurora if she believed Russians and Ukrainians would ever eat borsch together again. There was a long silence. Finally she replied, "Not until the Ukrainians who win this war and the Russians who lose it are long gone." Recently she'd driven to Tallinn, Estonia's capital, where for the first time in months she saw lots of Russians. "And everything inside of me just froze," she confessed.

So where then *was* my guilt in all this? Hanging up with Aurora, I thought again of a poem, the savagely offensive verse lamenting Ukraine's independence by Joseph Brodsky, exiled Jewish–Russian Soviet dissident and Nobel laureate poet. The one where he promises that on their deathbeds, Ukrainians will forsake the "bullshit" of their national nineteenth-century poet Taras Shevchenko for Pushkin; the one where he wants to go spit in Ukraine's great river, the Dnieper. Brodsky wrote this in 1992, deeply embittered by Ukraine's splitting away from Russia. He never published it, though he read it in public, but just twice. Recently, however, it had been resurfacing in various conversations about Russian imperialist arrogance, an arrogance that taints other anti-Soviet humanist dissidents; that towering moralizer, Aleksandr Solzhenitsyn, for instance, another Nobel laureate, was skeptical about the very idea of Ukrainian nationhood.

"I think I need to *decolonize* borsch from myself," I texted Aurora. "To stop thinking of *owning* it because of my Soviet-Russian personal history." Aurora texted back a smiley emoji. I wrote back now in Google-translated Ukrainian . . . As she replied in Ukrainian, the tension I'd felt during our conversation lifted a little.

ON A STORMY EVENING IN AUGUST, two old friends arrive at my apartment in Jackson Heights with an unruly armful of sumptuous marigolds.

"*Chornobryvtsi*—dark-browed, meaning beautiful." Andrei explicates the Ukrainian name for these sun-gold floral pompoms. "On the drive over," his wife, Toma, exclaims, "they perfumed our car with the scent of Ukrainian summer." Later I learn that Ukrainians plant marigolds by their houses to ward off the evil eye and misfortune.

Toma and Andrei are from Kyiv and live in New Jersey, and we haven't seen them for months. Since the invasion, Andrei—a documentary filmmaker whose works include an account of Ukraine's Orange Revolution of 2004—has been posting on Facebook with such all-encompassing raw anti-Russian passion, I wasn't sure if they'd want to see me again. In one post he talked about how his hatred, at first an "acute disease with fever, curses, and wishes for a painful death to you know who," had become "a chronic condition, always with me, day, morning, evening. And, of course, in my dreams."

Deeply worried about them, sheepishly I emailed my sympathies, kept suggesting getting together. Andrei would thank me for "reaching out" and leave it at that.

But now they're here, looking festive with their Ukrainian flowers and bottles and blue-yellow Ukraine solidarity bracelets. My mom, Barry, and I are overjoyed to see them. My anxiety about how the evening might go fades away in the hubbub of our greetings and chatter.

I thought long and hard about exactly what borsch I would serve for this occasion, this unexpected last national dish in my journey—a dish so familiar and yet so conflicted, my making of it here brought about by such wrenching circumstances. To decolonize borsch for and from myself as I promised Aurora, to make it truly Ukrainian, I purged all the recipes I knew as a Soviet and post-Soviet Russian. For days I researched the soup in Ukrainian, struggling with Google's translations at first, then eventually easing into this language so close to mine but now never more apart. What I found was a trove of regional recipes, recipes that would have once seemed merely ethnographic and curious but now read like an atlas of violence. Here was borsch ("prunes obligatory") from Vinnytsia, the west-central city with a long Jewish history where on a sunny July day Russian rockets killed twenty-three civilians going about their daily routines. There was a borsch based on dried fish from Mykolaiv, an industrial port city bombarded by Russians for months on end; there was a Tatar borsch with lamb, quince, and corn from Crimea. I discovered borsch aphorisms and cartoons, borsch proverbs and jokes, borsch poems newly composed in the noise of this war, personal borsch recipes triumphantly named for places where Ukrainians repelled Russian aggressors.

Sifting through all these, I would think of something Marianna Dushar, Aurora's coauthor, told me. "Borsch isn't so much a recipe as a national idea," she said, "an idea that all Ukrainians carry inside them. Borsch develops and changes—and it changes us in the process." In my own way, I felt that myself . . . that borsch was changing me, too.

Toma's and Andrei's eyes grow wide at my opening dish: a chilled borsch, for which I'd fermented the beet kvass myself, as it was done centuries ago, then added sour cherries and rhubarb for a classic fruity-tart flavor, per one of the Lviv recipes of Marianna Dushar. "In Kyiv," says Toma, "we'd use fresh gooseberries for that sour effect." "But we can never find them here," Andrei adds.

Just six months ago we were the same people, I reflect sadly, as my mom passes around her chopped liver, herring pâté, and a garlicky eggplant dip—Jewish appetizers iconic to her native Odesa. We were all former Soviets turned émigrés, Russian speakers of mixed ethnic backgrounds who'd read Pushkin, had the same cultural compass. "And now the invasion has divided us," Andrei continues my thought, his voice going quietly somber, "into those living in a daily personal hell, and the compassionate bystanders . . . who'll never truly understand our trauma."

Toma and Andrei have spent the past six months living and breathing nothing but Ukraine, waking up and going to bed checking the news and any updates from their Kyiv families. A fragile fatigue shades their bonhomie this evening. Toma has two sisters back home. Andrei's sister suffered such severe depression and panic attacks she was in Germany receiving treatment. "It's helped as well to get a break from the air raids," says Andrei. "But she can't wait to get back to her kids and grandkids."

I go and bring out my second borsch now, to the table my mom has decorated with sunflowers and Ukrainian flags. It's shocking pink, with blended-in sour cream, dusky with broth infused with smoked pork. It has no potatoes or cabbage and is meant to be sipped from cups at weddings. Nobody at the table has tasted anything like it. The recipe was taught to me by Maria, a recent refugee from Ivano-Frankivsk in the west of the country. "It will de-Russify you!" Maria promised only half-jokingly, as if casting a benevolent spell.

Inevitably the conversation turns back to our changed identities. Andrei—of Jewish-Polish-Ukrainian background, just like borsch, I note to myself—went to a Ukrainian school but now deeply regrets not doing a better job reading Ukrainian literature in its original language. Toma was born in Dresden (ex–German Democratic Republic) but lived in Kyiv since childhood. Though her entire family is ethnically Russian, her sister back home can't bear the sound of Russian anymore, can't look at Russians.

As they talk I think of the dream I've been having for weeks, one where I sit in my childhood Moscow apartment drinking sugary tea with my departed father and brother . . . and wake up feeling so homeless, sundered from my past. I want to tell them about it, but now Toma is proposing a toast.

"To borsch," she offers. "It's the color of pomegranate, bright as a Ukrainian folk song."

"To eating it often with people we love," my mother puts in.

Andrei raises his shot glass of Polish vodka. "Borsch is a generous dish," he declares, "a *Ukrainian* dish even if other people might claim it. I say: leave it to Ukrainians, please, and after they win this war they'll invite the rest of the world to the table."

"But *not* members of the Russian Federation," Toma adds tartly.

And we drink.

## Acknowledgments

Scott Moyers, my comrade, mentor, and brilliant editor, understood this book long before I did. It would have never happened without him and his wisdom and guidance. He is the champion an author dreams of. I celebrate and salute him.

Once the book journey began, I was beyond lucky to get to know so many remarkable people across several continents who so generously shared their tables, their scholarly acumen, their personal stories, and their countries' histories. Heartfelt gratitude to all those below, as well as people I might not have mentioned but whose kindness I'm ever grateful for nevertheless.

In Paris: *remerciements* to Bénédict Beaugé, Nicolas Chatenier, Mattias Kroon, Alexandra Michot, Alain Ducasse, Amy Serafin, Alec Lobrano, Monsieur Larbi Kechta, Meg Bortin, Lindsey Tramuta, Giles Pudlowski, Olivier and Martine Frayssé.

In Naples and beyond: *grazie* to Enzo Coccia, Antonio and Donatella Mattozzi, Elisabetta Moro, Marino Niola, Gino Sorbillo, Nunzia Rivetti, Tarantina Taran, Giuliana Bruno and Andy Fierberg, Livia Iaccarino, Amedeo Colella, Maurizio Cortese, Beatrice Cecaro, Fabrizio Mangoni, Mela Flauto, Antonio Tubelli, Davide Bruno.

In Tokyo: *arigato* to Naoyuki Yanagihara, Hiroko Sasaki, Maria Cobo, Abram Plaut, Tomoharu Shono, Hitomi and Harumi Yoshio, Masaki Funakubo, Brian MacDuckston, Kyoichi Tsuzuki, Motoko Watanabe, Shaul Margulies, Motoyuki Shibata and Hitomi Aoiki, Melinda Joel, Takashi Morieda, Ronald Kelts, Matt Alt, Craig Mod, Tsubasa Tamaki, Robb Satterwhite, Hamish Macaskill, Hiroyuki Kusunose, Akram Rahimov.

In Seville and beyond: heartfelt *agradecimientos* to Rafa Almarcha, Ana Valderrábanos, and Señora Mercedes Pardo López; Patxi Fernández Bengoa, Isabel González Turmo, Alberto Troyano, María Castro Bermúdez-Coronel and Severiano Sánchez at Cinco Jotas, Fernando Huidobro, Alejandro Antona Llanes, Eric Crambes and Ruth Rosique, Manuel León and Celia Macías, Shawn Hennessey, Alberto Candau, Javier Abascal, Antonio Zoido; Israel, Borja, David and other hospitable folk at Mercado de Triana; Emilio Vara at Casa Moreno plus other taberneros who keep the Sevillian spirit alive. In Córdoba: Paco Morales, and Almudena Villegas. In Jerez: Eduardo Ojeda. In Cádiz: Lourdes Acosta. In Madrid: Alberto Fernandez Bonbín, who opened so many doors.

In Oaxaca and beyond: *millónes de gracias* to Olga Cabrera Oropeza, Carlos, Miguel, Señora Evita, Abuelita Chonita, and the staff of Tierra del Sol; Celia Florián, Abigail Mendoza and her sisters, Cayetano Limón Sánchez and Natividad Ambrosio, Julio César Flores, Elmer Gaspar Guerra, Eufrosina Cruz Mendoza, Jorge Vera, Tucho and Daniel Hernández, Flavio Aragón Cuevas, Dr. Gloria Zafra, Thalía Barrios, Mari Paz Iturribarría, Estela Nolasco, Laura Martìnez Iturribarría, Alejandro Ruiz, Paulo Sergio, Ivette Murat, Graciela Ángeles Carreño, Salvador Cueva, Jonathan Barbieri and Yira Vallejo, Cuauhtémoc Peña, Amado Ramírez Leyva,

Jorge Leon, Coca Zarate. In CDMX: Rafael Mier of Fundación Tortilla, and Gonzalo Goût.

In Istanbul: *teşekkürler* to Gamze Ineceli and Arda Ipek, Deniz Alphan, Zafer Yenal, Özge Samancı, Meri Çevik Simyonidis, Takuhi Tovmasyan, Işıl Çokuğraş, Cemre Torun, Sabiha Apaydin and Gokhan Gönenli, Hülya and Adnan Ekşigil, Bahar Karaca, Mehmet Gürs, Engin Akin, Burçak and Murat Kazdal, Defne Karaosmanoğlu, Levon Bağış, Zeynep Miraç, Asiye Cengiz, Ihsan Karayazi and Armine Avetisyan, Şemsa Denizsel, Neslihan Şen, Haldun Dinccetin.

In Lviv: *dyakuyu* to Julia Aurora Ogorodnyk and Marianna Dushar.

At the dream house of Penguin Press, enormous kudos to Mia Council, Helen Rouner, Lavina Lee, Alyson D'Amato, Sarah Hutson, Jessie Stratton, and Mollie Reid. Special commendations to Sheila Moody for her eagle-eyed attention to detail.

A huge thank-you to the incomparable Roz Chast for making the book smile.

At the Wylie Agency in New York and London, profound gratitude to Andrew Wylie for his always-wise counsel, to Tracy Bohan for the global adventure, and to the entire team for never missing a beat.

Salutes to Julia Cosgrove, Jennifer Flowers, and all the wonderful folks at AFAR for sustaining and nurturing my wanderlust. And to lovely Sophie Brickman who commissioned stories on Seville and Tokyo for the much-missed *Airbnb Magazine*.

A book about food is pointless if you can't share it with friends. That truth became existential and urgent as we all emerged from the dark days of pandemic isolation and heartache. Cheers to

Defne Aydıntaşbaş and Mert Eroğul, Ursula and Jonas Hegewisch, Melissa Clark, Kate Sekules, Kate Krader, Anna Brodsky, Andrei and Toma Zagdansky, Sasha and Ira Genis, Sonya Gropman, Mark Cohen and Ivone Margulies, and so many other pals who lifted my spirits.

My mother, Larisa, is my role model, best friend, cooking and eating companion, and favorite book character. Her love is what kept calling me back from my travels.

Barry Yourgrau, my partner, improved every step of this journey and every page of the manuscript. He is my critic and confidant, my inspiration, my support—my one and only true love. No words of gratitude would be ever enough.

# Bibliography

**SOURCES CONSULTED**

Navigating between scholarly work on food and national identity, on the one hand, and the lived experience of eating, drinking, and talking with people at specific locales, on the other, has been both illuminating and challenging. While the many interviews I conducted during my research have been invaluable, the written sources below much informed and sharpened my understanding of the complex subjects at hand. In addition to academic works, these materials include cookbooks, travel writing, and social histories of the cities I visited.

**GENERAL**

Anderson, Benedict. *Imagined Communities: Reflections on the Origin and Spread of Nationalism.* London: Verso, 1983.

Appadurai, Arjun. "How to Make a National Cuisine: Cookbooks in Contemporary India." *Comparative Studies in Society and History* 30, no. 1 (January 1988): 3–24. https://doi.org/10.1017/s0010417500015024.

Bauman, Zygmunt. *Culture in a Liquid Modern World.* Cambridge: Polity Press, 2011.

Billig, Michael. *Banal Nationalism.* Los Angeles: SAGE, 1995.

DeSoucey, Michaela. "Gastronationalism." *American Sociological Review* 75, no. 3 (June 2010): 432–55. https://doi.org/10.1177/0003122410372226.

Erman, Michel. "What Is a National Dish?" *Medium* 28, no. 3 (2011): 31–43. www.cairn-int.info/journal-medium-2011-3-page-31.htm.

Hobsbawm, Eric, and Terence Ranger, eds. *The Invention of Tradition.* Cambridge: Cambridge University Press, 2002.

Ichijo, Atsuko, and Ronald Ranta. *Food, National Identity and Nationalism.* London: Palgrave Macmillan, 2016.

Jensen, Lotte, ed. *The Roots of Nationalism: National Identity Formation in Early Modern Europe, 1600–1815.* Amsterdam: Amsterdam University Press, 2016.

King, Michelle, ed. *Culinary Nationalism in Asia.* London: Bloomsbury Academic, 2019.

Porciani, Ilaria, ed. *Food Heritage and Nationalism in Europe.* Abingdon, Oxon., UK: Routledge, 2020.

Skey, Michael, and Marco Antonsich, eds. *Everyday Nationhood: Theorising Culture, Identity and Belonging after Banal Nationalism.* London: Palgrave Macmillan, 2017.

Smith, Anthony D. "Gastronomy or Geology? The Role of Nationalism in the Reconstruction of Nations." *Nations and Nationalism* 1, no. 1 (1995): 3–23.

## INTRODUCTION: *Paris: Pot on the Fire*

Adams, Craig. "The Taste of Terroir in 'The Gastronomic Meal of the French': France's Submission to UNESCO's Intangible Cultural Heritage List." *M/C Journal* 17, no. 1 (March 18, 2014). https://doi.org/10.5204/mcj.762.

Beaugé, Bénédict. "On the Idea of Novelty in Cuisine." *International Journal of Gastronomy and Food Science* 1, no. 1 (January 2012): 5–14. https://doi.org/10.1016/j.ijgfs.2011.11.007.

Bell, David. *The Cult of the Nation in France: Inventing Nationalism, 1680–1800.* Cambridge, Mass.: Harvard University Press, 2003.

Carême, Marie Antonin. *L'Art de la Cuisine Française au Dix-Neuvième Siècle. Tome 1.* Boston: Adamant Media, 2005.

Csergo, Julia. *Pot-au-Feu: Convivial, Familial: Histoires d'un Mythe.* Paris: Autrement, 1999.

Edwards, Nancy. "The Science of Domesticity: Women, Education and National Identity in Third Republic France, 1880–1914." PhD Diss., University of California, Berkeley, 1997.

Ferguson, Priscilla Parkhurst. *Accounting for Taste: The Triumph of French Cuisine.* Chicago: University of Chicago Press, 2006.

Gopnik, Adam. *The Table Comes First: Family, France, and the Meaning of Food.* New York: Vintage Books, 2012.

Ichijo, Atsuko. "Banal Nationalism and UNESCO's Intangible Cultural Heritage List: Cases of Washoku and the Gastronomic Meal of the French." In *Everyday Nationhood: Theorising Culture, Identity and Belonging after*

*Banal Nationalism*, edited by Michael Skey and Marco Antonsich. London: Palgrave Macmillan, 2017.

Kelly, Ian. *Cooking for Kings: The Life of Antonin Carême, the First Celebrity Chef.* New York: Walker, 2005.

Mennell, Stephen. *All Manners of Food: Eating and Taste in England and France from the Middle Ages to the Present.* Urbana: University of Illinois Press, 2006.

Poole, Benjamin. "French Taste: Food and National Identity in Post-Colonial France." PhD Diss., University of Illinois, 2014.

"Quels Sont les Plats Préférés des Français?" Elle à Table, *Elle* (France), December 16, 2016. www.elle.fr/Elle-a-Table/Les-dossiers-de-la-redaction/News -de-la-redaction/Quels-sont-les-plats-preferes-des-Francais-3401246.

Spang, Rebecca L. *The Invention of the Restaurant: Paris and Modern Gastronomic Culture.* Cambridge, Mass.: Harvard University Press, 2000.

Spary, E. C. *Eating the Enlightenment: Food and the Sciences in Paris, 1670–1760.* Chicago: University of Chicago Press, 2014.

Steinberger, Michael. *Au Revoir to All That: Food, Wine, and the End of France.* New York: Bloomsbury, 2010.

Tebben, Maryann. "French Food Texts and National Identity: Consommé, Cheese Soufflé, Francité?" In *You Are What You Eat: Literary Probes into the Palate*, edited by Annette Magid, 168–89. Newcastle, UK: Cambridge Scholars, 2008.

Tebben, Maryann. *Savoir-Faire: A History of Food in France.* London: Reaktion Books, 2020.

Trubek, Amy B. *Haute Cuisine: How the French Invented the Culinary Profession.* Philadelphia: University of Pennsylvania Press, 2001.

Weber, Eugen. *Peasants into Frenchmen: The Modernization of Rural France, 1870–1914.* Stanford, Calif.: Stanford University Press, 2007.

Weiss, Allen S. "The Ideology of the Pot-au-Feu." In *Taste, Nostalgia*, edited by Allen S. Weiss. New York: Lusitania Press, 1997.

## NAPLES: *Pizza, Pasta, Pomodoro*

Artusi, Pellegrino. *La Scienza in Cucina e l'Arte di Mangiar Bene.* Torino: Einaudi, 1974.

Artusi, Pellegrino. *Science in the Kitchen and the Art of Eating Well.* Toronto: University of Toronto Press, 2004

Belmonte, Thomas. *The Broken Fountain.* New York: Columbia University Press, 1989.

Benjamin, Walter, and Asja Lacis. "Naples." In *Reflections: Essays, Aphorisms, Autobiographical Writings*, 163–73. New York: Harcourt Brace Jovanovich, 1978.

Callegari, Danielle. "The Politics of Pasta: La Cucina Futurista and the Italian Cookbook in History." *California Italian Studies* 4, no. 2 (2013). https://doi.org/10.5070/c342016030.

Camporesi, Piero. "Introduzione." In *La Scienza in Cucina e l'Arte di Mangiar Bene*. Turin: Einaudi, 1974.

Capatti, Alberto, and Massimo Montanari. *La Cucina Italiana: Storia di una Cultura*. Rome: Laterza, 2014.

Caròla Francesconi, Jeanne. *La Cucina Napoletana*. Naples: Grimaldi, 2010.

Cavalcanti, Ippolito. *Cucina Teorico-Pratica*. Naples: Grimaldi, 2018.

Choate, Mark I. *Emigrant Nation: The Making of Italy Abroad*. Cambridge, Mass.: Harvard University Press, 2008.

Cinotto, Simone. *The Italian American Table: Food, Family, and Community in New York City*. Urbana: University of Illinois Press, 2013.

Dickie, John. *Delizia! The Epic History of the Italians and Their Food*. New York: Free Press, 2010.

Diner, Hasia R. *Hungering for America: Italian, Irish, and Jewish Foodways in the Age of Migration*. Cambridge, Mass.: Harvard University Press, 2001.

Gabaccia, Donna R. *We Are What We Eat: Ethnic Food and the Making of Americans*. Cambridge, Mass.: Harvard University Press, 2000.

Gentilcore, David. *Pomodoro! A History of the Tomato in Italy*. New York: Columbia University Press, 2010.

Goethe, Johann Wolfgang von. *Italian Journey*. Translated by W. H. Auden and Elizabeth Mayer. London: Penguin, 2004.

Hazzard, Shirley, and Francis Steegmuller. *The Ancient Shore: Dispatches from Naples*. Chicago: University of Chicago Press, 2009.

Helstosky, Carol. *Garlic and Oil: Politics and Food in Italy*. Oxford: Berg, 2006.

Helstosky, Carol. *Pizza: A Global History*. London: Reaktion Books, 2013.

La Cecla, Franco. *La Pasta e la Pizza*. Bologna: Il Mulino, 2002.

Lancaster, Jordan. *In the Shadow of Vesuvius: A Cultural History of Naples*. London: Tauris Parke, 2011.

Levenstein, Harvey. "The American Response to Italian Food, 1880–1930." *Food and Foodways* 1, no. 1–2 (January 1985): 1–23. https://doi.org/10.1080/07409710.1985.9961875.

Lewis, Norman. *Naples '44*. New York: Pantheon Books, 1985.

Mattozzi, Antonio. *Inventing the Pizzeria: A History of Pizza Making in Naples*. London: Bloomsbury Academic, 2015.

Montanari, Massimo. *Italian Identity in the Kitchen, or Food and the Nation*. New York: Columbia University Press, 2013.

Montanari, Massimo. *A Short History of Spaghetti with Tomato Sauce*. New York: Europa Editions, 2022.

Moyer-Nocchi, Karima. *Chewing the Fat: An Oral History of Italian Foodways from Fascism to Dolce Vita.* Perrysburg, Ohio: Medea, 2015.

Nowak, Zachary. "Folklore, Fakelore, History." *Food, Culture & Society* 17, no. 1 (March 2014): 103–24. https://doi.org/10.2752/175174414x13828682779249.

Parasecoli, Fabio. *Al Dente: A History of Food in Italy.* London: Reaktion Books, 2014.

Serao, Matilde. *Il Ventre di Napoli.* Milan: BUR Rizzoli, 2019.

Sereni, Emilio. *I Napoletani: Da "Mangiafoglia" a "Mangiamaccheroni": Note di Storia dell'alimentazione nel Mezzogiorno.* Naples: Libreria Dante & Descartes, 2015.

Serventi, Silvano, and Françoise Sabban. *Pasta: The Story of a Universal Food.* New York: Columbia University Press, 2002.

Snowden, Frank M. *Naples in the Time of Cholera, 1884–1911.* Cambridge: Cambridge University Press, 2002.

Twain, Mark. *The Innocents Abroad.* Berkeley: Mint Editions, 2020.

## TOKYO: *Ramen and Rice*

Bray, Francesca. *The Rice Economies: Technology and Development in Asian Societies.* Berkeley: University of California Press, 1994.

Bray, Francesca, Peter A. Coclanis, Edda L. Fields-Black, and Schäfer Dagmar, eds. *Rice: Global Networks and New Histories.* New York: Cambridge University Press, 2017.

Cang, Voltaire. "Policing Washoku: The Performance of Culinary Nationalism in Japan." *Food and Foodways* 27, no. 3 (July 3, 2019): 232–52. https://doi.org/10.1080/07409710.2019.1646473.

Cwiertka, Katarzyna. *Modern Japanese Cuisine: Food, Power and National Identity.* London: Reaktion Books, 2014.

Cwiertka, Katarzyna, and Ewa Machotka, eds. *Consuming Life in Post-Bubble Japan: A Transdisciplinary Perspective.* Amsterdam: Amsterdam University Press, 2018.

Cwiertka, Katarzyna, with Yasuhara Miho. *Branding Japanese Food: From Meibutsu to Washoku.* Honolulu: University of Hawai'i Press, 2021.

Dale, Peter N. *Myth of Japanese Uniqueness.* London: Routledge, 2012.

Farina, Felice. "Japan's Gastrodiplomacy as Soft Power: Global Washoku and National Food Security." *Journal of Contemporary Eastern Asia* 17, no. 1 (2018): 152–67.

Ishige, Naomichi. *The History and Culture of Japanese Food.* New York: Routledge, 2011.

Krämer, Hans Martin. "'Not Befitting Our Divine Country': Eating Meat in Japanese Discourses of Self and Other from the Seventeenth Century to the

Present." *Food and Foodways* 16, no. 1 (March 14, 2008): 33–62. https://
doi.org/10.1080/07409710701885135.

Kushner, Barak. *Slurp! A Social and Culinary History of Ramen—Japan's Favorite Noodle Soup.* Leiden: Koninklijke Brill, 2014.

Laurent, Christopher. "In Search of *Umami*: Product Rebranding and the Global Circulation of the Fifth Taste." *Food, Culture & Society*, April 13, 2021, 1–17. https://doi.org/10.1080/15528014.2021.1895468.

Lyon Bestor, Victoria, Theodore C. Bestor, and Akiko Yamagata, eds. *Routledge Handbook of Japanese Culture and Society.* Abingdon, Oxon., UK: Routledge, 2013.

Ohnuki-Tierney, Emiko. *Rice as Self: Japanese Identities through Time.* Princeton, N.J.: Princeton University Press, 1995.

Pons, Philippe. "Japan's Changing Food Tastes Are Hard to Swallow for Rice and Sake Enthusiasts." *Guardian*, June 5, 2015. www.theguardian.com/lifeandstyle/2015/jun/05/japan-changing-food-tastes-rice-sake.

Rath, Eric C. *Japan's Cuisines: Food, Place and Identity.* London: Reaktion Books, 2016.

Sand, Jordan. "A Short History of MSG: Good Science, Bad Science, and Taste Cultures." *Gastronomica* 5, no. 4 (November 2005): 38–49. https://doi.org/10.1525/gfc.2005.5.4.38.

Schilling, Mark. *The Encyclopedia of Japanese Pop Culture.* New York: Weatherhill, 1997.

Simone, Gianni. "The Future of Rice Farming in Japan." *Japan Times*, January 29, 2016. www.japantimes.co.jp/life/2016/01/29/food/the-future-of-rice-farming-in-japan/.

Solt, George. *The Untold History of Ramen: How Political Crisis in Japan Spawned a Global Food Craze.* Berkeley: University of California Press, 2014.

Takeda, Hiroko. "Delicious Food in a Beautiful Country: Nationhood and Nationalism in Discourses on Food in Contemporary Japan." *Studies in Ethnicity and Nationalism* 8, no. 1 (April 8, 2008): 5–30. https://doi.org/10.1111/j.1754-9469.2008.00001.x.

Tracy, Sarah Elizabeth. "Delicious: A History of Monosodium Glutamate and Umami, the Fifth Taste Sensation." PhD Diss., University of Toronto, 2016.

Vlastos, Stephen. *Mirror of Modernity: Invented Traditions of Modern Japan.* Berkeley: University of California Press, 1998.

Whitelaw, Gavin. "Rice Ball Rivalries: Japanese Convenience Stores and the Appetite of Late Capitalism." In *Fast Food/Slow Food: The Cultural Economy of the Global Food System*, edited by Richard Wilk. Lanham, Md.: AltaMira Press, 2006.

## SEVILLE: *Tapas: Spain's Moveable Feast*

Afinoguénova, Eugenia, and Jaume Martí-Olivella. *Spain Is (Still) Different: Tourism and Discourse in Spanish Identity.* Lanham, Md.: Lexington Books, 2008.

Alvarez-Junco, José. *Spanish Identity in the Age of Nations.* Manchester, UK: Manchester University Press, 2016.

Anderson, Lara. *Control and Resistance: Food Discourse in Franco Spain.* Toronto: University of Toronto Press, 2020.

Anderson, Lara. *Cooking Up the Nation: Spanish Culinary Texts and Culinary Nationalization in the Late Nineteenth and Early Twentieth Century.* Woodbridge, Suffolk, UK: Tamesis, 2013.

Anderson, Lara. "The Unity and Diversity of La Olla Podrida: An Autochthonous Model of Spanish Culinary Nationalism." *Journal of Spanish Cultural Studies* 14, no. 4 (December 2013): 400–414. https://doi.org/10.1080/1463 6204.2013.916027.

Arbide, Joaquín. *Sevilla, Siempre un Bar: De la Tiza al Ordenador.* Seville: Samarcanda, 2019.

Baztán, Maria Reyes. "Potatoes and Nation-Building: The Case of the Spanish Omelette." *Journal of Iberian and Latin American Studies* 27, no. 2 (May 4, 2021): 151–70. https://doi.org/10.1080/14701847.2021.1939529.

Burgos, Antonio. *Guía Secreta de Sevilla.* Barcelona: Ediciones 29, 1999.

Castro, Américo. *The Spaniards: An Introduction to Their History.* Berkeley: University of California Press, 2018.

Díaz, Lorenzo. *La Cocina del Quijote.* Madrid: Alianza, 1997.

Dursteler, Eric. "The 'Abominable Pig' and the 'Mother of All Vices': Pork, Wine, and the Culinary Clash of Civilizations in the Early Modern Mediterranean." In *Insatiable Appetite: Food as Cultural Signifier in the Middle East and Beyond*, edited by Kirill Dmitriev, Julia Hauser, and Bilal Orfali. Leiden: Koninklijke Brill, 2020.

Freidenreich, David M. *Foreigners and Their Food: Constructing Otherness in Jewish, Christian, and Islamic Law.* Berkeley: University of California Press, 2015.

González Troyano, Alberto. *Don Juan, Fígaro, Carmen.* Seville: Fundación José Manuel Lara, 2007.

González Turmo, Isabel. *Comida de Rico, Comida de Pobre: Los Hábitos Alimenticios en el Occidente Andaluz (Siglo XX).* Seville: Universidad de Sevilla, Secretariado de Publicaciones, 1997.

González Turmo, Isabel. *200 Años de Cocina: Historia y Antropología de la Alimentación.* Madrid: Cultiva, 2013.

González Turmo, Isabel. *Sevilla: Banquetes, Tapas, Cartas y Menús, 1863–1995: Antropología de la Alimentación.* Seville: Área de Cultura, Ayuntamiento de Sevilla, 1996.

Holguín, Sandie. *Flamenco Nation: The Construction of Spanish National Identity.* Madison: University of Wisconsin Press, 2019.

Ingram, Rebecca. "Spain on the Table: Cookbooks, Women, and Modernization, 1905–1933." PhD Diss., Duke University, 2009.

Kissane, Christopher. *Food, Religion, and Communities in Early Modern Europe.* London: Bloomsbury Academic, 2020.

"La Tapa." In *Revista Española de Cultura Gastronómica*, No. 0. Madrid: Real Academia de Gastronomía, 2018. https://realacademiadegastronomia.com/wp-content/uploads/2021/05/RAG_REVISTA-0.pdf.

"Las Tapas, Cada Vez Más Cerca de Ser Patrimonio Cultural Inmaterial," *La Vanguardia*, February 17, 2018. www.lavanguardia.com/comer/al-dia/20180217/44857743748/tapas-patrimonio-cultural-inmaterial.html.

Martínez Llopis, Manuel. *Historia de La Gastronomía Española.* Madrid: Alianza, 1989.

Menocal, María Rosa. *The Ornament of the World: How Muslims, Jews, and Christians Created a Culture of Tolerance in Medieval Spain.* New York: Back Bay Books, 2012.

Nadeau, Carolyn A. *Food Matters. Alonso Quijano's Diet and the Discourse of Food in Early Modern Spain.* Toronto: University of Toronto Press, 2016.

Nash, Elizabeth. *Seville, Córdoba, and Granada: A Cultural History.* New York: Oxford University Press, 2005.

"Origen y Evolución de las Tapas," ABC Sevilla, February 28, 2011. https://sevilla.abc.es/gurme/sevilla/sevi-origen-y-evolucion-de-las-tapas-201102282200_noticia.html.

Ortega y Gasset, José. *Teoría de Andalucía y Otros Ensayos.* Madrid: Revista de Occidente, 1952.

Pack, Sasha D. *Tourism and Dictatorship: Europe's Peaceful Invasion of Franco's Spain.* New York: Palgrave Macmillan, 2006.

Pardo Bazán, Emilia. *Cocina Española Antigua Y Moderna.* Donostia–San Sebastián, Spain: Iano, 2007.

Pardo, Mariano, Ana Palmer Monte, and Maria Fernanda González Llamas. *La Mesa Moderna.* Seville: Cerro Alto, 1994.

Riesz, Leela. "Convivencia: A Solution to the Halal/Pork Tension in Spain?" *Revista de Administração de Empresas* 58, no. 3 (June 2018): 222–32. https://doi.org/10.1590/s0034-759020180303.

Ríos, Alicia. "The Olla." *Gastronomica* 1, no. 1 (February 2001): 22–24. https://doi.org/10.1525/gfc.2001.1.1.22.

Romero de Solís, Pedro. "La Taberna en Espagne et en Amérique." *Terrain*, no. 13 (October 1, 1989): 63–71. https://doi.org/10.4000/terrain.2953.

Rosendorf, Neal M. *Franco Sells Spain to America: Hollywood, Tourism and Public Relations as Postwar Spanish Soft Power*. Basingstoke, UK: Palgrave Macmillan, 2014.

Savo, Anita. "'Toledano, Ajo, Berenjena': The Eggplant in Don Quixote." *La Corónica: A Journal of Medieval Hispanic Languages, Literatures, and Cultures* 43, no. 1 (2014): 231–52. https://doi.org/10.1353/cor.2014.0033.

Sevilla, María José. *Delicioso: A History of Food in Spain*. London: Reaktion Books, 2019.

Stillo, Stephanie. "Forging Imperial Cities: Seville and Formation of Civic Order in the Early Modern Hispanic World." PhD diss., University of Kansas, 2014.

Storm, Eric. *The Culture of Regionalism: Art, Architecture and International Exhibitions in France, Germany and Spain, 1890–1939*. Manchester, UK: Manchester University Press, 2011.

Venegas, José Luis. *The Sublime South: Andalusia, Orientalism, and the Making of Modern Spain*. Evanston, Ill.: Northwestern University Press, 2018.

Villegas, Almudena. *Gastronomía Romana y Dieta Mediterránea: El Recetario de Apicio*. Bloomington, Ind.: Palibrio, 2011.

Wild, Matthew J. "Eating Spain: National Cuisine since 1900." PhD Diss., University of Kentucky, 2015.

## OAXACA: *Maize, Mole, Mezcal*

Aguilar-Rodríguez, Sandra. "Cooking Modernity: Nutrition Policies, Class, and Gender in 1940s and 1950s Mexico City." *The Americas* 64, no. 2 (2007): 177–205. www.jstor.org/stable/30139085.

Aguilar-Rodríguez, Sandra. "'Las Penas con Pan Son Menos': Race, Modernity and Wheat in Modern Mexico." *Bulletin of Spanish Studies* 97, no. 4 (January 22, 2020): 539–65. https://doi.org/10.1080/14753820.2020.1701330.

Aguilar-Rodríguez, Sandra. "Mole and Mestizaje: Race and National Identity in Twentieth-Century Mexico." *Food, Culture & Society* 21, no. 5 (September 27, 2018): 600–617. https://doi.org/10.1080/15528014.2018.1516403.

Bak-Geller Corona, Sarah. "Culinary Myths of the Mexican Nation." In *Cooking Cultures: Convergent Histories of Food and Feeling*, edited by Ishita Banerjee-Dube, 224–46. New York: Cambridge University Press, 2016.

Barros, Cristina. *El Cocinero Mexicano: México, 1831*. Mexico City: Consejo Nacional para la Cultura y las Artes, Culturas Populares, 2000.

Bauer, Arnold J. "Millers and Grinders: Technology and Household Economy in Meso-America." *Agricultural History* 64, no. 1 (1990): 1–17. www.jstor.org/stable/3743179?seq=1&cid=pdf-.

Bonfil Batalla, Guillermo. *México Profundo: Una Civilización Negada.* Mexico City: Grijalbo, 1990.

Castillo Cisneros, María del Carmen. "En Mi Mero Mole: Una Lectura Antropológica de 'Mole' en Chapters of Food." *Entre Diversidades. Revista de Ciencias Sociales y Humanidades* 8, no. 1 (January 30, 2021): 164–85. https://doi.org/10.31644/ed.v8.n1.2021.a07.

Chapa, Martha. *La República de Los Moles: El Recetario Más Completo del Platillo Mexicano por Excelencia.* Mexico City: Aguilar, 2005.

Coe, Sophie D. *America's First Cuisines.* Austin: University of Texas Press, 1994.

Earle, Rebecca. *The Body of the Conquistador: Food, Race, and the Colonial Experience in Spanish America, 1492–1700.* Cambridge: Cambridge University Press, 2013.

*El Mole en la Ruta de Los Dioses.* Vol. 12 of Cuadernos de Patrimonio Cultural y Turismo, 29–53. Mexico City: Conaculta, n.d.

Esteva, Gustavo. *Sin Maíz No Hay País.* Mexico City: Consejo Nacional para la Cultura y las Artes, 2007.

Fitting, Elizabeth. "The Political Uses of Culture." *Focaal* 2006, no. 48 (December 1, 2006): 17–34. https://doi.org/10.3167/092012906780646307.

Fussell, Betty. *The Story of Corn.* Albuquerque: University of New Mexico Press, 2004.

González, Roberto J. *Zapotec Science: Farming and Food in the Northern Sierra of Oaxaca.* Austin: University of Texas Press, 2001.

Gutiérrez Chong, Natividad. "Forging Common Origin in the Making of the Mexican Nation." *Genealogy* 4, no. 3 (July 20, 2020): 77. https://doi.org/10.3390/genealogy4030077.

Juárez López, José Luis. *Nacionalismo Culinario: La Cocina Mexicana en el Siglo XX.* Mexico City: Conaculta, 2013.

Kennedy, Diana. *Oaxaca al Gusto: An Infinite Gastronomy.* Austin: University of Texas Press, 2010.

Keremitsis, Dawn. "Del Metate al Molino: La Mujer Mexicana de 1910 a 1940." *Historia Mexicana* 33, no. 2 (1983): 285–302. www.jstor.org/stable/25135862.

Laudan, Rachel, and Jeffrey M. Pilcher. "Chiles, Chocolate, and Race in New Spain: Glancing Backward to Spain or Looking Forward to Mexico?" *Eighteenth-Century Life* 23, no. 2 (May 1999): 59–70.

Lavín, Mónica, and Ana Luisa Benítez Muro. *Sor Juana en la Cocina.* Mexico City: Planeta Mexicana, 2021.

Lind, David, and Elizabeth Barham. "The Social Life of the Tortilla: Food, Cultural Politics, and Contested Commodification." *Agriculture and Human Values* 21, no. 1 (2004): 47–60. https://doi.org/10.1023/b:ahum.0000014018.76118.06.

Mann, Charles C. *1493: Uncovering the New World Columbus Created*. New York: Knopf, 2011.

Marcus, Joyce, and Kent V. Flannery. "Ancient Zapotec Ritual and Religion." In *The Ancient Mind: Elements of Cognitive Archaeology*, edited by Colin Renfrew and Ezra B. W. Zubrow, 55–74. Cambridge: Cambridge University Press, 2004.

Martínez, Zarela. *The Food and Life of Oaxaca: Traditional Recipes from Mexico's Heart*. New York: Macmillan, 1997.

Matta, Raúl. "Mexico's Ethnic Culinary Heritage and Cocineras Tradicionales (Traditional Female Cooks)." *Food and Foodways* 27, no. 3 (July 3, 2019): 211–31. https://doi.org/10.1080/07409710.2019.1646481.

Méndez Cota, Gabriela. *Disrupting Maize: Food, Biotechnology, and Nationalism in Contemporary Mexico*. London: Rowman & Littlefield, 2016.

Morton, Paula E. *Tortillas: A Cultural History*. Albuquerque: University of New Mexico Press, 2014.

Núñez Miranda, Concepción Silvia. *DISHDAA'W: La Palabra Se Entreteje En La Comida Infinita: La Vida de Abigail Mendoza Ruiz*. Oaxaca: Fundación Alfredo Harp Helú/Proveedora Escolar, 2011.

Overmyer-Velázquez, Mark. *Visions of the Emerald City: Modernity, Tradition, and the Formation of Porfirian Oaxaca, Mexico*. Durham, N.C.: Duke University Press, 2006.

Pilcher, Jeffrey M. "The Land of Seven Moles: Mexican Culinary Nationalism in an Age of Multiculturalism." *Food, Culture & Society* 21, no. 5 (September 27, 2018): 637–53. https://doi.org/10.1080/15528014.2018.1516404.

Pilcher, Jeffrey M. *Planet Taco: A Global History of Mexican Food*. New York: Oxford University Press, 2017.

Pilcher, Jeffrey M. *Que Vivan Los Tamales! Food and the Making of Mexican Identity*. Albuquerque: University of New Mexico Press, 1998.

Pollan, Michael. *The Omnivore's Dilemma: A Natural History of Four Meals*. New York: Penguin Books, 2016.

Poole, Deborah. "Affective Distinctions: Race and Place in Oaxaca." In *Contested Histories in Public Space: Memory, Race, and Nation*, edited by Daniel J. Walkowitz and Lisa Maya Knauer, 197–226. Durham, N.C.: Duke University Press, 2009.

Restall, Matthew. *When Montezuma Met Cortés: The True Story of the Meeting That Changed History*. New York: Ecco, 2019.

Stephen, Lynn. *Zapotec Women*. Austin: University of Texas Press, 1991.

Thomas, Hugh. *Conquest: Montezuma, Cortés, and the Fall of Old Mexico*. New York: Simon & Schuster, 1993.

Villafaña, Hana Xochitl. "The Global Reach of the Mexican Corn Revolution." *Perspectives: A Journal of Historical Inquiry* 45 (n.d.). calstatela.edu/cen ters/perspectives/volume-45.

## ISTANBUL: *The Ottoman Potluck*

Ágoston, Gábor, and Bruce Masters. *Encyclopedia of the Ottoman Empire.* New York: Facts On File, 2009.

Alphan, Deniz. *Dina'nın Mutfağı: Türk Sefarad Yemekleri.* Istanbul: Boyut, 2012.

Aslan, Senem. "'Citizen, Speak Turkish!': A Nation in the Making." *Nationalism and Ethnic Politics* 13, no. 2 (May 17, 2007): 245–72. https://doi.org /10.1080/13537110701293500.

Aykan, Bahar. "The Politics of Intangible Heritage and Food Fights in Western Asia." *International Journal of Heritage Studies* 22, no. 10 (August 25, 2016): 799–810. https://doi.org/10.1080/13527258.2016.1218910.

Brodsky, Joseph. "Flight from Byzantium." In *Less than One: Selected Essays*, 393–446. New York: Farrar, Straus and Giroux, 1987.

Cevik, N. K., ed. *Imperial Taste: 700 Years of Culinary Culture.* Ankara: Ministry of Culture and Tourism Publications, 2009.

Douglas, Mary. *Food in the Social Order: Studies of Food and Festivities in Three American Communities.* London: Routledge, 2009.

Elliot, Frances Minto. *Diary of an Idle Woman in Constantinople.* London: J. Murray, 1893.

Erdemir, Aykan. "The Turkish Kristallnacht." *POLITICO*, September 7, 2015. www.politico.eu/article/the-turkish-kristallnacht-greece-1955-pogrom -polites-orthodox/.

Fisher Onar, Nora. "Echoes of a Universalism Lost: Rival Representations of the Ottomans in Today's Turkey." *Middle Eastern Studies* 45, no. 2 (March 2009): 229–41. https://doi.org/10.1080/00263200802697290.

Göktürk, Deniz, Levent Soysal, and Ipek Türeli, eds. *Orienting Istanbul: Cultural Capital of Europe?* London: Routledge, 2010.

"Interview with Zafer Yenal: On the Connection between Nationalism and Cuisine." Qantara.de—Dialogue with the Islamic World, 2007. https:// en.qantara.de/node/786.

Işın, Priscilla Mary. *Bountiful Empire: A History of Ottoman Cuisine.* London: Reaktion Books, 2018.

Karaosmanoğlu, Defne. "Cooking the Past: The Revival of Ottoman Cuisine." PhD Diss., McGill University, 2006.

Karaosmanoğlu, Defne. "From Ayran to Dragon Fruit Smoothie: Populism, Polarization and Social Engineering in Turkey." *International Journal of Communication* 14 (2020): 1253–74.

Kia, Mehrdad. *Daily Life in the Ottoman Empire*. Santa Barbara, Calif.: Greenwood, 2011.

King, Charles. *Midnight at the Pera Palace: The Birth of Modern Istanbul*. New York: W. W. Norton, 2015.

Mango, Andrew. *Atatürk*. London: John Murray, 2004.

Mansel, Philip. *Constantinople: City of the World's Desire, 1453–1924*. London: John Murray, 2006.

Mills, Amy. "The Ottoman Legacy: Urban Geographies, National Imaginaries, and Global Discourses of Tolerance." *Comparative Studies of South Asia, Africa and the Middle East* 31, no. 1 (January 1, 2011): 183–95. https://doi.org/10.1215/1089201x-2010-066.

Mills, Amy. "The Place of Locality for Identity in the Nation: Minority Narratives of Cosmopolitan Istanbul." *International Journal of Middle East Studies* 40, no. 3 (August 2008): 383–401. https://doi.org/10.1017/s0020743808080987.

Navaro-Yashin, Yael. *Faces of the State: Secularism and Public Life in Turkey*. Princeton, N.J.: Princeton University Press, 2006.

Necipoğlu, Gülru. *Architecture, Ceremonial, and Power: The Topkapi Palace in the Fifteenth and Sixteenth Centuries*. New York: Architectural History Foundation, 1991.

O'Connor, Coilin. "Food Fight Rages in the Caucasus." Radio Free Europe/Radio Liberty, January 17, 2013. www.rferl.org/a/food-fight-rages-in-the-caucasus-coilin/24840815.html.

Öncü, Ayşe. "The Politics of Istanbul's Ottoman Heritage in the Era of Globalism." In *Cities of the South: Citizenship and Exclusion in the Twenty-First Century*, edited by Barbara Drieskens, Franck Mermier, and Heiko Wimmen, 233–64. London: Saqi Books, 2007. https://research.sabanciuniv.edu/id/eprint/9395.

Öney Tan, Aylin. "Empanadas with Turkish Delight?" *Hürriyet Daily News*, December 9, 2013. www.hurriyetdailynews.com/opinion/aylin-oney-tan/empanadas-with-turkish-delight-59222.

Örs, İlay Romain. *Diaspora of the City: Stories of Cosmopolitanism from Istanbul and Athens*. New York: Palgrave Macmillan, 2018.

Özyürek, Esra. *The Politics of Public Memory in Turkey*. Syracuse, N.Y.: Syracuse University Press, 2007.

Pamuk, Orhan. *Istanbul: Memories and the City*. New York: Alfred A. Knopf, 2017.

Pamuk, Orhan. *The Black Book*. New York: Vintage International/Vintage Books, 2006.

Pultar, Gönül. "Creating Ethnic Memory: Takuhi Tovmasyan's 'Merry Meals.'" In *Imagined Identities: Identity Formation in the Age of Globalism*, edited by Gönül Pultar, 59–67. Syracuse, N.Y.: Syracuse University Press, 2013.

Salmaner, Muge. "The Bittersweet Taste of the Past: Reading Food in Armenian Literature in Turkish." PhD Diss., University of Washington, 2014.

Samancı, Özge. "The Cuisine of Istanbul between East and West during the 19th Century." In *Earthly Delights: Economies and Cultures of Food in Ottoman and Danubian Europe, c. 1500–1900*, edited by Angela Jianu and Violeta Barbu, 77–98. Leiden: Koninklijke Brill, 2018.

Samancı, Özge. "History of Eating and Drinking in the Ottoman Empire and Modern Turkey." In *Handbook of Eating and Drinking: Interdisciplinary Perspectives*, edited by Herbert L. Meiselman, 55–75. [Cham, Switzerland]: Springer, 2020. https://doi.org/10.1007/978-3-030-14504-0_154.

Samancı, Özge. "Images, Perceptions and Authenticity in Ottoman–Turkish Cuisine." In *Food Heritage and Nationalism in Europe*, edited by Ilaria Porciani, 155–79. Abingdon, Oxon., UK: Routledge, 2019.

Samancı, Özge. "Pilaf and Bouchées: The Modernization of Official Banquets at the Ottoman Palace in the Nineteenth Century." In *Royal Taste: Food, Power and Status in European Courts after 1789*, edited by Daniëlle De Vooght, 111–42. Abingdon, Oxon., UK: Routledge, 2011.

Simyonidis, Meri Çevik. *İstanbulum: Tadım, Tuzum, Hayatım*. Yenibosna, Istanbul: İnkılâp Kitabevi, 2015.

Singer, Amy. "Serving Up Charity: The Ottoman Public Kitchen." *Journal of Interdisciplinary History* 35, no. 3 (2005): 481–500. www.jstor.org/stable/3657036.

Tovmasyan, Takuhi. *Mémoires Culinaires du Bosphore*. Marseille: Parenthèses, 2012.

Tovmasyan, Takuhi. *Sofranız Şen Olsun: Ninelerimin Mutfağından Damağımda, Aklımda Kalanlar*. Istanbul: Aras Yayıncılık, 2004.

Türeli, İpek. "Ara Güler's Photography of 'Old Istanbul' and Cosmopolitan Nostalgia." *History of Photography* 34, no. 3 (July 12, 2010): 300–313. https://doi.org/10.1080/03087290903361373.

Yenal, Zafer. "'Cooking' the Nation: Women, Experiences of Modernity, and the Girls' Institutes in Turkey." In *Ways to Modernity in Greece and Turkey: Encounters with Europe, 1850–1950*, edited by Anna Frangoudaki and Caglar Keyder, 191–214. London: Bloomsbury, 2020.

Yerasimos, Marianna, and Sally Bradbrook. *500 Years of Ottoman Cuisine*. Istanbul: Boyut, 2005.

Zat, Erdir. *Rakı, Modern and Unconventional*. Istanbul: Overteam, 2014.

Zubaida, Sami, and Richard Tapper, eds. *A Taste of Thyme: Culinary Cultures of the Middle East*. London: Tauris Parke Paperbacks, 2011.

# Index